Through the Fires

The Wizard's Way

A Book of the Old Religion

*Written for gay men...
and other happy people*

by Lou Percus

**COPPER
CAULDRON**
PUBLISHING

Credits

Author: Lou Percus
Foreword: Raven Grimassi
Cover Art & Design: Rory McCracken
Transcription: Karen Ainsworth
Layout & Publishing: Steve Kenson

Copyright ©2018 Lou Percus and Raven Grimassi. All Rights Reserved. No part of this work may be reproduced, stored in a retrieval system, or transmitted in any form or by any means, without the prior permission in writing of the Copyright Owner, nor be otherwise circulated in any form other than that in which it is published.

ISBN 978-1-940755-10-6, First Printing, Printed in the U.S.A.

Disclaimer

This book and all spells, rituals, formulas, and advice in it are not substitutes for professional medical advice or psychological care. Please confer with a medical professional before using any herbs, remedies, or teas in any manner. Unless specifically indicated, formulas are not intended to be consumed or ingested. The publisher is not responsible for the use of this material.

Publisher's Note

Through the Fires is a work of the time in which it was written and it is presented as we received it as a legacy of that time and the author's life, untouched save for formatting and copy editing, in order to preserve the author's original intent, tone, and style as much as possible.

TABLE OF CONTENTS

FOREWORD 7
THE "GAY" WORD 11
   The Wizard's Way 11
INTRODUCTION 13
   What is the Old Religion? 13
   What Are the Gods? 14
   What is The Spiritual Path? 15
   The Masters of Old 15
   A Religion Without Congregations 17
   Very Traditional Values 18
CHAPTER ONE: THE GODS 19
   Choosing a Divinity 19
   Religious Control vs. Spirituality 19
   Rejecting Domination 20
   The Nature of the Gods 22
   What is True Worship? 23
   Forming Personal Rapport 24
   Invocations To The Gods 40
CHAPTER TWO: TOOLS 54
   Dirk 55
   Sword 55
   Wand 56
   Mirror 56
   Comb 57
   Chalice 58
   Thurible 58
   Pentacle 58
   Bolline 59
   Staff 59
   Moon Bowl and Sun Bowl 59
   Pouch 60
   Cingulum 61
   Figurines 61
   Robes 61
   Amulets or Talismans 62
   Altar 63
   Flute 63

    Masks 63
    Consecration 64
CHAPTER THREE: THE MYTHS **66**
    The Reason for Myths 66
    Reincarnation 66
    The Rituals of Myth 68
    Myth and The Human Psyche 69
    Concerning Sexuality 83
CHAPTER FOUR: THE RITES **90**
    Temples 90
    The Guardians, Or The Lords Of The Elements 91
    The Four Elements 93
    The Globe Casting 93
    Full Moon Ceremony 100
    Rites 113
    Traditions 128
    Magical Personality and Illusion 136
    The Magical Voice 137
    Cleansing 138
    General Guidelines For A Worship Ceremony 139
CHAPTER FIVE: THE EIGHT-FOLD PATH **141**
    Basic Principles 141
    The Eight-Fold Path 144
    Priesthood Spirituality 147
    Star Aspects of Bride and Angus Og 149
    Concerning the Union of the Sexes 151
    The Expansion of Awareness 154
    The Path of the Red God, The Green God, and The Rainbow 163
    Nature Spirits 165
    Numen 168
    Transformation and Evolution 169
    Culture, Society and The Gods 172
    The Return of Balance 172
    Relinquishment 173
    Past Lives 174
CHAPTER SIX: MAKING YOUR OWN MAGIC **176**
    Element of Spells 178
    Self-Responsibility 182
    How To Do It 187
    Natural Magic 196
    Dissolving Objects by The Elements 197

Sigil Making 198
Smoke Spell 199
Power 199
Elemental Workings 199
Chapter Seven: The Ancestral Altar 204
Ancestral Invocation 205
Personal Altar 205
Teaching 206
Chapter Eight: Animal Guides 211
The Egotism of Being Human 211
The Role of the Animal Guide, or Familiar 212
Animal Telepathy 213
Other Uses of an Animal Guide 213
Animal Magic 215
Chapter Nine: Groups 217
Leaders 217
Power Madness 220
Council 221
Group 222
Chapter Ten: Rites of Passage 229
Rite of Manhood 231
Rite of Womanhood 232
Group Dedication Ceremony 234
Self-Dedication Rite 236
Instinctual Needs 238
The Rite of Acknowledgement 239
Marriage Instructions 241
The Nature of These Rites 242
Gay Homophobia 244
Handfasting Ceremony 246
Ceremony of the Wedding Vows 247
A Child's Acceptance into the Clan 248
The Rite of Divorce 249
Funeral Rite 251
Chapter Eleven: Meditation 253
Ecstatic States of Consciousness Through Meditation 253
Past Life Meditation 255
Goddess Meditation 256
Sparkles 259
Love Meditation 259
Power Symbol and Power Animal 259

- Animal Meditation 260
- Aura Cleansing 260
- Action and Inaction 261

Chapter Twelve: Wisdom and Study 262
- Sacred and Mundane 262
- God and Goddess Metaphors 263
- Wisdom 267
- Areas to Study 268

Chapter Thirteen: Psychic Self-Defense 272
- Dealing with Idiots 272
- The Pentagram 275
- Black Magic Prayer Groups 275
- Psychically Charged Oils 277

Afterword 278
- A Word for Pagans of Other Systems 278
- The Old Religion's View of Gay People 279
- The Origins of Religious and Spiritual Systems 281

References 288
- Recommended Reading 288

FOREWORD

The author of this book was a very dear friend of mine. He was also one of my initiates in the Arician Tradition of Italian Witchcraft. Lou was born on June 13th, 1953 and was arguably the most classic Gemini I have ever known. He died on September 15th, 1994 from complications due to AIDS, which he contracted during a vacation in Greece. In those days the diagnosis of AIDS was a certain death sentence. He fought bravely and outlived his prognosis of remaining time. When death finally arrived, Lou died in the arms of a friend who came to pick him up for a doctor's appointment. It was a quick and merciful death.

The book you now hold was passed to me in manuscript form not long before he died. My intention was to publish it for him, but things did not work out for a variety of reasons. The manuscript was tucked away until it recently resurfaced. I felt it should be published, and I am grateful to Copper Cauldron Publishing for accepting the manuscript for publication.

I first met Lou in the late 1970s at a shop in San Diego called Ye Olde Enchantment Shoppe. He was a silent partner with co-owner Judith Wise (founder of the Wise-Rhodes Tradition). I taught several classes there over the course of time, and it was here that I also met Scott Cunningham (who was later to enter Lou's life). Scott attended several of my classes and we became friends, and then later he was also initiated in the Arician Tradition. He remained a first degree initiate for several years, and then drifted away after becoming a published author.

The material in this book, *Through the Fires*, was crafted over several years. It was written by a man whose passion for Witchcraft was unequalled by anyone I have ever known. He believed in Witchcraft as "The Old Religion" of Europe. His belief did not originate from books written during the 1960s and 1970s that promoted this idea. It didn't arise from a love of subcultures or Lou's predisposition to rebel against those who presented themselves as authorities. It came instead from a personal gnosis; it was a feeling he held that, to him, was past life memory.

In the years that I knew him, Lou spoke very little about his personal past and his background. He was from the Midwestern part of the United States, was an only child, and he served in the Navy. He told me that his Witchcraft background came from two women, both of whom were named Ruth. I was never able to sort out one from the other. One of the women lived in Oklahoma and practiced some form of Conjure Witchcraft. The other lived in Hawaii and taught a traditional system of Witchcraft. I believe this was "Ruth P." as Lou called her. He and Scott Cunningham eventually created a system together based upon her material. Sadly, the joint venture eventually led to irreconcilable differences and they parted ways on less than favorable terms.

Lou's life was a long struggle against mainstream society. He was a gay man in a time when most gay people felt the need to keep it a secret from everyone. In the early part of our friendship he even kept this from me. When he finally confided in me that he was gay, I asked him why he never told me. He replied that he was afraid I would stop being his friend. It was a painful moment for both of us, and I then realized that we didn't know each other as truly as we had thought. Our friendship continued on and strengthened over the years.

In the 1970s it was still being taught that Witchcraft was an ancient fertility religion. It was presented as a gender-based system. Lou believed that Witchcraft was fertility-based, and it caused him great personal challenges (particularly in coven practice). He felt disenfranchised from the very thing he loved most, and he felt not truly accepted as an equal in the Craft Community as it was in the day. This sadness later turned to anger.

Lou held a strong belief that gays and lesbians were instrumental in the "survival" of the Craft over the centuries. The theme of Witchcraft as a surviving tradition was very common at the time. He was the first, in my circle of Witches, to state a belief that the Goddess could be invoked in a man. This idea was extremely controversial at the time and resulted in a great deal of heated discourse within the Community. We sat many nights discussing his views about Witchcraft, and I am happy that at least some of those views are now preserved in this book.

In the pages of *Through the Fires* you will find a wealth of sound basic tenets, foundational concepts, and useful techniques. Lou writes with the certainty and confidence of his long training and practice in the ways of Witchcraft. This can be off-putting to some, particularly those with an unfavorable view of authoritative statements. Lou did not come across in person as someone displaying authority, but he did easily evoke the air of someone with profound knowledge and personal power. There is a lot to be gained in reading this book, and sorting out the gems will be a worthwhile endeavor.

Lou presents the pantheon of deities used in the system he writes about. He also includes important myths. The gods and goddesses are of Northern European culture. Lou viewed them as very archaic and powerful in their primal state. In talking about the old gods, he had the ability to make them feel tangible. I was fortunate to be initiated by him into the Pictish-Gaelic tradition, and I learned a great deal from him. When he went overseas with the Navy into a war zone, Lou asked me to be the steward of his Book of Shadows in case he did not return. I came into possession of this and other materials he passed to me at the time.

Through the Fires essentially consumed his time during the last year and a half of his life. Unfortunately, Lou developed dementia near the end of his life, and this made communication difficult for those of us helping him with the project. One night he lamented to me saying "I've forgotten more about Witchcraft than most people will ever learn." It wasn't egoism; it was a testimony to his intense study and practice over several decades. His collection of books contained some very rare occult works along with the largest assembled collection of books by Austin Spare I have ever seen in one place. Sadly, Lou had to sell off his personal library to pay for his healthcare.

Lou was more than a Witch; he was a serious occultist. In his book you can read about some of the principles and teachings he felt strongly about. There are also messages in his writings. Unlike many authors today Lou does not present a technique and then assure the reader that there are many other ways to perform it. He does not down-play his role as a teacher or practitioner by presenting his instructions as optional or something to cherry-pick. Instead Lou writes with personal conviction. Let that be okay in this book, and you can learn much. No mystery is closed to an open mind.

Raven Grimassi
September 2017

The "Gay" Word

The words *homosexual*, *gay*, and *faerie* each have a slightly different connotation. *Homosexual* speaks strictly about sexual acts, while *gay* refers more to a lifestyle and politics, and *faerie* refers to a type of spirituality and social consciousness.

This becomes a problem as all of these terms manifest from a unified consciousness. This is like trying to name the base substance of a rainbow, which is water, by calling it by the different colors it appears to be. In the end, none of these terms are really appropriate, as they are manifestations of a type of consciousness, and what we are dealing with here is a consciousness itself, which cannot be defined or limited to social, political, spiritual, or sexual contexts.

Therefore, any of these terms may apply as manifestations of a primal causal consciousness. None of them are wrong, but a deeper, undefined meaning is intended.

I have decided to use the term "gay" simply because it is quicker to write and includes most of the other definitions as well. If you wish to substitute another definition, such as homosexual or faerie, that is fine, as long as the term refers to the type of awareness intended.

The Wizard's Way

Much thought went into what this system should be called, and finally the Wizard's Way won out. Often it was stressed that what was being taught to me was not exactly Wicca, as Wicca was Anglo-Saxon, and this system is from a very different lineage. Parts of this predated the invasion of the Anglo-Saxons and Celts into Scotland and parts of it had no relation to the Germanic races at all. This system is composed of a number of older systems that have been updated, as well as some modern additions that were found appropriate for the times. It is therefore eclectic, but based upon the hereditary elder ways. To have drawn too heavily upon any one system that was shared with me would have violated trusts and released too much to the public of what is a very private and personal family matter. Respect is required as the sincere feelings of love are more important than information, and friendships more important than the dissemination of information.

Many of the older systems did not usually use the term "witch" to describe themselves. They always used other terms, and although this system has similarities to Wicca, I technically cannot class it under that heading. I have therefore decided to use the term wizard rather than witch as it is more appropriate for the lineage from which I draw this. This is not meant to be divisive within the pagan community, just more accurate for the information I am putting forth.

Many times, the older systems and clans had no names for themselves except for maybe "The People." Mine did have specific names, but often when the people in the older systems saw the similarity to Wicca, they said "Oh, we must be witches" because of the closeness of some of the rites. This may not have been entirely accurate, but it was the best they could do, as they were very scattered and secretive. They had very little contact with each other. They simply had no other references.

So, "the Wizard's Way" it is, and the people who would practice this should call themselves "wizards" if they wish to use any term at all. It is the most appropriate. So be it.

INTRODUCTION

This book is written for gay men seeking a spiritual path. It is not that it cannot be used by others. No truly spiritual path can be discriminatory as awareness itself has no boundaries; but it is written specifically for gay men by a gay man.

The function of a spiritual path is the psychological evolution of awareness towards the realization and experience of Union with deity. The main function of religious institutions is to maintain social structure.

WHAT IS THE OLD RELIGION?

The Old Religion is a religious and spiritual system that arose out of shamanism and has survived from ancient times. Its adherents were severely persecuted during the Middle Ages by the Inquisition and the ensuing hysteria. Those who followed the Old Way were forced underground to avoid a horrible death. This ancient European spiritual path survived only through the incredible courage and love of the old people.

Essentially, the Old Religion teaches that deity manifests in a monistic form, similar to the Hindu God, Brahma. Everything is an aspect of deity. You, the rock next to you, the tree over there, those are all manifestations of deity; each being deity complete in itself. In taking this concept of an all-pervading Unity, it is brought into the level of physical manifestation in the form of a duality, like the Chinese concept of Yin and Yang. So, we have the polarity of a divine Mother Goddess and a divine Father God. This is an expression of the duality of existence, as negative and positive. This is not an ethical judgement such as "good" or "bad." Those are concepts limited to moralistic patterns of social structure and are not universally useful. This is more like the positive and negative poles of a battery. Using those two points of difference, energy flows. You must have a difference in potentials or it won't work. Energy, as physics demonstrates, flows on the basis of universal principles, not because of ethical judgements. If something is a universal truth, it is true on a mathematical, physical, and spiritual level. This is of course, what makes it a universal truth.

WHAT ARE THE GODS?

From these two aspects of one divine force, come all of the other beautiful gods and goddesses. Yes, there are many gods and goddesses in the Old Religion, it is an ancient system and it is pantheistic. It is a polytheistic monism, with a multiplicity of gods arising from the single divine force or principle. That is because there are many kinds of people and not everyone finds one individual deity perfect for them. All of the Gods are aspects of this one masculine force, as all Goddesses are aspects of this one all-pervading feminine essence. The separate Gods and Goddesses were created (I'm not saying whether they were pre-existent to man or not), because it is difficult to have a fulfilling spiritual relationship for most people with these vast universe filling energies. Instead, individual aspects of these two great universal energy patterns are what we usually experience and come to know on a personal level.

To make it clearer, even though we're the Universal Being ourselves, it is easier to have a conversation with the handsome man next to you, than to transform into a galactic presence. It is the same with our Gods and Goddesses. We can get to know them on a personal level and so They respond to us. So, we work to establish a relationship to Apollo, Hercules, or Gaith, for example. These in many cases are the personifications of natural forces, yet that doesn't mean that there is not a form of intelligence behind these things. So what we try to do is come into harmony with the natural world around us.

How is this done? By starting to observe and come into tune with the wholesome natural cycles of nature. Consequently, days on which there are solstices, equinoxes, full moons, etc., are the days that are observed as holy, and on which rites or festivals are celebrated.

Through personal devotions and ceremonial rites, we try to align ourselves with the most natural and healthy forces that are expressions of ourselves and the world around us.

What is The Spiritual Path?

By aligning ourselves with that which we are the natural manifestations of, we come closer to deity. And so begins the path for the final goal in the direct realization of deity itself. As I said, it is experimental, and not solely intellectual, although if you don't use your head, you'll get nothing out of this book or life for that matter. The realization of deity is accomplished through learning how to change your level of consciousness naturally, not through artificial means. But first we need to give you a firm foundation. Changes in levels of consciousness can often leave you feeling disorientated and without a suitable anchor to hold you to your place and time, you can run into trouble.

Therefore, we use the religious tradition as the anchor to return us to our own level of reality and proper perspective. The tradition of the western path has been to remain connected to the larger society and to deal with its issues and problems, not to withdraw from them. This is very important.

The Masters of Old

One of the major differences between the ancient Eastern and Western paths was that of ego. The Eastern traditions have often sought to eliminate the ego or lessen its importance. The Western path teaches us not to identify with ego or destroy it, but to use it as a tool to survive normally in our culture and world. Yes, the ego can be a tool to help you relate in a positive and beneficial manner to the world around you. It permits you to appear like everyone else and lead, to all other eyes, a perfectly normal and ordinary existence. Of course, you can see how useful this was during the times of bitter persecution. A Wizard knows the ways and customs of his times and does not necessarily seek to stand out.

To be perfectly honest, the real masters of the old traditions are nearly impossible to identify unless they wish you to know. They usually don't wear metaphysical jewelry because they carry the spiritual and religious precepts in their hearts, not around their necks or fingers. They don't wear robes in public or run around acting secretive and mysterious. To do so is considered childish, immature, and somewhat ludicrous. They are serene. They wear suits and ties or dresses and blouses because they know the ways and customs of their times, and to a certain extent, wish to be in harmony with this.

Psychically, they are so well cloaked that even for someone who is well trained it would be hard to detect them, if not impossible. So, if you want to wear robes, tons of metaphysical jewelry, and freak out the neighbors, this is probably not the path for you. I would discourage it as it draws unnecessary attention to yourself in an unbalanced manner. That is not to say that attention is bad; there is a proper time and place for everything and sometimes attention is necessary.

If you haven't guessed it already, I am obviously speaking from a Traditionalist point of view. One of our most powerful concerns has been for secrecy. It is how we have survived the persecutions and murders of our people that are within living memory for us. To preserve ourselves, our ways and traditions, we have sought total anonymity.

A Religion Without Congregations

The Old Religion, now, is really a priesthood without a congregation. In the old days, these people were the priests and priestesses of the religions of the people. During times of the Inquisition, the Old Religion was violently suppressed. This was not for reasons of spirituality, it was for social control and wealth. It was during this period that the people were forced to convert to Christianity, many times against their will. In order to perpetuate the Old Religion, the priesthood taught only others who would become priests or priestesses as it was simply too dangerous to have too many people involved.

While in Europe I went to one of the displays of torture instruments put on by a group of pacifists to inform people of the atrocities that were and still are being committed by secular and religious institutions. It was truly horrifying. There were special instruments of torture used by the Christians for women and passive homosexuals that were inserted anally or vaginally and then screws which opened up the sides and ripped the people apart internally. Many were absolutely fiendish in design and I was filled with revulsion. Many were old and had been used by the Inquisition on the Old Religionists and others, and there seemed to be piercing screams that still echoed from them. I left the exhibition physically ill, but full of respect for the people who, to preserve these truths for us, had faced these horrifying male inquisitors and their instruments of terror.

Knowing how little human nature changes through the years, I realized theses tortures again wait for us if our vigilance of religious and secular authority lapses. In all times, it has taken courage to follow your own truths and freedoms. In these times, we are very fortunate to have the freedoms that we do have, for we no longer face the physical terror and horrors of the tortures of the church. The horrific tortures have continued on a psychological and spiritual level against gay people and women by the church however, and have never been stopped. Who is to say if they are not more damaging than the physical torture? Who is to say that they are not as scarring or soul murdering? On these levels the Inquisition has never been discontinued or apologized for and has directly or indirectly caused the degradation, physical and spiritual deaths of millions even after secular authorities put a stop to the direct physical torture.

For people anywhere, it is madness to support any institution which oppresses, suppresses, or excludes you. Any institution, secular or religious, does not deserve the support of the people whom it oppresses, suppresses or excludes.

VERY TRADITIONAL VALUES

Obviously, I am breaking with our basic traditional values in writing this. At this time there is a desperate need for a workable, non-biased spiritual and religious tradition which heals, embraces and empowers gay men. I have tried to give something to those people who, because of orthodox religious traditions, have felt that deity has turned its back on them. For many of us it is our most desperate hour and it is necessary for gay men to know and experience the total love and acceptance of deity. Gays and members of the Old Religion were burned in the same fires, but the "faggots" like wood, were thrown directly on the fire. They never got the chance to breathe the smoke and die of asphyxiation like the Old Religionists. Their deaths were much more painful and horrible.

The Old Religionists and gays suffered together, died together, and have been reborn together. The Old Region traditionalists, recognizing the need of their still persecuted brothers and sisters, return to them now what remains they have been able to preserve through time of the lost gay spiritual traditions. They have been kept safe for you through the fires and beyond. We have tried to place them once again in your hands. With this in mind, we begin the aspects of the religious tradition.

Chapter One: The Gods

Choosing a Divinity

Deity by its nature is undifferentiated, an all-pervading Unity. To define it by a name places limitations on it. To truly speak to deity, one does not speak. When you choose a god or goddess, you are choosing an aspect of this one universal force. When you form a rapport with a differentiated deity, what you are doing is forming a bond with a doorway to the ultimate divinity. However, because it is aspected or differentiated, it is a doorway leading to the undifferentiated and unaspected.

Why choose an aspect of divinity? Because they are easier to relate to on a personal and psychological level. A gay person will feel more comfortable with a gay god, a straight person will feel more comfortable with a straight god. A white, black, yellow, or brown person will generally feel more comfortable relating to a god they can personally identify with. Personal as well as tribal gods are formed in this way. Totem gods fall into this category, as well as some nature gods. Each one of these is valid as they are aspects of one undifferentiated force. To say any of them is invalid is to misunderstand the nature of undifferentiated deity.

Religious Control vs. Spirituality

If one group tries to restrict access to deity, it shows that it is interested in social control rather than illumination. All of deity is valid, not only parts. If a particular group can cause others to feel that the deities they are able to form personal bonds with are invalid or wrong, they are teaching that all other peoples are invalid and inferior as well. If you stop a person from forming a personal rapport with a deity that he can relate to on his own terms, you disempower the person. Other social structures are dismantled eventually as well and if the affected people believe or accept the foreign teaching, that their personal god is wrong or evil, they become subjugated.

If all heterosexual people were forced by social structure to worship a gay differentiated god, they would become a subjugated people, placing themselves as second best or second class citizens as they are not able to psychologically identify or access divinity through this aspect. Following generations would be brainwashed from birth, but would remain (and view themselves as) second class. Having difficulty with this, they would have to trust that someone else would have greater ability to do this for them, as their self-esteem would be damaged. It would make them feel that they must depend on someone outside of themselves for their personal relationship to God. In many cases this would bring on great frustration and the only outlet for this frustration would be others, who like themselves are viewed as inferior or tainted. It would make some turn away from their very identity and try to turn into something that they were never intended to be, making them live a lie. This would also be incredibly damaging to the individual and other people. Because of their low self-esteem, the people would believe that it is permissible to be treated in an abusive fashion, as this would then appear to be the divine will put forth by the control group, and would probably not resist, or resist as much. In certain respects, this is how the caste system of India works, as well as the caste system in the Christian hierarchy.

REJECTING DOMINATION

If you empower these people who have been taught to disown or reject their own personal relation to the differentiated aspects of deity, you will cause social upheaval for the controlling groups. It is therefore not surprising to find the most heinous punishments in this world and the spirit world for establishing rapport with a personally empowering deity outside a control structure created for social domination. The greatest threats or warnings are directed at the people most feared by the control structure and people most able to destabilize them.

In ancient times, the punishment most often imposed for forming a personal rapport outside this control structure was death. Often the death of the entire family unit resulted, or at least lowering the family's social position through confiscation of property or social discrimination. To maintain their social control and wealth, the control group will do everything including social purges, using their false belief system to justify murder, defamation, and discrimination. The myth that a particular god is the only valid one is a myth developed for social domination and is not in harmony with divine laws or principles.

It becomes necessary therefore to find a deity that you can personally bond with and communicate with. This system has its own pantheon, but if you do not find a deity in this system to form a personal bond with, look elsewhere for one until you do. If you cannot find one in any other pantheon, invoke your own personal deity and ask its name. Your own god or goddess is as valid as anyone else's no matter how popular or how old in human history. Just because something is older does not mean that it is necessarily right for you, and if you think about it, all of the gods were accessed by someone in another time in the same way. They were frail human beings just like you, who lived in an earlier time. They were still subject to the same doubts, hopes, and insecurities that you yourself experience; this is part of the human condition that we all share. Do not place these people on a pedestal or give them more authority than you give yourself, as that only shows low self-esteem and a lack of understanding of how the human condition affects every one of us. This will empower you and lead you on the steps of your own personal realizations.

THE NATURE OF THE GODS

Now let us focus on different aspects of the Gods. The legends of the Gods are marvelous and wonderful things. As you come to investigate the stories of the Gods, you come to realize that They represent things that are very real, if in some way intangible. Take Venus for example, the Roman Goddess of Love. Venus corresponds to our emotions of love. If you have ever felt the emotion of love, you have felt the essence or emanation of Venus. If you have ever thought about love, you have meditated upon Venus. In this sense then, Venus represents a psychological and emotional function. If you have ever made love to someone, you have manifested the divine influence of Venus. Venus does not only represent love, but the force that caused love to come into being, just as Her son Eros caused passion to come into being. In many ways the ancients expressed these things in beautiful humanized analogies. It did not however mean that these things were not real. If that were so, your emotions of love would not be real. Venus arises in every human heart and to say She does not exist, or that she is not worshipped in some way in every human heart, is falsehood, whether you are pagan or not.

The Gods however are not just simply psychological functions. They are multi-faceted existences and awarenesses. If for example, you take the concept that in the Old Religion all things are interlinked, and the causes of love are interlinked, and love itself is interlinked, there arises out of this a very powerful primal cause that interpenetrates all of us, but is also beyond all of us. If this force or energy or vibration or whatever you wish to call it passes through every one of us and is interlinked through every one of us, then a great deal of energy is accumulated and it is conceivable that after thousands of years this energy would develop its own consciousness, since it arises out of consciousness. Then we have the existence and creation of a God or Goddess. The power of such a thing would be incredible, and if then this interlinked energy pattern went beyond our planet to other beings of consciousness, the buildup of energy and power would truly be awesome.

The ancients wished to express this and so came about the myths of the Gods that can be used to cover psychological functions but also much more. It was in an attempt to understand a universal principle and to gain rapport with these consciousnesses, that worship was instituted.

WHAT IS TRUE WORSHIP?

It is in coming to recognize these patterns in your own life and beginning to expand your awareness along these lines that the recognition of deity is found. As you expand your awareness, you actually follow in the footsteps of the Gods. This is what is meant by having a God in your life and in your heart, and in the end, you become a reflection or a channel for that energy to manifest itself. You come to have a small understanding of the being of a God or Goddess and so She or He becomes a personal matter to you, and this is true rapport. Through this rapport, great energy can be channelled as you link yourself to the great energy patterns of an immanent and transcendent being.

These energy patterns do have their own consciousness, so in that sense although They are a part of you, They can also be separate from you. They also have their own level of existence and being and it is for these that the ancient temples were built, that They would come and be present in the rites and ceremonies dedicated to Them. Don't think of the Gods as unreal or that even this is the only type of God that there is or that it is only a myth. Their powers have not faded or receded over the years, only our acknowledgement of Them and consequently the knowledge of our own selves.

FORMING PERSONAL RAPPORT

Naturally one of the most important aspects of the Old Religion as a religious and spiritual path is to come to know a personal deity. A list is given after this exercise to help you choose one specifically to come to know.

Before you go to bed at night, light a candle for that God. Say aloud or silently, "This candle is for _____." Sit in meditation on the attributes and myths of that God or Goddess if you know any, and call Them to come and visit you. You might find it beneficial to surround yourself through visualization with lavender or violet light. An aid in this process is to go into your bedroom, keeping the heat up a little so that you are not uncomfortable when you are undressed.

Make sure that there are just sheets on the bed and that they are pulled very tight so that you are comfortable but have as little relaxed body contact with anything as possible. You should be naked when you do this as this involves sensory deprivation in the best way that we can do without a tank or special apparatus. Either dim the lights or be in a room totally dark, and as you lie there meditate on your body becoming numb as though there is no feeling and that you are in a state of floating darkness at the beginning of time. Visualize yourself floating in a gray void, weightless and unattached to anything.

Stop the internal dialogue as best you can and call the name of the God or Goddess you wish to establish a rapport with, and wait expectantly. Hold this state for about fifteen minutes. This is a meditation; prayer is talking to deity, while meditation is listening to deity. If this does not work the first time just try later on or the next day.

It is wise to trust yourself if you begin to see or hear something in your mind. You may ask that They also appear to you in your dreams and guide you. Eventually you will see a light or something appear to you as you float in this gray void. This is a guide or God come to you. You'll hear their voice speaking to you. Listen and respond. Don't be frightened by your first contact. Then start to talk silently to your God and express how you really feel. After all, how can you expect to get to know someone at all on any level, much less form a close personal bond, unless you talk or communicate with them? After you have done this, it is also imperative to still the internal dialogue and listen for an answer. Indeed, if you listen hard enough, you'll stop the internal dialogue automatically. It's hard to get to know someone if it is only a one-sided conversation. If you do this every evening and are truly sincere about it, you will start getting a response soon.

Believe it or not, this is what worship is all about. What is worship, you ask? It is not bowing down and giving oblation, it is an act of love and accord with deity. When you feel the presences come (and They will), you won't feel so alone. You can ask for help and many times help, if appropriate, will be given.

When you truly come to love your deity, you'll know you've formed a true relationship and rapport with your God. This is both appropriate to the path and personally fulfilling. The answers will come in your heart and mind. Strive to listen and remember that if you go and ask a big favor of the person on the street you don't know, you probably won't get it. If you ask a close friend who is truly a friend, you are more likely to get a favorable response, and that's true in this case as well. (Also remember, to have a friend you have to be one.) But really, we're not talking about doing this to get something. That is pretty insincere and the wrong motivation and it will be seen through even by most people, much less a God. Don't plan on being just a user in this type of situation. If that is your pattern you are going to have to change it as this is about your evolution, not your acquisition.

Let's face it though, if you really do need something and you are sincere in your heart with the Gods and do form a close personal loving bond, They'll hear you. They are not judgmental. They are loving and want to be loved. They are formed in our image, after all. They abide by Their own laws that we may have little or no understanding of. But you are precious to Them, and in all fairness, They should be precious to you. After you come to form your bond with Them, that should be no problem.

Worship is to experience the divine.

Daga

The Daga is not a being with whom to form a rapport. The Daga is the foundation of all being, awareness, energy, matter, all that is, and all that is not. It is the undifferentiated manifest and unmanifest totality. It is listed here as a God concept, but no one can totally realize it. It must be approached through Bride or Angus Og.

Bride (pronounced "Breed")

Bride is the Mother Goddess of this system. She is often called Bride the Calm, as this is Her nature. She presides over all art and beauty beneath the sky and sea. Since man is the highest ideal of beauty, Bride presides at his birth. She is also a Goddess of milk and healing, as well as a Moon Goddess and Star Goddess.

Her long curly hair hangs down to her waist and is such a light golden as to almost silver, decked with fair spring flowers. Her eyes are a deep violet and where Her tears fall, there spring up violets as blue as her eyes. Her face is of peerless beauty and grace. Her garment is a white robe with shining silver spangles. Her mantle is a deep purple. Her symbol is the Moon. Over Her heart gleams a star-like crystal that is called the Guiding Star of Bride. It is as pure as Her thoughts and as bright as the joy that Angus Og gives Her.

In one hand, She carries a clear comb of silver adorned with gold and a silver mirror with four golden birds chased around its edges. In the other hand, she carries a white wand entwined with golden corn stalks with the tip glowing almost like a star. Her mantle is held in place with clasps of gold and silver. Her teeth are like pearls and She is as pure as the fresh fallen snow.

The linnet and the crane are Her special birds, the Unicorn her steed, and Her flower is the wild rose. All white animals are sacred to Her. Bride, unlike some other Goddess, has no dark or negative side. When Her symbol, the Moon, became dark, it simply meant that She had fallen asleep as it was thought that even a Goddess must sometimes sleep. Bride always remains pristine and pure and this is a constant state of being. In certain respects, this represents our own conscious awareness of being.

Angus Og (pronounced "Angus Og")

Angus Og is the lover of Bride. He is a Sun God and the Sun is His symbol. It is said His beauty is more beautiful than all beauty. His hair is golden and His eyes are violet. From His shoulders hangs His royal cape of crimson that the winds lift up and spread across the sky. He dresses in gold and white and wears greaves of silver with precious stones on His legs with shoes of gold. His shirt is embroidered with dragons and griffins. In His hand He holds a red gold harp with strings of silver. Carved over the harp are two birds that seem to be playing on it. About His head fly four birds that are His transformed kisses which He sends to men. His sword is also of gold. He is a Love God and the Father God of this system. He is a special patron of beauty and when He plays His harp, it is sweeter than all the music under the sky. He has a cloak of invisibility and is forever young. In certain respects He was similar to Pan, for He was called the Frightener or Disturber, for the plough teams and every sort of cattle that is used by men would make away in terror of Him. He is the God of the Mystery. His sacred animals are His birds and his two oxen.

Midhir (pronounced "Meath-ear")

Midhir is the God of Death and Transformation. He wears a long black cloak with shining silver threads woven through it, that gleam and sparkle and a brooch of gold that reaches across His shoulders on each side. Underneath He wears a purple tunic, with threads of red gold woven in. On His arm is a shield of silver with a golden rim and boss. Gems of gold are scattered upon it. His hair is fair yellow, shoulder length, with a band of gold to keep it from loosening.

He appears as a young warrior, with luminous gray eyes that shine like the flame of a candle. In His hand is a five-pronged spear covered with rings from heel to socket. He is represented by personal splendor in apparel and appearance.

He rides a black horse with a curled mane and tail. He also carries a dark sword. He guards the gates of death as Angus Og guards the gates of life. He is known as Midhir the Proud. His symbol is the night sky. His sacred animal is the elk.

Aidche (pronounced "Ithkheh")

Aidche is the Owl Goddess and all owls are sacred to Her. She is the Goddess of secret and silent wisdom. She is associated with Midhir as She knows and remembers His secret identity. The horned owls are especially sacred to Her.

She dresses in a brown mantle made of feathers, has golden eyes with feathered brown hair that streams down Her back and is enchantingly beautiful. Often, She questions more than she reveals, but Her questions are revealing in themselves. She is invoked for discovering lost or hidden knowledge, channelling information or writing magical workings. She is not lightly invoked, requiring much forethought. She is called by saying Her name three times while lighting a candle and waiting in silence.

Artio

Artio is the Bear Goddess and all bears are sacred to Her. She is invoked for protection of the clan and for the strength and power of the bear. She is especially close to Bride and acts as a protectress of Her. Woe betide the one who gets too close to the children of the Bear Goddess with evil intent for She can be very fierce. Mostly She is soft and gentle but is dual aspected in that She can also be raging, persistent, and dangerous if She is angered. Generally, She is retiring and does not like to be roused or disturbed unnecessarily. She is the patron of the Bear Warriors, and the special patron of gay women to whom She lends her strength. She wears dark colored skins and robes. She has brown eyes, black hair and bear ears. She is a rather solitary Goddess and appreciates time alone or with Her children or Her human female lovers. The men who form a rapport with Her are Her children, while the gay women who form a rapport become lovers. It is all love, but different kinds. She appreciates a fresh offering of the first fruits of spring. She is invoked with the posture of the bear that is standing with both hands raised in front, as though a bear was standing upright, and calling Her name three times.

Bogha Frois (pronounced "Boa-froish")

Bogha Frois is the Rainbow Goddess. She is a Love Goddess and is invoked for happiness. She is the blending of colors into one thing and as such is the reflection of enlightenment, and is composed thereof of pure beauty.

She is flaxen haired, blue eyed, and wears a many-colored cape with a white iridescent robe. She is very beautiful and very young. She has a somewhat changeable, very ethereal nature and sometimes has sisters. Her lover is Broen and She will not appear unless He is there. She is invoked with light through a crystal prism if there is no rainbow about. The bluebird is Her sacred bird. She speaks through the heart with the language of love.

Broen (pronounced "Broyne")

Broen is the Rain God. His head has a nimbus of clouds around it as he was created by the Daga from the clouds. He is invoked for rain and for the rivers of Life. He is also a Healing God as He washes away impurities. His garments are silver gray and He is black haired with gray eyes. He does not have a beard or mustache and He is quite young. He is changeable and can be gentle and soft, or He can be black visage and stormy. He therefore has a dual nature as He is light or heavy, heavy rain. This also hints at bisexuality. His weapon is the thunderbolt. He is invoked by the sprinkling of pure water upon the earth and speaks through the sound of the falling rain and thunder. The otter is His sacred animal.

Cron

Cron is the Goddess of Mischief. She is very small and childlike but She creates chaos and confusion. She has curly bright red hair, green eyes, and always dresses in reds and blacks. She is invoked to stop harassment. If She takes something, She leaves something in its place, something gold. She is not all bad, just mainly interested in excitement and basically causes problems. The magpie is Her sacred bird and the packrat her sacred animal. She is invoked by the calling of Her name.

Cruinda (pronounced "Croontha")

Cruinda is literally Mother Earth. She is the great pervading Goddess of beast, man, field, and forest. She is invoked for skill in harmonizing one's actions with all things and especially invoked at planting time. Most rituals to Cruinda were done in the latter part of April and most of these were for fertility. She is invoked for magic as well. She is seen as a buxom woman, flaxen haired, brown eyes, dressed in forest green homespun. Her complexion is dark brown and She can be recognized in the Black Madonna of Christianity. The Church could not eradicate Her worship and so included Her. Her color comes from the rich loam of the earth. Cruinda is a Goddess of Magic. All creatures are sacred to Cruinda. Her voice can be heard by laying and listening to the sounds of the earth near a cave or hollow in the ground. You can create this hollow yourself as this gives Her voice.

Dubro

Dubro is the Beaver God. He is Guardian of all Beavers and the creator of refuges. He is invoked for sanctuary, virility, and retribution. He brings beauty and peace where before them were strife.

He is blustery and rotund. He has brown bushy hair and a beard, brown eyes, with small beaver teeth in front. He dresses in browns with silver threads woven in. He is the guardian of the creatures of the rivers and pools, as well as children. He is invoked by the slapping of water.

Elanti

Elanti is the Deer Goddess. She is the Guardian of all Deer. She is invoked for food, clothing, peace, fulfillment, generosity, freedom and beauty, as well as the hunt. She is also invoked for gracefulness of movement, and is therefore the Goddess of Dance. She has brown eyes, brown hair, very small stag horns, long hair, and dresses mainly in browns with white or black trim, or furs. She is very gentle, beautiful, and doe-eyed. She is the special patron of magic taught in this system, and so of course of gay magic. She is invoked by the clicking of two antler horns together.

Fogamur (pronounced "Foa-mor")

Fogamur is the Goddess of the Harvest. She is invoked for a bountiful harvest, and the abundant fruition of one's efforts. She has golden hair, tawny skin, and brown eyes. She wears garments of yellow and green cloth. She is very generous and loving, bestowing many blessings upon Her people. She is invoked by the shaking of grain from its sheath, and

She speaks through the sound of the wind blowing through the dry corn. Her sacred animal is the partridge.

Gaith (pronounced "Gah")

Gaith is the Wind and the Storm God. He is very mischievous and is invoked for gentle winds or gales. He has brown hair, gray eyes, a beard and mustache. He is tall and handsome and wears a gray cloak that billows out behind Him. The garments that He wears are normally dark blue and grays. He is a wild God, but loving and is especially fond of gay men. They are His special children and He is greatly concerned for their welfare. His consort is Vroiko, but he is sometimes seen with Broen. His animal is the blue jay. The special means used to invoke Him is to take some incense and gently blow it in the air with your breath or burn it while breathing upon it, or barring that, to whistle an invocation to Him. This is done by giving three strong whistles while facing north, the end note dropping low. He speaks through the sound of the wind and can be heard if listened for.

Ghiuthais (pronounced "Yoo-hes")

Ghiuthais is the Pine God, the Giver of Gifts. He gives beauty, wood, pine nuts to eat and so forth. He is an important God of Yule as the presents placed under His tree are under His protection. He is the guardian spirit of all pine trees.

He wears a cloak of green and a tunic of brown, has brown eyes and hair. He is happy, serene, and generous. The pine is the tree of illumination on a physical and spiritual level as He can be the Torch of Knowledge. His blood is pure incense and as such the pine is a holy tree. He has great generative power and the power to purify. His consort is Guithas. He is invoked when walking among the pine trees or when burning pine incense. His sacred animal is the squirrel.

Guithas (pronounced "Gew-has")

Guithas is the Fir Goddess. She has green eyes and brown hair. She wears a dark green cloak and a brown gown. She is invoked for life, fertility, strength, and shelter. She saw Her peoples through dark and hard times and gave them warmth. Ghiuthais is Her consort. All forest animals are under Her protection, but the robin is Her sacred animal. She is invoked by the shaking of a fir cone or when walking among the fir trees.

Katto

Katto is the Cat Goddess and all cats are sacred to Her, especially orange or "marmalade" cats. She is very loving and independent. She is invoked for comfort and contentment. She is also invoked for warnings of harm to come and thus protective. She has orangish hair, green eyes, and the ears of a cat. Her gowns are oranges and yellows which sometimes are striped. She is also Goddess of the Hearth. She takes who She wants when She wants a lover. She is invoked with a special offering of milk.

Kavaro

Kavaro is a Provider God. He is the Hero God. He is invoked for skill or help in any form. He is a great protector of His people and never lets them starve. He is invoked for justice and is associated with safety and abundance in general. Because of His good deeds and heroism, He was rewarded by the Daga at Bride's request with invincibility. His arrows always hit their mark. He has a small round shield that swells when He is in danger until it covers Him. His shield cannot be penetrated. He is very stern and strict and seen nearly always in furs or red clothes. He has brown eyes with red hair and a beard. He is in the peak of physical condition, and is mentally brilliant. He is a perfect example of manly and godly beauty. He has one rule and that is that nothing at all be wasted. Bones were used for utensils, hide for covering, meat to eat. He is somewhat of a rascal but is courageous and important. All the Gods and

Goddesses love Him as well as His warriors, but His special lover is Cruinda. He was known to have affairs, as He was a polygamous God. This comes from the times when the old clans were nearly wiped out and there were very few men left after the battles to re-establish the tribe. Sadly, polygamy was mandatory or the tribes would have ended for the lack of children. He is invoked whenever you are in need. His voice can be heard in your heart in special moments requiring courage. The badger is His sacred animal.

Laku

Laku is the Goddess of Lakes and Rivers. She is the Goddess of all fresh water as Manannan is the God of all salt waters. They meet and kiss on the beaches and inlets where the streams and rivers meet the sea. She is the consort of Manannan. She is very beautiful, with clear blue eyes, black hair and fair skin. She wears a blue gown that sparkles and dazzles the eye. She is invoked for food and for life and protection on rivers and lakes. She is also the one who grants rulership or authority, for whoever controls the waters controls the lands. Her nature is purifying and She is also invoked for healings. She is invoked by the pouring of pure fresh water into a stream. The salmon and trout are Her sacred creatures. She speaks through the sound of falling waters.

Lukot (pronounced "Lûkot")

Lukot is the Mouse God, and all mice are sacred to Him. Lukot is the smallest of all the Gods and Goddesses. Lukot is invoked to protect the stored grain. He is therefore a God of sharing and preservation during hard times. Make no mistake, He is a good God of subtle but powerful magic. The story of the Mouse and the Lion in Aesop's fables is a good representation of His nature. He has rescued His people many times. He dresses mainly in gray and is very shy and retiring. He is rather sneaky, like a field mouse. His appearance is like an elf, with large ears that are rounded, not pointed. He wears a pointed hat, has beady eyes, wears a gray tail coat, gray knee britches, gray socks and shoes. He wears white ruffles at His throat. He is the guardian of all field mice. It was thought that if a little grain was shared with the field mice, Lukot would keep them away from the rest. He is invoked with an offering of grain.

Manannan (pronounced "Mahn-ah-nan")

Manannan is tall and beautiful, with eyes as blue green as the sea. He wears a cloak of every changing color, which could make Him invisible at will. He is the Lord of the Sea, beyond or under where the Evergreen Isle (the afterworld) is. He is therefore, the guide to this land.

He has a boat called Ocean Sweeper that moves merely by thought, and his steed, Aonbarr (Splendid Mane) which can travel alike overland and sea. He has a number of swords and spears. No weapon can hurt Him through His magic mail and breastplate. If He shakes His mantle, a storm will arise on the sea. If He shakes His cloak between two people, they would never meet again for eternity. His helm is crested like the white horsehair (or sea foam) blowing in the wind, but with a blueness in it. It also has two magic jewels on it that are as bright as the sun. There is a cold curling flame under the soles of His feet. He is the Guide of Souls, the Initiator. He is the patron of sailors and merchants. He has a brown beard and hair, with webbed fingers and toes. The dolphin is His sacred animal and the albatross His sacred bird. He is invoked by calling with love for, and over, the sea. His voice can be heard in the sound of the waves.

Oeng

Oeng is the God of Fire. He is the Master of All Crafts. He is the son of the Fire Bird (the Sun), hatched from an egg that is laid. He has bright red hair that is feather-like, blue eyes with a beard and mustache and a ruddy complexion. He dresses mainly in yellows and reds with blue trim.

He is able to withstand fire as did the phoenix. He is friends with Katto and is very beautiful, but He can touch no one as He is so hot that anything he touches will be destroyed by His heat, so He must love only from afar. He is loved by Laku and He loves Her back, but They can never meet, and thus their love is unrequited. He is invoked by placing frankincense in a fire, and He speaks through the crackling of the flames.

Ostara

Ostara is the Hare Goddess and all hares are sacred to Her. She is invoked for fertility, renewal, new beginnings, and joy. She is especially associated with springtime, the moon, the resurrection of vegetation, and new birth.

She is quite small, very quick, and dresses mainly in soft brown furs. Her eyes are dark brown and She is very pretty in a gentle feminine way. She is very shy and retiring and has small rabbit ears which do not detract from Her special beauty. Her sacred symbol is the egg which denotes life and fertility out of barrenness, as well as the world. Her love is all life and She is invoked by concern for life.

Reothadh (pronounced "Row-thath")

Reothadh is the Frost Goddess. She is usually invoked to depart and take away the bite of frost and cold. She is very beautiful with white silvery hair and light blue eyes. She dresses in white furs and Her enchantments can turn ugliness to beauty. Consequently, when She is invoked, She is invoked for beauty like that of frost patterns or snowflakes. Her lover is Snechta. She can represent the fading away of life and as such is hardly ever invoked. She comes when there is a frost. The goat is sacred to Her. She speaks through the crackling of the frost.

Sebac

Sebac is the Falcon Goddess. She is a Goddess of the Sky and of the falcons and hawks. Like the incense smoke, She carries your prayers to the Gods. She is invoked for safe journeys and hunting, as well as clear vision and farsightedness in the sense of prescience and understanding the responsibilities and the outcome of one's actions. Since Her area of influence is the sky, She is invoked for weather magic. She can appear as a beautiful woman with a falcon's head, or as a woman whose hair is brown and feathery, which extends down to form wings with hands at their ends, dressed in a brown robe with a white mantle made of feathers. She is invoked by calling Her name three times with the hands raised, tips of thumbs touching, and fingers splayed.

Snechta

Snechta is the Snow God. He is very powerful and is invoked for protection and also for a hiding place. He protected His people by burying their pursuers in a blizzard. He is similar to a very kind old Father Winter and as such was the giver of surcease from work, many gifts and rest. He can also be very fierce when angry. He, like His lover, Reothadh, dresses in white furs, has white hair and light blue eyes. He is present in the snows and most often is invoked to leave. His voice can be heard in the crackling of ice. The white fox is sacred to Him.

Torko

Torko is the Boar God, and all boars are sacred to Him. He is invoked for the hunt and for battle. Consequently, He is also a War God, known for perseverance, speed, and cunning. The boar warriors were masters of disguise and escape and used the power of Torko for super human strength and power.

He is short and fat, a great eater, and has bristly hair and a beard. When He shaves, bristles immediately reappear. Torko has boar tusks, but is still very handsome. He has brownish gray hair and brown eyes. To be under His protection a boar's tusk is worn. He is called upon for courage and resourcefulness. He wears a black cloak and gray clothes or furs and can be very fierce or the truest friend known. He is the guardian of all boars and forest creatures. He taught men the ways of tilling the earth. His only lovers would perhaps be warrior brothers or sisters. He is invoked by the turning over of a small piece of turf.

Vailo (pronounced "Wye-low")

Vailo is the Wolf God and all wolves are sacred to him. He is invoked for organization, strength, protection, and focus on a goal. The Wolf God is closely associated with Angus Og and is considered as one of the family by Bride and Angus Og. He is invoked also for battle and is an aggressor of the clan and is very fierce. If He is invoked unjustly however, there is a chance that He will turn upon the invoker, therefore He is invoked for battle only, with great solemnity, thought and care.

Wolves were accepted into the clan by the Old Wizards for hunting, stalking, and protection. The wolf is an extremely psychic animal and can also communicate well with humans if the wolf chooses to and the person listens. The Wizards are conversationalists, but the wolf should be of special interest as it is a cult animal and an ally. In other words, it is still clan and is loved as such. He was the patron of the Wolf Warriors.

Vailo is very sociable with both Gods and men, although He approaches warily and waits in silence to see if someone is trustworthy. He is incredibly protective once a rapport is established. He is cunning, wise, and very loving. He has wolf ears, golden eyes, but is very handsome. He dresses mainly in gray wolves' furs with skin shoes and leggings. He tolerates no disrespect, but loves His people. He is invoked with the voice of a wolf's howl.

Veikos (pronounced "Way-kos")

Veikos is the Raven God, thus He is the Guardian of all Ravens. He is a god of wisdom and of guidance. He teaches the stepping forward into new opportunities and situations, walking closely in front of you. He relays messages to and between the gods if asked. He is a regal and beautiful god and can appear with a strong and graceful man's body with a raven's head, or as a handsome man with black eyes and black feathery hair that extends down over His shoulders to form winged arms ending with hands. He opens to you doorways of the mind, forgotten and lost to peace and freedom. He is associated with the stars. He dresses with a black robe or sometimes just a black loin cloth made of feathers. He is invoked generally at night by gazing at the stars and seeing ravens' wings behind them in the blackness, while calling His name three times.

Vroiko

Vroiko is the Heather God. He wears the purple of the heather and has black hair and violet eyes, and is stunningly beautiful. He is the God of the fields, flowers, and moors. He is a Love and Peace God, as well as a Warrior God, guarding peace through strength and was thus invoked to stop quarrels. He is also invoked to hasten spring back to the moors and to end the coldness of winter because when the heather blooms, the crops and animals are safe from the cold. He is also the God of Self-worth, so it is very wise to have good self-esteem when invoking Him. If you invoke Him without a good sense of self-worth, it can be perilous, because self-doubt or low self-esteem is not something He tolerates.

He is very beautiful and His spirit is as sweet as the glorious scent of the heather. Gaith is His consort, although Vroiko has also taken worthy men as lovers. He represents the beauty of love, as Fogamur represents the fruition of love. He is invoked by the offering of flowers. He is actually the Gay God in this system, although Gaith fulfills this function as well.

Vroiko is really an androgynous God and can also be referred to as Goddess, as this deity can appear in either male or female form. In either case, this God/dess carries the gay function and is the special patron of the gay people in this system. The hummingbird is sacred to Vroiko.

A special note from the author must go with this deity. Having an experience with this deity taught me several things. When He looks at you, He truly looks to the very core of your being, which can be terrifying. He can appear during periods of self-doubt and if He finds you unworthy, you may find yourself in trouble. The old legends state He won His battles by just talking with the enemy before battle, and His self-confidence and strength were so great that His enemies fled before Him even before battle was enjoined. Thus, He is a warrior God never known to have actually engaged in battle. When a warrior appeared before Him with self-doubt and He accepted him, the warrior knew that he had worth or Vroiko would not have permitted him to remain. He tolerates no one in His presence who does not feel or have self-worth and to approach Him without it invites peril. I feel it only ethical to include these comments about this God here, and to say that this deity is not one to be invoked thoughtlessly or carelessly, or without major amounts of introspection.

INVOCATIONS TO THE GODS

Invocation to Bride

O great and gracious Goddess, Mother of us all, hear me.
Let Your influence be felt across the lands. Gift us with
Your wisdom that teaches the connectedness of all things.
Help us on the path of spiritual illumination in Your
gentle evolving way. Bless Your children who honor You,
and rise again to Your ancient place of honor, for
until You do we shall not be free. Reinstate Your ancient
worship and let Your influence once again be felt
in the kind actions and compassion for all.
Free us of the bonds and hatreds of institutions
who would sell people's spirits and souls for
greed and gain.

*Let us feel Your influence in our lives so that we accept
Your qualities in us as holy and perfect in their own right.
Assist us to integrate these in our minds, hearts,
and actions understanding their correctness, beauty and
sacredness.
We love You, Beloved Mother, and we need You to manifest
in our culture and our lives, for if You do not we shall
not survive. Bless us and be with us, Beloved Bride.
So be it.*

Invocation to Angus Og
*Oh bright and shining Angus Og, God who brightens
our days, and gives us strength and warmth. O ancient
God of illumination and brightness, teach us to shine
as brightly and as beautifully as You. Grant us Your
strength and bravery in battle. Teach us what to
strive for, and to see through the darkness of deception.
Show us what is worth protecting, and what is worth
letting go. Teach us to accept help from others, as
You accepted it of Bride, and not be ashamed.
You learned proper values and priorities through trial and sorrow.
Teach us this knowledge, that we might learn without pain, if it may be,
Protect us, O great Protector.
So be it.*

Invocation to Midhir
*O great Midhir, God of Endings and Transformation,
guide us through all of the transformations and endings
in our lives without fear or pain. Help us to
recognize that out of each change, good comes even if
it seems dark for a moment.*

Through the Fires

O God of Relinquishment, help us release our limitations
and narrow self-concepts to a greater field. Help us
to realize You as a friend and gracious conductor, giver
of peace and releaser of our pain.
O Shining Midhir, God of Personal Splendor, welcome
us with gentle grace as we tread the path towards renewal
on a personal level.
Permit us to see that You walk with us at the close of each
moment, each day, each year, and each life as a friend
and companion.
Let us know You as someone who is interested
in the best for our personal evolution.
Bless us Midhir, that we appreciate life, friends, and all
creation, for it seems these things last for but a moment
then we pass away, and are reborn from the arms of Bride and
Angus Og. Things seem of more value when they are limited
Midhir, it is no wonder you are a God of Wealth.
Be our friend and teach us Your Wisdom.
So be it.

Invocation to Aidche
O wise and beautiful Aidche, Goddess of the Owls
Silent Goddess of darkened forests
Come to us in our moments of darkness
And give us Your counsel and wisdom.
Speak to our hearts in our moments of quandary
And show us how to see through the shaded veils
That may obscure our lives.
Gift us with Your hidden wisdom,
Teach us of the ancient knowledge and hidden ways.
Show us how to approach power with wisdom and knowledge

That we may be like You.
Bless us with Your presence and guidance,
O wondrous Aidche, fly with us through our lives
So be it.

Invocation to Bogha Frois
O iridescent-robed Bogha Frois, Beautiful Goddess of the Rainbow, bless us with Your radiant beauty. Remind us that there is great beauty in diversity. Each color of the rainbow, Your garment, is filled with beauty, but behind the garment we find You, whole and complete. Assist us to find the beauty in our own divergent qualities, and recognize behind all these qualities, there is only Us, our being, our awareness. Help us to see that our different qualities, our different tribes and our different preferences are all coming from the one awareness behind you all. We ask You to send us beauty, make us as beautiful as You, as gracious and as full of hope and love. Let us take joy in our differences, as You in Your robe of many colors. Bless us, Transcendent Goddess, and let us manifest as You.
So be it.

Invocation to Broen
O mighty Broen, God of the Sky Waters,
Send Your sky streams down to quench the parched earth
Let the rains fall down so that the rivers of life may flow freely once more. Our crops and our animals need water. Hear the cries of the clan that honors thee.
Bless us, O great Broen, and let our crops and our lives be plentiful and good. We love You for the beauty You create.

Through the Fires

So be it.

Invocation to Cruinda

*O Sublime Cruinda, Goddess of the Earth, bless me
O Great Mother, with the realization necessary for
survival, not only for my clan, but for all others.
Give me the realizations that when You are harmed, I am
harmed on a personal and individual level.
O Goddess who is blood of my blood, flesh of my flesh,
bone of my bone, heart of my heart, and hope of my
hopes, hear me. When you are poisoned, I am poisoned,
when you are burnt, I am burnt, when you are raped, I
am raped. Help me, O great Mother,
to stop these violations, for have you not taught us
that there is no person nor institution, no matter
how great, which has the right to rape?
Grant me the visions of Your enduring grandeur uncorrupted.
Lavish upon me the visions of the glory
of all the tribes in harmony with You.
Keep these visions within me, Your child, that I create them.
Bless all Your children and preserve us,
we who shall try to return to harmony the evil done.
Give us the strength to confront the small hearted people
of personal greed. Aid us Cruinda, as we strive to aid You.
So be it.*

Invocation to Dubro

*O great Dubro, Creator of Refuges and protector
of the weak, grant us Thy wisdom to understand that
refuges are a necessity for all of us to build strength.
Teach us to find the refuges in our minds, spirits,*

*and hearts. Help us to find these places in the
world around us, not only for ourselves and for others
in our tribes who may be upon the catastrophic brink
of total destruction.
Help us to realize that a refuge should not become a prison,
but a place to heal before the struggle is carried on again
to our eventual victory.
Bless us, O great Dubro, that we know when to come, and
know when to go, for among the dangers are also others
who may need to know the way to safety, and they may
not find it without us. Guide us to You and your ways,
and know in Your own peace, that we love and honor You.
So be it.*

Invocation to Elanti

*O beautiful Elanti, Goddess of the Deer,
Teach us grace and beauty, in our movements,
thoughts, feelings, aspirations, hopes and relationships.
Teach us to use all of our senses to enjoy life
to its fullest, and avoid the errors
that lurk in life's path.
Make us aware of the dance of being, that we may find joy
and join in it fully, realizing each movement we make
affects our future, and all others around us.
Show us how to trust our perceptions, and act with
integrity and responsibility, responding in a healing
and healthy manner with understanding towards all.
Teach us to be great wizards, unfolding within us
the abilities granted to Thy children by Thy grace.
O great Elanti, instruct us how to live our
lives in a peaceful, non-aggressive way,*

*and how to defend this in a correct manner
when called upon to do so.
Bring us personal serenity, joy, and vitality
so that we may be strong when others come to us
weak from the world's cares.
Instruct us in Your Wisdom, ways, and power.
So be it.*

Invocation to Gaith

*O most free of all the Gods, Beloved Gaith, bless us and hear us. Teach us to be as free and wild as the winds, bound by nothing, strong and unrestrained. Show us how to evade our oppressors, and to slip through their fingers and around their grasp as does the wind. Let us rise up above limitations and restrictions to simply manifest as we are, as who we truly are. Special patron of my people, reflect in us Your freedom, Your rejection of confining situations which become a slow death. Let us, just for a moment, taste the heights and the depths of the world around us so our experiences are complete, and thus achieve wisdom. Free us from the walls of bound oppression and false conceptions that we must stay within. Help us to be free enough to achieve our greatest goals and aspirations. Help us touch the roof of the heavens in our achievements and realizations. Teach us the freedom of the mind and spirit, which can only be bound by our agreement. Teach us to be as limitless and as flexible as You.
So be it.*

Invocation to Katto

O beautiful green eyed Goddess
Lady of peace and contentment
Defend our home against discord and pain.
Let Your gentle soothing influence flow
throughout our home, like the comforting sound of your purring contentment.
Fierce protectress that You are, hold at bay any unwanted invasions of our home, Your territory, by evil forces.
Let the warmth of our hearts be as a hearth to You, that You may come and warm Yourself.
We receive Your love, even those of us who are as outcasts to our own kind, You nestle firm against us in Gratitude. Bless us and ours with peace, we ask it of Thee.
So be it.

Invocation to Kavaro

O great Kavaro, Hero God of our people.
Lend us Your strength against adversity,
against injustice, and against untruths.
Let Your shield swell around us, that we
Be protected against the cruel points of those who would suppress our freedom.
Teach us, O great Kavaro, to use all of our resources both within and outside of ourselves, to stop the destruction of Your people, places and times.
Show us the right goals to strive for, and let us gently reflect this wisdom to others.
Give us the courage to go against great odds and overcome them. Give us the courage in our own

daily lives to let us live our truths.
Truly, many of the greatest moments of courage are the
ones that no one else sees or knows about. Let us face
these knowing that we have Your support and guidance.
Let Your grace fall upon us as the personal fortitude
to live our lives richly, honestly,
hopefully, and fulfillingly
on all levels, and accept nothing less.
Give us the grace to show mercy and compassion,
as any great hero does.
Let us be secure in our own self knowledge and self-esteem,
and to cure what is wrong if there be ill.
Help us, O great Kavaro, to be as Thee.
So be it.

Invocation to Oeng

O brilliant Oeng, long have the days been dark and cold.
Yet during this time You have warmed our hearts and souls.
You have given us companionship and comfort. Your
Promise that we shall survive, and even thrive.
Teach us the ancient fire magic that once graced our lives.
Instruct us in passion and fervor so that we live
life fully and richly, sharing with all around.
Shine within our souls with the fire of joy and life
and let not the hard days of darkness dampen Your influence
in our lives. Shine forth through us with the job and
happiness of being. Bless us, oh great Oeng.
So be it.

Invocation to Ostara

O beautiful Ostara, Goddess of the Hare, bless us with

*the birth of creativity and renewal. Touch and draw
forth from the well springs of our beings, the creative
solutions to our problems. Let flow up the creation of
beauty, for beauty's sake alone. O shining Goddess of
Fertility, sweet bringer of youth and splendor,
manifest through us your qualities of regeneration.
As You spring forth You renew all around You, refresh also
our hearts, our minds, and our spirits. Bring forth
into the world the new born of all tribes, in their
perfection and helplessness, reminding us we are
their protectors against the adversity of life, and the
trusted keepers of their inheritance and future.
Let us hold the newborn of each tribe with reverence, for
it is through Your grace that there is continuance. Life
is sacred to You.
How Your heart must grieve for all the children, now lost
forever, of the tribes that are no more. O Ostara, show
us the priorities necessary, and the heart
and love to stop this from happening more.
Grieve for the lost babies of other tribes ended;
for some there is no one to grieve them but You.
Forgive us and bless us with wisdom. We love you.
So be it.*

Invocation to Sebac
*O powerful and regal Sebac, Goddess of the Falcons.
Give us clear vision and far sightedness in our works.
Teach us to be as sharp and alert as Yourself,
Warding us from pain and danger on our journeys
through life.
When we are depressed, let us meditate upon you.*

*Bear us high above the pain and trials to see the
clear skies above. Give us your overview so that
We shall know what is ahead and prepare.
Bless us with Your presence, O great Sebac,
Teaching us that above the clouds, there is
Clear skies in all things.
So be it.*

Invocation to Ghiuthais

*O Ancient God of the Pine, we come to honor Thee.
Long have You sustained Your people of the clan, with
food, shelter, beauty, incense, and inspiration.
No longer may the ways of men be to make Your charges just
a commodity to be bought and sold. To do so is a violation
of the Law of Life, for to take life without honor or
remorse is evil. You are our life, for we cannot live
without Your purifying, beautifying force.
Accept again, Your ancient place of honor and reverence,
not only once a year at Yule, but throughout the year.
Let your greenness and stark presence teach us illumination
by the light and love that You graciously surrender to us.
Teach us holiness, and the correctness of harmony as we
breathe Your essence. Guide us to the truth of being
with the Aid of Elanti, and show us how to live in peace,
purifying all around us just by our existence.
As you give us food, let us feed others nourishment on all
levels like You. Let us find and cultivate this quality
within ourselves. Guide us with Your wisdom, O Ancient
God of the Pine, Giver of the Gifts, and teach us to live
the right way, unashamed, in beauty and with sacredness.
So be it.*

Invocation to Torko

O brave Torko, Boar God supreme, cultivate in us the strength to persevere. When the way looks endless, give us the wisdom to approach this in the best way and to realize that there is an end of every road if the first step is taken. When the road looks hopeless, find within us the courage to hope and to dare, for nothing is truly hopeless if You are with us. When obstacles block our way, let nothing deter us, but find a way through that is best for all. If others make war upon us, O brave Torko, lead us with strength, victory, care, and let our oppressors know that we shall never surrender our dreams and aspirations, no matter the cost, no matter the wait, no matter the persecutions, until we achieve our goal. We will be free. Teach us to integrate the clan, that if one falls, another answers, and that if there is a loss to one, it is a loss to all, and let the knowledge and realizations be real. Show us personal and integrated strength, for together and with you, Torko, we shall not fail, no matter the odds. Always we can know we are not alone if You are with us.
So be it.

Invocation to Veikos

O great and gleaming Veikos, Messenger of the Gods
The Raven God whose eyes reflect the world as it is.
Chart the paths that lead us to our proper goals,
And shield us with Your great wings from the trials along the way.

*Teach us to communicate well, and to understand clearly.
Show us how to reach our enemies and make peace.
Guide us through the darkness to the shining points of light
that are our desires as though You guided us
among the Stars.
Lead us Veikos, in the ways of the Gods.
So be it.*

Invocation to Vroiko

*O handsome Vroiko, God of the Heather, with Your
black hair and violet eyes, teach us of beauty.
Let us see the beauty of our own souls, and those
of the clan around us.
Show us the perfect beauty of nature, untouched
and unharmed by man, and that this perfect nature
lives within us harmed only by our misconceptions.
Indeed, that nature is ours by right and by love
Share with us Vroiko, the love You carry within You.
Let the same love manifest within us, Vroiko, expose it to the light
of day, and let our emotions manifest
in beauty perfect as the flowers. Let the one who would
crush the love of others heal and put forth beauty, harmony,
and blessedness. Let him learn self regard and self respect,
so that he respects others, and we respect ourselves.
Teach us how to be immune to the poisons of others
Vroiko, and as the forest overgrows the wood cutters ax,
teach us to heal from harm so that our beauty may once
again manifest, to be seen by all. Lead us into the
mysteries of beauty, by this way we shall learn perfection.
So be it.*

Invocation to the Gods to Bless the Feast

O Gracious Goddess and Gentle God
We thank Thee for this bounty spread before us.
Send upon us Your blessings and grace. We thank Thee,
O Cruinda, Fogamur, and all of the beautiful Goddesses
and Gods who make our existence and happiness possible.
We shall honor the law of Kavaro, and we shall remember
To return something to You, O Cruinda, for what is given.
Bless us one and all.
So be it.

Chapter Two: Tools

This chapter discusses all of the tools that are used in this system. As far as the strictly ritual tools, first and foremost it should be remembered that they are objectified symbols. There is no inherent magic power in any tool in its natural state, yet there can be great power or energy in the concepts the tools symbolize. Changes in awareness and the manipulation of energy is done with the manipulation of concepts on a mental level, and indeed, you cannot truly master what I am hoping to teach you here unless you can manipulate these concepts without tools. However, if you are beginning these practices you *must* have these tools. Don't consider yourself so advanced that you do not need them if you have never worked with them. Even if you feel you do not need them, perhaps the person you pass your experience onto will need objectified concepts in the form of tools to begin to understand the manipulation of concepts. I usually get a lot of flack on this from the few people I have taught because they usually consider themselves too advanced to need them. If they're that advanced, then they shouldn't need me either, so I end up being very firm. After years of experience, they usually end up agreeing with me, and they realize why. Besides that, there is great beauty to be expressed by the using of beautiful objects in a ceremonial form, if properly understood. So, with all of this said, we shall begin with a list of tools and what they represent.

It should be remembered that all of the tools should be consecrated to the Gods, and used only for ritual or personal religious use, absolutely nothing mundane.

DIRK

The first tool that we shall cover is called the dirk. It is a black handled double-edged knife. Its handle is made of a natural substance, either wood or bone. According to tradition if you buy it you must not haggle over the price, but it's best if you make it yourself. Although buying it is easier, if you make it yourself, you can make it just how you want it to be, which is best. Your tools should all be very pleasing to you. It doesn't have to be sharp because it is never permitted to cut any material whatsoever, but I have also known people to keep it very sharp for symbolic reasons. Its use is purely and solely symbolic. On this level it symbolizes your will and is a tool representing force. The two edges represent the two polarities, both positive and negative, or spirit and matter. It can be used in creating the boundaries of the globe and in summoning the Watchers, or Lords of the Elements. It also symbolizes the power to protect from evil and to protect justice and peace. It symbolizes courage. If you wish to direct personal power or energy to a friend in dire need of it, many times the dirk is used. It is a tool of personal power and it demands, it does not request. It came into use during the Middle Ages. Prior to that, only the wand was used magically.

The dirk is sacred to the Moon Goddess and if it cuts anything or touches the earth it must be reconsecrated. Don't drop it during a ceremony. It is worn hanging from the cingulum in its sheath on the right side of the robe.

SWORD

The sword has the same associations as the dirk but it is wielded only by the Servant of the God as a symbol of his authority in the group structure. It is wielded by no other with ancient penalties for this violation. There were also sociological reasons for this, as in times of history it was illegal to own a sword unless you were a member of the nobility. It is in the histories of the hereditary systems that did survive, that they survived among and because of the nobility. Contrary to modern thought, our systems did not survive among the peasantry, but because of the nobility of the family. It was these families which politically could not be touched by the Church, and which could afford to buy their way out of harm's way. It was because of this that the hereditary systems came down much more complete and intact than most other systems. Virtually all hereditary systems that I know of have ties to the old nobility, and the fact that the sword is found here is a remnant of that fact. Its use was incorporated during the medieval period, borrowed mainly from the ceremonial magicians.

Wand

The magic wand has been the most noticed of all the tools of magic in the Old Religion. Indeed, it can be the most beautiful. Traditionally the wand is made of willow, elder, hazel wood, mountain ash, or oak, but it can be made of any wood. Again, the tool is purely symbolic. It represents the power of request, persuading, and reasoning, rather than demanding like the dirk. Actually, the wand can be the most powerful of all of the tools as it is used in invoking the God and Goddess and channelling their power. Since the dirk represents personal power or ego-focused power, the wand represents divine power which is actually far stronger than personal power. It is one of the oldest magical tools in existence.

Mirror

This arose originally out of the reflective quality of the Moon Bowl. It has been adapted for modern use.

From the most ancient times, the mirror has been an attribute of the Goddess. The symbol of Venus, for example, is Her small hand mirror. In this system however, it is used to symbolize the Daga, which is neither male or female, but comprised of both.

Since there is nothing solid found on the other side of the mirror, it is as if you are looking directly into the realm of spirit. That is one of the reasons why it was bad luck to break a mirror, as you broke your spirit if it was reflected in the mirror. A mirror has a clean light that reflects everything as it is. It symbolizes the stainless and serene mind of the Daga. In ancient times it was an object of ceremonial and religious significance rather than of personal use. In many ways the mirror hides nothing. It shows everything exactly as it really is, good or bad, right or wrong, everything is reflected without fail. The mirror is the source of honesty because it has the virtue of responding according to the shape of objects. It points out the fairness and impartiality of the divine will. It shines without a selfish mind. It symbolizes the underlying power in nature, of the underworld, and of enlightenment. It is symbolic of hidden knowledge.

Usually a small round mirror is used in this system, and placed in the center of the altar.

COMB

The comb frequently accompanies the mirror on ancient carved standing stones. It was sometimes viewed as a feminine symbol but later it became an object of consecration. Objects connected literally or ideally with the hair of the head acquired a certain sanctity, the hair itself being peculiarly sacred as typifying from the earliest times the rays of the sun and moon. It can also be viewed as aligning energy patterns, thus making them positive or purifying them. Hence its reason for being a tool of consecration. It is made of wood or bone.

CHALICE

The chalice is traditionally made of silver, but a crystal or glass chalice will serve as well. Although I find that silver is more appropriate personally, I think that crystal is better because it does not corrode. Usually the chalice holds wine or salt water and salt does eat away at silver. So, unless you plan on putting away your tools and altar immediately after use, you may find that a crystal chalice will be more practical for you. Its most ancient form was that of a hollowed wooden burl.

The chalice holds water purified by salt to represent the feminine principle and also to represent the western quarter of liquid.

THURIBLE

The thurible is really just an incense burner. It should have a handle so that it can be lifted and moved. Many find the shape of a small cauldron the easiest to use and I would encourage it. It can be made of any heat withstanding material. It should be large enough to hold a small odorless charcoal briquette used for burning incense with some sand under it so that you do not burn the altar you set it upon, or enough sand to put some stick incense in it if you have no other kind of incense. Usually these briquettes are found at any religious supply house.

It represents the element of air or gases, and is placed in the eastern quadrant of the altar. Incense is considered the breath of the Gods, carrying your prayers and invocations to them.

PENTACLE

The pentacle in this system is usually a small dish with a pentagram or five pointed star inscribed upon it. It is used to hold salt generally, or small ceremonial cakes. In many traditions this is just a small bowl with no special ornamentation and in others it is used differently as it can be a magical shield. It represents the element of earth, and is placed in the northern quadrant of the altar. It symbolizes earth or solid matter and stability.

BOLLINE

The bolline is a sharp white handled knife. It really has no symbolic value like the wand or the dirk, its uses are actual. It is used to carve or cut symbols on handles, wood, cut string or cord, or whatever it needs to be used for in practical matters. It can even be used to draw symbols on the ground. It is also a necessary tool even though it has no symbolic value.

STAFF

The staff is used by the Servant of the God to stop talking in the globe. It is tapped three times. It is about six feet long. The staff can also be used to draw the Globe. If you wish it to just mark the globe, attach it to a nine-foot cingulum which is fixed to the centre of where you wished the globe to be. When it is used in this way its end is allowed to touch the ground.

MOON BOWL AND SUN BOWL

The Moon Bowl is the most ancient tool of the Old Religion. It belongs to the first mysteries of the Goddess coming from the shadowy mists of time. Because of the antiquity of this tool, I wished to include a place for it in this tradition. Much lore of the Moon Bowl has been forgotten. Once it was the only tool of the Old Religion. Its mysteries were tied to the blood, rebirth, and the Moon. In later times it was replaced by a reflective mirror, or other items which usually had clear or reflective qualities. Since this tool is of such great age, it was especially sacred to the Goddess. It was originally a large white shell, and later earthenware, but modern times have made it more often of metal. Often it has been silver, the moon metal, but earthenware is just fine. It was filled with salt water.

The Moon Bowl is always present when the Goddess is invoked to descend, and hopefully a reflection of the moon will also be showing in it when She is called down. If you are indoors or the sky is overcast, a silver coin, a white round stone or shell should be placed in the water of the bowl to represent the moon in the waters.

Three drops of red food coloring may also be added to activate the power of the bowl even more, although this is not necessary.

If a gay man chose to draw down the Goddess, instead of a silver mirror, a polished bronze mirror was used. He gazed upon the Moon in this golden colored mirror as he invoked Her. If She did not find him worthy as an individual to contain Her, She descended into the mirror and he gave oracle from this. This takes us back to something called the Sun Bowl. This is a polished bronze or gold bowl filled with salt water with a bronze or gold coin in the bottom, or filled instead with fire to represent the sun.

The Sun Bowl must be present for the descent of the God, and the Moon Bowl must be present for the descent of the Goddess. The Moon Bowl is the elder of the two. The appropriate bowls are placed at the feet of the person doing the drawing down of the Goddess.

POUCH

The pouch is worn on the cingulum. It was made of deerskin leather in the old days. Usually the pouch holds personal power objects or papers. Its use is like a pocket and you may use it to carry whatever you wish to take with you into the globe, including medication.

CINGULUM

This is the cord which is tied around the waist. It is used as a belt and is used to hold the dirk's sheath and the pouch. It was also measured out to make the ritual globes, being fixed to the center of the globe and used as a line to show how far out the globe should extend. It should be measured out to be nine feet long, or longer if you wish. Simply make knots farther down the cingulum to measure out a bigger globe, the first knot being at nine feet. The cingulum colors originally had reference to specific parts of the Myth or to what level you had progressed in the Wizard's Way but that must be dropped for public dissemination. Therefore, let the cingulum be of the color that matches your robe or to your own desire.

FIGURINES

There is usually on the altar an image of the God and Goddess. They are usually nude sculptured figures but can be a painting or drawing.

ROBES

We always work clothed in this system. Robes were worn and these were woolen, heavily padded or lined with sheepskin when they began keeping sheep. This was to keep out the bitter cold of northern Europe. The robes worn were loose and non-confining for comfort. If one goes back far enough they become the dress or cassock of the priestess and this has remained so even in the Catholic Church and among the Protestants usually in their choral groups. A robe is worn to take off the mundane world and put on a spiritual mentality, so it is something used only for sacred ceremonies. Since it is the wearing of a mentality, it is the body of the Goddess. They may be embroidered in any way you wish, the more energy you put into it the better.

The Wizard's Way does not really consider robes per se essential. This is a modernization. A jogging suit with a hood is just as good nowadays. As long as what you wear is loose and comfortable and used for no other purpose than ritual work, it is acceptable. If you wish to wear pants and a shirt, do so as long as they fit the requirements above. It is best if the whole group decides to wear the same thing as one reason that robes were also worn was to stop any differences in wealth or rank from being noticed, and to make sure everyone was the same as all are the same in the sight of the Gods. Under the ritual dress there is nothing worn, so the only thing you have on is your robe. The globe is always entered barefoot by everyone.

It is not incorrect to work nude but it is not traditional in this system or preferable. To be purely traditional, white robes are worn with pointed hoods by everyone except the Servants of the God and Goddess, who wore black. That was so that if the persecutors came upon them they would notice the white robed ones first and the Servants would have a better chance to flee as everyone else would act as decoys. Often times everyone wore black because it was easier for everyone to get away as well. Hoods have a psychic effect as it narrows your vision to a narrow focus during ritual work but also served to hide the faces of the people should the inquisition happen upon them. If you do not wish to use white, lavender the gay color, green the fairy color, or black will also do.

Amulets or Talismans

Among the old Wizards a piece of jewelry was usually worn during the ceremonies. Women wore a necklace of beaded jet, often with 13 beads, to represent the moons of the year. The men wore the tips of the tines of antlers as a pendant to represent the horns of the God. It would be good in this system for men to wear the tine of an antler around their necks as a pendant. If the group chooses a special symbol to represent their personal group, that can be worn or the Wizard's symbol can be worn. Actually, what is really important is the leather thong which it is placed upon for the thong represents the sacred circle and that philosophy.

ALTAR

The altar is a small round table upon which are placed the consecrated tools and holy objects of the tradition. When used in ritual context it is also considered a portal or opening to the realm of the Gods. It is placed in the exact center of the globe and is thus considered the heart and soul of the temple dedicated to the Gods. It is usually covered with an altar cloth which can be white, black, violet or red. Flowers were placed around the altar depending on the season. In the east were spring flowers, south, summer flowers, west, autumn flowers, holly and berries were always used at Yule in the north.

FLUTE

A flute is used in this system for ritual purification upon the entrance to the globe. The Wizards perceive the purifying qualities of music. The flute is played in a seven-note tonal scale upwards to achieve this effect. We do not believe in pain, or the semblance of pain, so achieve purification ritually.

MASKS

Masks are encouraged in the Wizard's Way. Each person should begin to feel a personal rapport with one of the spirits of the animal tribes and begin to study them. Creating an atavistic nostalgia is also encouraged when working with your animal guide. The creation of a mask to represent your animal guide is a good thing to work upon. These masks should only be worn for ceremony and personal meditation, never at any other time. It should not be used for parties, pagan get-togethers, or at any other time, period. These are sacred objects and as sacred objects they should not be exposed to general public view or laid upon the ground.

It was the old way for all to have a mask on of their totem animal while in the globe and during the rites. They are not necessary but they would be a good thing to bring back for a number of reasons. Check your local library for books on mask-making. Masks originated from face painting, so if you prefer, face painting may be used in place of masks (for convenience, collect greasepaints available at Halloween, or at some toy stores).

Consecration

This is a general ceremony for the consecration of sacred objects which will be placed upon your altar. This not only includes the tools which we have already gone over, but other small bowls or personal objects that you may wish to place upon your altar. The oils for anointing objects are sandalwood and frankincense. This consecration moves the object from mundane vibrations to spiritual vibrations, and the object should not be used again for mundane purposes.

Anoint the object with the first two fingers of the right hand with the consecrating oil while holding the object in your left hand. Hold the object aloft with both hands and say:

(Face east)
"In the names of the Guardians,
"Lord of the Eastern Reaches,

Through the Fires

(Face South)
"Lord of the Southern Reaches,
(Face West)
"Lady of the Western Reaches,
(Face North)
"Lady of the Northern Reaches,
"And by the power of this sacred oil, I invoke thee,
Gracious Goddess and Gentle God, imbue this _____
with the power needed to aid me in the performance
of my religious rites and magic. This is my will, so be it."

 Now sprinkle the object with salt water, pass it through the flame of a candle quickly, and then pass it through incense smoke (a floral one, if possible). This purifies, seals, and censes the object, making it holy. The consecration is finished.

 If the consecrated object is broken, it should be buried and returned to the earth, or burned. It is used no more.

Chapter Three: The Myths

The Reason for Myths

Usually the focus of the rituals in traditionalist Old Religion is based upon a main myth. The myth is always an allegory about the sun's procession through the cycle of the seasons. Other meanings and applications can apply as well.

In Old Religion theology time is seen as cyclical, not linear. In other words, creation is not seen as having a beginning, middle, or end, but is an endless cycling of day after day – not starting or stopping at midnight but continuing endlessly. In the Old Religion this view shifts the way that life and death are viewed from the way that is it generally viewed in this society.

Reincarnation

Reincarnation is one of the major tenets of the traditions. Just as the year has a continuously renewing of seasons, so we have a continuous renewal of life in different bodies. The period of transition of death is a resting period from the vicissitudes of life and a preparing place for another life. There the soul reviews what it has done and what it hopes to achieve under the gentle and careful guidance of the Gods. Every person has his or her own spiritual vibration as a person which manifests eventually in actions. Because of the high or low vibrations of the person, it is the intent with which something is done, not always the actual action, which determines the karmic flow. For an example, if a person pays a religious institution a great deal of money in hopes of buying a place in the afterlife which might be better than what their actual vibrations align to, it won't do any good because their intent is not to help others but to secure for themselves something that they know inside they don't deserve. In this case, it is the intent which determines the positivity or negativity of the actions.

When the body dies, the spirit, soul, or consciousness of the person ascends out of the body to the non-material or astral level of existence. Now this level of existence has many rates of vibration and while they interpenetrate each other, they are imperceptible in most ways to each other. The person's rate of vibration will determine which level that person goes to. You are still responsible for all of the unkindness or kindness you have done on a karmic level. They are not just wiped away. No, if you have done some unkindness, you must try to right your wrong but by the same token, you won't be sent to an eternal place of punishment either. You will simply return to right the wrongs you have done. This is not cause for personal despair or major guilt. What is done is done and cannot be changed. You can change your life so that you won't do the wrong thing again, in which case you have learned from your mistakes which is essential for growth. In a cyclical time view, remember, your past becomes your future.

To invoke divinity to assist you to the higher levels can be helpful, but as in most things in life, you are the one ultimately responsible for your own situations. Where you sit right now reading this is a culmination of every decision you have ever made. If you don't like where you are at, you must change your way of thinking and being.

After the spirit of consciousness or the person has learned and reviewed its own actions, it is again permitted to rebirth to correct the mistakes made or to help mankind on its evolution to eventual unity with deity.

THE RITUALS OF MYTH

Returning to our subject of myth, many of these points are represented by an allegory. The solar year is viewed as a wheel, turning from season to season, rite to rite. Yule (which actually means "wheel'), is the time of the 'birth' of the sun. It was thought that on the winter solstice the sun "died" at midnight, but was instantly reborn, just as we will be. At the solstices and the equinoxes, as well as the first day of each season, feasts and religious rites are held to celebrate the sun's progress. There are eight of these days, and they are called the High Days. The full moons were also celebrated as natural cycles of nature, and were for the celebration of the Goddess, as the High Days were for the celebration of the God.

The mythos then generally is solar orientated, although the religion in general is more lunar orientated.

Generally, the pagan myths represent a love story or companion or consort type of story, with a protagonist and an antagonist, with the Goddess usually not harmed or hurt, but always remaining stable through the myth. The Sun God may be wounded or killed, usually on October 31, or Samhain. He is taken into hiding to be cured by the Goddess or is killed. A part of the God is preserved and hidden from which eventually in the spring, the Goddess (or Mother Nature) brings forth or heals the Old One. Thus, the God is resurrected. This not only applies to the sun becoming stronger, but also to vegetation, which is resurrected from the dead, or dormancy.

Usually there is a ritual re-enactment of each part of the myth, either as a passion play, or as a liturgy describing the symbolic actions of the myth. For example, there is the wounding of the god, usually by His dark half, and this is enacted or described in ritual on Samhain. The other ceremonies are similar.

The purpose of the rituals is not only to celebrate the celestial events and seasons, they are there for us to see the cycles and events in our own lives and minds. The cycles you see around you are really the cycles of your own life. The acknowledgement of these outer cycles is also an acknowledgement of you and your inner processes as you progress.
The rituals in many ways form a spiral, just as our own lives do, towards illumination. As Yule celebrates rebirth, there are also many rebirths in our lives. Samhain also represents endings in our personal lives and evolution. Each ritual and mythic story refers not only to the passage of time, but to the events and passages in our own lives. Understanding that you are the myth is essential to the understandings of their correct use and the human condition as well.

Myth and The Human Psyche

The myths also represent psychological functions which are present in all of us. The antagonist who wounds or kills the Sun God, in many respects represents the dark side of our own psyche, while the Sun God represents our brightest ambitions and gentleness and kindnesses to the weak and helpless. He represents love as the Dark God represents greed. Don't make the mistake that that is all that the Gods represent. They have many levels as do all truths. Please don't think that the Dark God is all negative, it just is not so. It is a necessary part of ourselves that makes us complete. The Gods are multi-level beings, They don't just exist in your mind. They exist inside of us and outside of us, both.

The thing to remember about the dichotomy of the Sun God and the Dark God is that they are really one. Janus, for example, is represented by a door which has two sides representing both life and death. Metaphorically speaking it is two sides of the same coin. The Sun God generally represents life and the positive aspects of our own psyche, just as the dark side of the God represents death and the negative qualities in each of us. This may have no moral or social analogy, but simply be a state of the form of energy. Yet in the end through the beauty of the soul, represented by the Goddess, the positive qualities of the Sun God always prevail. The positive aspects of our own psyches always prevail just as the sun rises every morning.

This sets a positive view of our own evolution as people, and shows that eventually the positive aspects of life always prevail.
Generally speaking the High Days are almost strictly for worship rites, whereas the full moons were more often used for the manipulation of energy and consciousness usually termed "magic". Make no mistake, the full moon rituals show devotion to the Goddess, but generally the main works done are magic and meditation. Also, the High Days can be used for great magic as well, depending on the wishes and desires of the people participating.

These are not the only myths that are in the Old Religion. There are myths of how the world was created, how the Gods were created, myths about spiritual evolution, and myths that showed the Gods approval or disapproval of certain acts. Indeed, certain myths showed the natures of individual gods and considering the myth of Actaeon and the Virgin Diana, it would be most unwise to dedicate a sex spell to her. Instead of a blessing, in Her case you might get something back rather unpleasant. However, if you do a ritual or spell that has something to do with chastity, you might well be rewarded. Leave the sex magic to Venus, that delightful Goddess of Love. There seems to be a God or Goddess appropriate to most every type of rite you may wish to do, but do not annoy the Gods with things they may not like. It is wise to seek out the myths of the God or Goddess you wish to do a ritual to so that you don't make a major faux pas.

The myths also set out prescribed ways for the clans' social behavior in many ways.

The Myth of Bride and Angus Og

My brothers, let me tell you a story of what befell Bride and Angus Og. One afternoon long ago when Goddess and Gods walked the earth among men, Bride was walking through Her gardens with Her unicorn. Angus Og was a short ways away from Her as He was never far from His lover. She was smelling and enjoying Her sacred wild roses. As evening's shadows grew longer, She did not notice a darker shadow following closer and closer behind Her. Her unicorn noticed Him first, and screamed a warning as a dark form sprang forth towards Her. In a moment, Angus Og was there and intercepted Midhir, God of Death, as He sprang to carry Bride away. Long They fought and Angus Og fought well, but in an unguarded moment Midhir threw his spear and tabbed Angus Og in His chest. Angus Og looked at His wound in surprise, and then looked at Midhir as He slowly fell to His knees. When he had toppled to the ground Midhir turned and fled unable to bear the look in the eyes of Angus Og.

Bride cried out and rushed to His side and tore Her gown for a bandage to staunch the deadly wound. Realizing Her deadly peril, for it would be but a moment before Midhir returned to claim His prize, She managed with great difficulty to get Angus Og on Her unicorn's back and climbed up as well to hold Him.

"Flee!" She gasped, and the unicorn ran. Bride could hear the crashing and smashing of Her roses as Midhir returned and He caught a glimpse of Them as They rode away. When He saw this, He grew very angry and called His horse which was a black as night. Swiftly He mounted and rode after Them calling for Bride to stop.

"Faster, faster," She cried to Her unicorn and anxiously tried to think of a place to escape to. Finally, She cried to Her unicorn to take them to Manannan, the Sea God. The unicorn plunged on through the forest with Midhir in hot pursuit towards the West. At last the woods thinned and Bride saw the glinting of the ocean peering through the oak trees. The unicorn's chest was heaving and he was beginning to stumble as the weight of Them both was something he was not used to. Angus Og slumped heavily in Brides arms and droplets of blood seeped from His chest and down Her arm.

When They burst through the trees She saw the God Manannan with His chariot on the beach. He beckoned to Her and the unicorn bore Them to Him.

He helped take Angus Og from the unicorn and gathered Them in His chariot and let the unicorn go free. The unicorn waited momentarily for Them on the beach as They rode out over the water. When he heard Midhir crashing through the last few trees to the beach and knowing Bride was now safe, he turned and fled to the deep forest to wait for Her return.

Bride told Her story to Manannan as She held Angus Og against Her, His head to Her cheek. Manannan's visage grew grim and after a moment He told Them what He would do. He had seen omens that Bride would be in peril and had gone to look for Her and had met Her on His way.

"I shall take you to the Evergreen Isle," He said. "Midhir shall not think to look for You there. He shall look for You in My kingdom."

Indeed, as They had ridden away, They had seen Midhir thunder down the strand into the water and roar His curses after Them. They all knew He would not give up easily. They rode and rode across the waves in Manannan's magic chariot and finally the secret Evergreen Isle rose out of the sea in front of Them.

"Go and see the Daga," Manannan advised Her, "She may be able to heal Angus Og." He assisted Angus Og and Bride to a thicket of trees where They would be hidden. He rode away to try to stop or divert Midhir. Bride was alone with Angus Og and She let Him rest for a moment.

"Come, We must find the Daga," She said to Angus Og, but Angus Og knew He could rise no more.

"Beloved, You must go on alone for I can go no further, but take My four birds with You. As long as they live I shall be thinking of you. If they fail, so shall I." He lightly kissed Her four times and as He kissed Her, four small golden birds appeared and flew to Her. They glowed like beams of the Sun and they sang beautifully.

Bride begged Him to try to come but finally He urged Her on alone saying that He could not survive long, and Their only hope was for Bride to find the Daga,

So Bride with an anguished heart set out to find Daga, Queen of the Evergreen Isle. She walked for about a mile and a half. The birds were singing for Her as She went and they lightened Her heart because She knew Angus Og lived. She crossed a small stream, which cooled Her feet. Finally, She spied a fortress on a hill and made Her way towards it. It sat upon a hill for all to see but it looked forbidding and She was not at all sure it was even the right castle. It seemed very plain and unadorned. She noticed a door but it looked ominous to Her and so She walked on. She found another door but it was like the first and closed. Round the castle She went and in all She counted eight doors before She came back to where She had started.

She noticed that the birds had begun to falter in their songs, so gathering Her courage, She stepped up to the door and knocked. The door swung open before Her at Her first knock and She saw a passage way extending before Her. On all sides were wondrous pictures and tapestries and they slowly moved bedazzling Her. Looking neither to the left or right She moved on through the passage way that slowly curved. Before long, She came upon a Guardian robed in silver who was standing guard before a door.

"Is this the castle of the Daga?" Bride asked.

"Yes," the Guardian replied.

"I must see Him," Bride said, "It is most important. Please let Me pass, I'll pay You anything You ask," Bride replied desperately.

"Relinquish to Me Your blouse," the Guardian said.

Bride surrendered this without a word, and passed it to Guard who opened the door, and She passed through. She progressed down the corridor about 50 yards when She came to another closed door with another Guard, this time dressed in a robe of pale blue.

"Please let Me pass," said Bride, "I must see the Daga."

"I will let You pass if You surrender to Me Your necklace," said the Guardian. Bride took it off without regret and passed it to the Guardian, who opened the door. She walked down the corridor another fifty yards intent solely on what was ahead of Her and ignored the dazzling pictures around Her. She came upon another door with another Guardian dressed in a yellow robe.

"Please let Me pass," said Bride, "I must see the Daga."

"I will let You pass if You surrender to Me Your bracelets," said the Guardian. Bride took them off without remorse, and passed them to the Guardian who stepped forward and opened the door. As the Guardian did so, one of Angus Og's small birds dropped to the floor and was silent. Bride continued down the corridor until She was stopped again by another door and another Guardian, this time dressed in a golden colored robe.

"Please let Me pass," said Bride, "I must see the Daga."

"I will let You pass if You surrender Me Your brooch," said the guardian. Bride undid the clasp and handed it to Guardian. She held Her mantle together with Her hands. The Guardian opened the door, and let Her go through. Bride continued on down the corridor another fifty feet ignoring moving sculptures that tried to catch Her attention. Before Her came another door, with a Guardian dressed in black, one of the most terrifying that She had seen.

"Please let Me pass," said Bride, "I must see the Daga."

"I will let You pass if You permit Me to have Your cape," said the Guardian. Bride unflinchingly took it off and passed it over to Him. He opened the heavy arched wooden door and let Her pass through. One of the birds that Angus Og had sent with Her dropped to the floor and was silent. It became gray and then faded from sight. Bride was alarmed. She hurried down the passage and came to another barred door. In front of it stood another Guardian this time dressed in purple.

"Please let Me pass," said Bride, "I must see the Daga."

"I will let you pass if You permit Me to have Your skirt." Bride quickly undid it and passed it to the Guardian hurriedly. He opened the door and She quickly passed through. She nearly flew down the corridor ignoring all about Her until She was once again stopped by another door and another Guardian, this time dressed in red.

"Please let Me pass," said Bride, "I must see the Daga."

"I will let You pass if You surrender to Me Your encircling crown," said the Guardian. Bride reached up and took it off and handed it to Guardian, now completely naked. The Guardian opened the door for Her and She passed through. As She did so, the third small bird of Angus Og dropped to the floor and slowly faded from sight.

After the last Guard has taken Her crown She entered the chamber of the Daga. She felt no insecurity in approaching a great king in this way and Her love and terror at the thought of losing Angus Og moved Her as She walked boldly into the chamber. At first, She could see nothing for all was gray, not light and not dark. Her steps echoed across the seeming emptiness. As She slowly walked forward She looked about Her and finally looked up. Towering high above Her She saw a gigantic head and shoulders watching Her and She realized the She had been walking on Its robe. She was stuck dumb with astonishment and wonder. She stood there forgetting Herself at the enormity of the Daga which the Daga calmly gazed back. At last She found Her voice and quietly asked the Daga to heal Angus Og, Her Beloved. The Daga continued to gaze upon Her without a response. She finally repeated Her request but again seemed to get no response.

Suddenly all of the floor around Her faded from view except the small area that She was standing upon. Before Her appeared an image of Midhir showing no expression on His face, hovering without support in the smoky air before Her. She looked into an immense chasm of light and darkness that disappeared into the distance with no bottom in sight. Bride huddled down on the floor because the heights made Her dizzy and Midhir in His silence terrified Her. A voice whispered to Her, "To save Angus Og, you must accept Midhir and jump into the Abyss." Bride froze at the words. The image of Midhir waited impassively, not moving.

"I am terrified," She thought. "I can't do that. I just can't! I can't! I can't!" On the fourth denial the last small golden bird of light of Angus Og fell dead at Her feet. For a moment Bride went numb with the realization that by Her delay She had lost Her lover. She gazed at the small gray dead bird which began fading from sight and for the first time She knew the sorrow of the gift of men. She wept bitterly as the life that She had always cherished grew as gray and joyless, vanishing as the little bird before Her. In Her deepest moments of wild grief, She learned true compassion, and was never to forget the experience. The soft sounds of a flute began to play in the distance but it was lost on Bride at that moment.

"All is lost," She wept, "everything."

"All must be lost to save anything," the voice said next to Her. As Bride looked up through Her tears and pain, She asked, "Do I still have to jump and enfold Midhir?"

"You never had to," the voice replied.

"What will happen if I do so?"

"You will then Know," came the fading answer.

Bride slowly picked up what remained of the small bird in Her fingers, which was only a shadow and with nothing now left of importance to Her, with nothing to lose, She stepped from the floor into the Abyss and past Her deepest fears and into the arms of Midhir Who faded then from view. Instead of falling, She found She stepped beyond the earth, beyond the sun and the moon and stars, and communed with the being of the Daga. There She found the bright being of Angus Og, and with a joy greater than She had known possible, She caught It to Her and It flowed into Her and She became both and knew ecstasy.

When She took Her next step, She found Herself next to the silent form of Angus Og. She knelt and held Him and breathed His life back into Him with a kiss.

His eyes fluttered open, and He looked upon Her as a new born child. Bride smiled and Her joy knew no bounds.

She held Him in Her arms and loved Him with all of Her heart.

"Thank you Daga," Bride whispered, because She saw that Angus Og was healed although He was still weak.

"I walked beyond the earth, the moon and the sun, even the stars," Angus Og whispered to Her, "And there I found You."

Bride knew in Her heart that He would be well. She would stay and nurse Him to health in the Evergreen Isle.

Meanwhile, as Angus Og had weakened, Midhir had also found Himself growing weaker and weaker from an unknown malady. He cursed in His anger and growing frustration. As the world grew colder and darker without Angus Og, and as the days went by and no cure was found, Midhir began to be afraid. On the shortest day of the year, Midhir felt in some unknown way, Angus Og surrendering His life. When He felt this, He became so dizzy that it was as though He would fall into the unknown, and He screamed so loudly that the world moved and He drew Himself back from the Abyss with all His might and lay panting in a fear greater than any He had ever known. Desperately He had clung to His life and He had won! But in some way, He knew He had also lost for in that one fleeting moment He knew Bride and Angus Og had surpassed Him in knowledge and power. He had been too afraid to follow Them. When the day came that Bride and Angus Og, missing their children, returned from the Evergreen Isle, Midhir fled into the woods to hide. He feared Them now and hated them with a new born passion. He would wait for His next opportunity to do Them harm.

The Ascent of Bride and Angus Og

Bride and Angus Og lingered on in the Evergreen Isle, enjoying the beauty of the eternal land. Both Bride and Angus Og knew that it was just a resting place, a place of renewal before They once more ventured out to meet Midhir. There the land was neither bright nor dark, but is ever a land of twilight, the twilight beginning or ending was never known. Bride laid Herself down to sleep, for even a goddess must sometimes sleep which is why the Moon sometimes becomes dark. Bride is asleep.

As She slept, She heard the voice of Midhir asking Her to return with Angus Og back to the world. His strength was fading and He was afraid and wished all had been as it was when He was hale and hearty.

When She awoke, Angus Og (who had been at Her side guarding Her) spoke, and said that He wished to return to the world and asked if She would follow Him. Bride agreed, and followed Him once again to the world. They called to Manannan to bear them back and He came for Them and once again carried them back to the world of men where They were received with much joy.

Of Midhir, He fled at Their coming to the far reaches of the north and was not to be found again during their reign.

The Creation of Myth

In the beginning was the Daga, and the Daga sat alone and in silence. The desire for creation arose in the Daga, and so It stretched forth Its hands. From Its right hand manifested the God and, simultaneously, from Its left hand manifested the Goddess. Each of these retained the essence of the Daga in Them, and thus part of each other was the same. These Gods were the first created and remain forever the favorites of the Daga. Now the Goddess was called Bride and the God was called Angus Og. For a long time, They dwelt together, but Bride and Angus Og began to be lonely for Their own kind and asked the Daga to create others like Them for companionship. The Daga then drew forth from Bride and Angus Og the essences of the other Gods, and gave Them Their attributes. Thus were Broen and Bogha Frois created, as well as Cruinda and Oeng and the other Gods and Goddesses. One by one the Gods and Goddesses were created to ease the loneliness of Bride and Angus Og. After a time the Gods decided to create the Earth as a place for manifestation, and They began to create the beings of this plane.

Now the animals and the creatures of the light were created first. All things that fly through the air, all things that swim through the waters, all things that walk and crawl upon the earth, all things that climb the trees, and all plant life were created upon earth. Thus these beings became our elder brothers and sisters. Now all of these beings were created long before the humans were, and at that time the world was a paradise.

Finally, Angus Og and Bride spoke unto each other and said, "All of these things are lovely and beautiful to behold, but why don't We create something that appears as We do?"

"Yes, We shall create some like You, the male," said the Goddess.

"And We shall create some like You too, the female," said the God. Now they both began creating the human spirits together. From the Goddess flew the flame of the essence of Herself and from the God came the flame of the essence of Himself. This was done exactly at the same time by both of Them and the flames separated from the God and Goddess and danced together finally joining, thus creating one individual human spirit. Thus, each human spirit was created by both the God and Goddess and the human spirit contains the essence of both. This was done each time for each human spirit, and the remnants of this creative act rests in the male and female hormones that are in all of our bodies. In some the power of the flame of the God was stronger and the spirit manifested in a male body, and in others the flame of the Goddess was stronger and the spirit manifested in a female body. Thus, it is that we are the essence of the spirits of the God and Goddess and equally partake of their natures and powers. So it is that we are all equal, for we all come equally from the dust of the galaxies by which we were formed, nor was one intended to be less than another, otherwise we would have been created differently.

Thus, it is understood that we are all created equal, none greater nor none lesser among all of the creatures of the earth. In obeying the law of nature and the universe we come to live a good life. We become one with nature, not seeking to dominate or to harm, but to seek union as we are truly children of nature, and of Bride and Angus Og.

Now all creatures have their own way of working their own magic but naturally their way of creating their magic is different from ours. The wild animals' needs are taken care of by the Lord and the Lady, as well as our own.

Finally, the Lord and the Lady gave different tongues to all creatures and peoples so that it would all be unique, and thus be more beautiful. Each language was created differently and this was how it was intended to be by the Gods.

The Myth of the Beginning

In the beginning, the Gods descended to teach people how to work, play and enjoy life. The goddesses taught the women how to cook, sew, and all of the things that they should know. The Gods took the men out to teach them how to hunt, how to clean their kill, how to cook it, and show proper respect for it, and all the others things that they should know as well. They were taught all of these things and given the gift of fire.

They were given also a sexual desire and taught how to copulate, male and female. They were given this drive so that they could create through pleasure and bring forth more members of the clan.

One time when the men had gone off hunting for about three weeks, their desires became aroused because they had not been with their women. Consequently, they began to experiment with sexual gratification between themselves instead of just with the women. The Gods observed them and saw that they were having complete sexual gratification, but They did not condemn them. After They had observed them for a while and saw that they were not going to harm each other, the Gods went away to confer among Themselves. They spoke of the advancement of these people that had been created in Their image, the way they had swiftly learned to ask permission before they hunted, to kill their food painlessly, how to clean their foods, and how to cook it. They were well pleased with the things that the clan was learning. They did not condemn members of the clan for their activities in sex between each other. Some of the men liked it much more than they did sex with the women.

Back in the camp where the women were, they also had begun experimenting one with the other in the ways of sexual gratification between themselves. The Goddesses observed but did not stop them nor condemn them for it. Naturally, They watched to see that they did not hurt each other and when They saw they didn't, the Goddesses went away and conferred among Themselves. They did not condemn the women for their activities, and it was with the women as it was with the men. Many of them enjoyed it much more with their own kind than with the men they had known.

When the Gods returned back to the camp and brought the men, the Gods and Goddesses went away and conferred among Themselves. They spoke of what had gone on in the camp and what had happened on the hunt. When They had finished Their conference, They called all of the clan into the centre ground of the camp to talk about what had happened. They spoke plainly and openly about the sexual activities that had gone on between the same sexes, and wished to know the thoughts of Their people in the clan. The women that had preferred a woman told the Goddesses that they enjoyed such and such a person much more than they did any man, and then the men who felt the same likewise told the Gods that they enjoyed sex with each other much more than they did a woman. The Gods and Goddesses then spoke among Themselves again, and then turned to the clan and told them that if that was their desire and their pleasure in the gratification and the ecstasy of the earth plane, then the ones that enjoyed the male to male or the woman to woman to a greater extent were at liberty to do so.

No one must try to force themselves upon another who chose a different gender, but to choose the ones that would have the greatest gratification with themselves. The men and women who chose their own gender were told in doing this there would be no conceiving and bringing forth offspring. It took both male and female to create human flesh such as theirs, and that if they chose their own gender for gratification there would be no children between them to bring into this world. They wanted them to fully understand this and not wonder why not one or the other had not brought forth a child. Then the Gods and Goddesses further instructed all that it would be better if they could find their own chosen mate and to stay with this chosen mate, and not scatter their energies from one person to another. They told them to find their own special chosen mate whether it be male to male, female to female, or male to female. They were to stay with that person and as a result they would grow so close together, so close until it would be as if they were one. Their powers would be much stronger and they could utilize their works and find out that the world consists of great and mighty magic through the union as one with nature and the Gods. All are equal and one regardless of the sexual preference. The clan was told that their sexual preference was of their own choosing and that as long as there was no harm one to the other that there would be no retribution nor any breaking of the Laws of Life.

They again repeated that they should stay with their chosen mate, whomever they chose, as long as there was one speck of love left. They further instructed that if love died within one person for the other, that the other is to let them go freely and not to try and bind him or her to them. Consequently, there would be an even greater love sent, and they would have the marriage ceremony. This was the same for all the people, not just for the people who were man to woman, but to all of the people of the clan, whomever they chose.

CONCERNING SEXUALITY

As a spiritual and religious system there are people who might look to this for guidance in setting the pattern of personal sexuality. First, the morality of a spiritual system must be based upon the health of its people on all levels and not upon their control or domination.

Our sexuality resides in the core of our beings. It is the most intimate and personal side of ourselves and most of our actions and ego definitions are expressed in ways that are appropriate to this idea. The Wizard's Way considers this to be a fundamental right to be secure in this definition and expression of ourselves as it goes to the very center of our being, and any repression creates an illness on a mental, physical, or spiritual level. As long as the law that no one be harmed is remembered, or the lesser of two harms chosen if there is no one perfect way, then there is nothing that is considered inappropriate between two consenting adults.

If someone attempts to control your sexuality or reproductive processes over your own will, it is an attempt at social control no matter what else is said. Any attempt to define or control what aspect of a person's sexuality or reproductive process will be permitted, is a fundamental blow to a person's sense of self. This is essentially a psychological violation amounting to rape against the person on the most intimate and personal level. This aggressive warfare achieves nothing but the degradation of an individual by making them feel helpless and exposed. This is exactly what it is intended to do. This means of social control is used extensively by church and state for the destruction of a self-minded individual.

If the society and cultural system does not permit freedom of sexuality expressed without harm, then the system is creating mental, physical, or spiritual illnesses among the people and should be changed. A spiritual system cannot do this evil. Self-responsibility must come into play on an individual level when one addresses these issues, and all life must be taken into consideration, not just human life, needs, or desires.

Monogamy

Within the Wizard's Way, monogamy is encouraged for several reasons. One is that in a closed society as some of the clan systems where there was less likelihood of social problems arising, such as violent competition for a male or female. The second was for magical reasons, because close unions cause the blurring of ego definitions and the intense love that can be generated between two people can cause spiritual evolvement to take place. On an emotional level it can be more satisfying as well.

Everyone owns their own sexuality and there are few rights and wrongs. The only injunction is that no one be hurt. That is for the health of the people.

In ancient times orgiastic rites were not only permitted, they were encouraged. May 1 was an important High Day in this respect as these rites were held to give fertility and energy to the earth. November 1 was also important in that orgiastic rites were held as the spirit of death was very close and the sex act was performed as an act of life affirmation to halt the power of death. Generally speaking there were always orgiastic rites held on the high days as well as the full moons. Sex magic is one of the most powerful types of magic known. The symbolic fertility act is a remnant of these ancient practices. Sex was used after the ceremonies to ground the power raised as sleep could be a little difficult to get after generating all of that energy. Indeed, one of the charges most often raised by the Inquisition was one of orgies and sodomy. That is in the history of the old traditions. Times have changed however, and although it is recognized that this was a part of the old ways it is not appropriate now. To be valid a system must be in tune with the times and so this is not recommended now.

It must be stated that as long as two or more consenting adults want to do this safely, and there is no harm to anyone else, there is no religious or spiritual reason in this system not to do so. It is certainly not wrong but it is their own responsibility for the safety and well-being of their loved one and themselves.

It should also be remembered that these rites that took place at certain times, not all the time and that the orgies were held for the rites, not the other way around. Orgies were not a total way of life but were a free acceptance of sexuality without restrictions, shame, embarrassment, or apologies, something we could learn from today. If one finds only this way of life pleasing, then perhaps the individual has not come to grips with his or her own instinctual needs on all levels, as relationships are encouraged as well as freedom of choice.

This system recognizes the state of bi-sexuality as most balanced. Your people, prior to the commitment of a handfasting or marriage, may experiment with relationships of both sexes. If one is not drawn to one of one's own sex or the opposite, they are free not to pursue it. It is a freedom, not an obligation. It is however acceptable as the acknowledgement of the ability to have close relationships with persons of both genders.

A system must be responsive to the events of the times, and safety is a must. Monogamy is the most desirable form of relationship in the system in these times, but it is not required. Safety however is a must, both in the area of conception and in the transmission of diseases. Safe sex on the part of both sexes is required until safety is assured and monogamy established.

Once a person feels free to express his or her desires truthfully and sincerely, a much happier permanent Union is possible. Suppressed desires and feelings will eventually have to be dealt with either directly or as side effects in behavior.

After a union is made it is a commitment of love and should not be violated with another.

The History of Religious Bans on Homosexuality

The religious injunctions against homosexuality in the Judaic based traditions began politically. Small tribal bands were moving into the land of Canaan which was already occupied by a high culture with city states. Since the land was already prosperous the invaders wanted it. They claimed that their tribal god had given them the land. That was not readily accepted by the indigenous people as they already had their own gods and their gods had said nothing about giving their land and homes away.

To increase their war making ability and assume more political control, the invading people named Habirl, meaning "wanderers," needed to increase the numbers of their tribe's people. The ban was put on homosexuality as it did not increase the number of the tribesmen to make war, and also because homosexuality was honored and accepted in the temples of the highly civilized cultures around them. They wished to distinguish themselves culturally for political reasons as they were basically from the same genetic stock. The reason for the ban on homosexuality in religious law was based upon land grabbing and social and political control, not for any spiritual reason whatsoever.

The Christian ban on homosexuality comes from this ancient conflict, is talked about in the Bible, and carried on down to the present day. This also gave Christianity a scapegoat for its own abuses, and added members to its structure with little or no effect on its part in the way of conversion. This policy easily added to the Church's power, wealth, and social control; thus, any ban to fertility was to be rigidly suppressed for reasons of wealth and control by the institutions intent upon these purposes. True spirituality has nothing to do with it.

The Wizard's Way and other spiritual traditions of the Old Religion must reject this corruption of religion and the religious control over the reproductive processes. Sex is of great power both in magic and social control, and if a person can gain control over your sexual impulses they have control over you. Again, a spiritual tradition involves the evolution of awareness, a religious tradition is used for the maintenance of social structure. If a religious institution is corrupted by greed or has something to hide, its nature is to institute repressive control for its own gain instead of maintaining a healthy society.

It is natural for religious institutions to exclude or banish a people who might actually intuit, show, or reflect a true path to deity based upon experience, especially if the institution's main motivations are the manipulation of political or temporal power. Gay people, who often fit into these categories, are a prime target. It is in their best interests to keep people ignorant and under their control. If innovative or creative people, or people who think for themselves are permitted in these institutions, such people will point out the abuses of the priests, which would cost the priests temporal power and expose their greed and manipulation. Obviously, the institution cannot allow this and would begin to discriminate, thus reflecting their divergence from true spirituality into corruption.

On Being Gay

If you are not happy about being gay, that is truly unfortunate because you cannot be recognizing the special beauty that you are and carry within you. You have a place outside of the desires and expectations of others that is unique to you alone. To glory in your own being, gay or otherwise, is to uplift a beautiful reflection of the true nature of deity, which transcends sexuality to the essence of being. Even though the path may be hard, consider yourself personally blessed by deity if you are gay. You must graciously accept and endure the adversities of life, as well as the beauty of achieving true maturity by doing the best you can with what you have without regret, guilt, remorse, envy, or shame. True spiritual beauty can be achieved by focusing on what you can do and doing that in the best way you know how.

For gay people, our art and creativity in most cases are our children. Our beauty in words, pictures, and essence is truly the wonder of the whole world. Our thanks should be to the gay people who managed to transcend and left a testimony of it in art, literature, or whatever creative methods that they used. In these things rest an immortality not of the body, but of the consciousness and soul, signposts which direct us to follow in their spiritual footsteps. The gay path is the path of innovation and beauty. It is important to understand that your children and inheritors are young gay people, although not of our bodies, they are the children of our spirits and consciousness. Since they are our spiritual descendants they will enrich art and culture as well as spirituality after us. Therein rests our immortality as gay people show up in every culture and genetic group. We will continue on despite the horrific persecutions, no matter what is done, we will manifest in every race and generation on earth, we always have, and we always will. This is obviously the will of deity. Nothing will stop us from appearing. Nothing.

The term kinship becomes of special importance in this regard. It comes from the work 'to ken' or 'to know'. Therefore, kinship was originally a relationship with someone who understands you. Later it came to mean blood relative, but if you are gay, gay people are true kin.

Always remember that you are not alone, but a member of a very large extended family which extends into every culture, race and tradition.

Diversity

According to Old Religion myth, when the Gods created the world, They created many things to be different intentionally. They created the different peoples, the different languages, and arts and cultures with the specific idea of diversity. It was through the diversity of things that all was made unique and beautiful. An analogy is that through differences, music and harmony are created, instead of just a single note. This is true today. Imagine the world if there was only the color blue. Think what it would be like if everything was one shade of blue. The world would seem much more dreary than it is. Change that to red, make everything in the universe red in your mind. What a sad loss it would seem to be.

See the world around you as beautiful because of the diversity. See the other cultures and peoples around you perfect in the way that they are and don't be threatened by it. If you are really secure within yourself, you're not really intimidated or frightened by new experiences. Understand that because they are different, it makes you yourself more unique and precious yourself. Joy in diversity, it is the Gods intent. There is no need to make everything just like you and yours. That is only manifesting your own insecurities.

Chapter Four: The Rites

Temples

One of the most important aspects of our religious tradition is the erection of our temples. In the old times special places were chosen for our religious ceremonies. These were places of earth energy flux points, or points where the energy of the earth seems to accumulate much like chi does in the human body. This was often by wells, springs, caves, certain shaped mountains, or things of this nature.

When Christianity gained ascendency, we lost our temples, much like what has happened to the American Indians. Our sacred places were desecrated, most of our temples pulled down and ruined, and the beautiful art of centuries ruthlessly destroyed. In many cases Christian churches were built on top of the older temples or their sites as people still came to these sacred places even though the buildings were gone. These places were then taken over by the Christians and that is why the Church built their cathedrals there. Notre Dame in Paris is a good example of this. It was erected over an older temple dedicated to Cernunnos, Lord of the Animals of the Celts. The Vatican was also built upon an older pagan site.

During the periods of persecution like the Inquisition, the Old Religionists learned to create a temple wherever they were and to take it down immediately after the ceremony. It could not be seen by an outlander, or one not learned in the system, since it was created out of energy with symbolism Christians usually did not understand.

What was created was what they called the globe. In other systems it has been referred to as the circle, but the circle only represents the line on the ground where the globe went into the earth beneath us and the sky above us. Our temples are in the shape of a sphere.

If it was safe, a line was laid out of white satin, flowers, or whatever greenery there was available at that time of year. It was laid out nine feet from a centre point forming a circle, or a larger amount depending on how many people were attending. A round table or cloth was placed in the exact center of the circle with the ritual items laid out on it. The images of the God and Goddess were placed on the altar as well as the four elemental symbols and the ritual tools. The globe was never violated or stepped across after it was set, as this could cause astral damage, or damage to the energy body or chi of the offender. This could cause physical illness later on.

During the days of persecution this was sometimes carried out as a family picnic with a piece of kindling for the wand, the knife for cutting the bread the dirk, a tankard of ale for the chalice, etc. These were placed around the outside of the globe instead of all together so that if others came by, everything could be quickly kicked away and out of order to avoid discovery. Other groups went deep into the caves at night to practice the old rites.

It is due to the remarkable courage of these peoples who braved unspeakable tortures of the Inquisition to preserve the old ways of illumination that this information still exists. Let us honor them upon our ancestral altars.

THE GUARDIANS, OR THE LORDS OF THE ELEMENTS

No one really knows what the Guardians are. They are clearly intelligences and energies, but of their history or origin there are only hazy legends which in different traditions contradict each other. Perhaps they were created by ancient Wizards or are a race of beings that have evolved beyond the need of bodies. We do know however, that they do exist and aid us in our rites.

In this tradition they are called, not commanded. They are called with love and respect and work should be done to create a rapport with them. To make a rapport with the Guardians you must speak to them as you would your Gods and wait for their responses to come to you. They are the Guardians of your globe and a proper globe cannot be created without their help. They do correspond to the four states of creation and this should help with your meditations upon them. One is never called alone; if one is called they are all called and they are never left alone undismissed after the globe is taken up. To do so is to court disaster for your possessions and possibly sanity. They are incredibly powerful and like anything powerful, if they are not handled correctly they become dangerous. Treat them with great respect, they deserve it. After all fire is our servant, not our master if properly handled. Therefore, the Guardians come at our call as we are their masters, but this mastery is granted through love alone and must not be abused either emotionally or through neglect or improper conduct.

When you have created your globe reach out with your antlers (see the chapter on the eight-fold path for a clearer explanation of this technique) and if you feel a pressure, a presence, or a solidity after you have given your invocation to them, they have come. If you feel nothing, they probably have not come and your invocation must be repeated until they do. They are very powerful beings and if you have established a good rapport with them, then you must ask them to lend their energy to help you with your workings. They are very important to the Old Religion workings and should be honored as friends and protectors. They are like the Guardians of the four quarters of the American Indians.

THE FOUR ELEMENTS

The four elements are 'pure' as they are the pristine or primal elements manifesting from deity in order to form us and our world. The tools are representatives of these four elemental concepts and it is through their manipulation that the material world is affected by the fifth force, or consciousness.

Being that these four emanations of deity are pure and make the fundamental building blocks of our world, they are used in their pure form to create a place for deity to manifest on our plane. This holds true for our globes and our own bodies as well.

Earth	Matter	All solid substances
Air	Gases	All matter in a vaporous state
Fire	Energy	All matter in a super excited state
Water	Liquids	All matter which takes the shape of its container

THE GLOBE CASTING

In this system the globe casting is done in this way. The altar is set up first in the exact center of the globe, orientated to the north. In the northwest quadrant of the altar is set a white candle to represent Bride. In the northeast quadrant is set a yellow candle to represent Angus Og. In between these two candles are set statues or pictures of the God and Goddess. The pictures and statues are optional as the candles alone can represent Them. In the very center of the altar is placed a small round hand mirror with a wooden or bone comb placed right beside it. To the east is placed a flute, or failing that a harmonica.

The outside perimeter of the globe is set up nine feet from the center where the altar is. If the globe needs to be larger because of the amount of people attending, make it in multiples of nine, such as eighteen or twenty-seven feet. The perimeter is usually laid out with a white satin ribbon but if this is too light and you are outside where the wind moves it, a white rope may be used. At each quadrant if possible, place a white candle. These are lit as each guardian is invoked. If the area is too small, omit these, as they can be a danger in a small confined area. It is nice if there is room for them as they give also more light for the rites and add beauty and signify that the Guardian is there, but they are not mandatory.

In the north point of the altar is placed a small dish or pentacle of salt. In the west point is placed a chalice containing water, in the east is placed the thurible, at the south point the fire candle.

After the altar and the elements have been set up in proper order the casting of the globe may be started. All movements within the globe should be in a clockwise direction. Light the Goddess candle and say:

"O Gracious Goddess, let Your thoughts rest upon us, who seek to honor Thee in this rite."

The God candle is then lit and this invocation spoken:

"O gentle God, let Your thoughts rest upon us, who seek to honor Thee in this rite."

The south or fire candle is then lit. Light the incense and put salt in the chalice of water to purify it. Tap each element three times with the comb as a consecration. The altar is also tapped three times with the wand to activate the altar. Walking in a clockwise direction, the Servant of the Goddess sprinkles the area around the altar lightly with salt water. The Servant of the God follows and censes the area with incense smoke. This purifies the area of unwanted vibrations. All of the rites, high days and full moons, are celebrated within the globe. On full moons the Servant of the God casts the globe, on the high days the Servant of the Goddess casts the globe.

This is an example of a full moon casting. The Servant of the God stands before the altar, arms raised above his head. He then makes this invocation:

> "O Great Bride and Angus Og, hear my words, attend to me. Bring through Yourselves the power of the Daga and cause it to manifest from the Evergreen Isle through this mirror, that we may draw upon this power for our globe and temple."

Visualize the power of the Daga manifesting through the mirror, which begins to glow with a blue violet light. The Servant of the God takes his wand and lowers it into the blue violet glow he is visualizing coming through the mirror. He draws this light into his wand and goes to the east point. He sees the blue violet glow come from the tip of the wand and go up and below him as he treads the circle in a clockwise direction making a sphere or globe around the altar area going into the earth at the point of the satin ribbon or rope, the temple being completed when he returns again to the east. It is important that the circle be totally closed so it is sometimes wise to go just a little past where the globe was started.

The Servant of the God now picks up the thurible. He takes the thurible to the eastern quadrant of the circle and censes the east. If the globe is large a person may carry the four elements on a tray with the comb for convenience. He sets the thurible down and draws his wand. He raises it and draws the antler symbol of the God. As he does this, he repeats this invocation:

> *"O great Lord of the Eastern Reaches,*
> *King of all Sylphs, Come!*
> *I call you in the name of Gaith!*
> *Draw close to us the power of your realm."*

He then lowers his wand after the Guardian has come, and lights the point candle. He can sense this by extending his antlers and feeling a resistance or wall or body if the Guardian has manifested. If this pressure or resistance does not come, he should redo the invocation and gesture, visualizing strongly the Guardian coming from his realm.

Next the Servant of the God goes to the south. He holds the candle aloft as though presenting it to the south, and then sets the candle down. He again takes his wand and draws the antler symbol and says:

> *"O Great Lord of the Southern Reaches,*
> *King of all the Salamanders, Come!*
> *I call you in the name of Oeng.*
> *Draw close to us the power of your realm."*

He waits for the Guardian to manifest and then lowers his wand and lights the point candle. He then continues on to the west quadrant. He takes the chalice and then holds it up in presentation towards the west. He then sets the chalice down and takes his wand. He draws the mirror symbol with it and says:

> *"O Great Lady of the Western Reaches,*
> *Queen of all the Merfolk, Come!*
> *I call you in the name of Manannan*
> *Draw close to us the power of your realm."*

He waits for the Guardian to manifest, lowers his wand and then lights the point candle. The Servant of the God proceeds onto the north. He then takes the pentacle and holds the plate up as if presenting it to the north. He then sets the plate down and takes his wand and traces the mirror symbol in the air to the north. As he does this he says this invocation:

> *"O Great Lady of the Northern Reaches,*
> *Queen of all the Dwarves, Come!*
> *I call thee in the name of Cruinda.*
> *Draw close to us the power of your realm."*

He waits for the Guardian to manifest, and then lowers his wand and lights the point candle. He then walks to the north-eastern quadrant of the globe and creates a doorway in the globe. He takes his wand and starting near the ground, traces an arch going counter-clockwise. For this procedure the wand is held in both hands. He then places the tip of the wand in the center of the arc and holding the wand horizontally tips his wrist so that the wand is moved to a vertical position as it turning a knob and pushes it outward as he would a door. The people of the group then enter the globe with their hands crossed over their chests, thumbs interlinked with their hands flat on their chests (it is also acceptable to cast the globe with the group within it). This is the ancient prayer posture. The Servant of the Goddess plays the flute low to high as a purification for each person who enters the globe. After all have entered and formed a clockwise circle around the altar, the Servant of the God closes the door by bringing his wand in sharply and moving the wand from a vertical position to a horizontal position visualizing the door being closed and resealed. He then proceeds to the altar and says:

Through the Fires

"The presence of our Gracious Goddess and Gentle God reaches throughout the worlds. The globe is sealed and we are separated from the outside world that we may glorify our beloved Bride and Her Lover, Angus Og. May They shed their illuminating light upon us all. So be it."

He then salutes the Goddess candle by holding his wand straight up towards the Goddess candle and then does the same for the God candle. Now whatever needs to be done in the globe can be done. If it is a high day then the rite is performed and magic done if there is need. On the full moons the power is raised and sent from the globe, and meditations performed.

After the ceremony is completed again the people of the group go out through a doorway created by the Servant of the God in the south east, and the globe is resealed.

The dispersal of the globe is accomplished in this manner. The Servant of the God starts in the eastern quarter of the globe and saluting the Guardian by holding out his wand, point straight up, says this invocation:

"O Great Lord of the Eastern Reaches,
King of all the sylphs,
Hail to thee and all thy kingdom.
Return now to thy lovely realm and return again
When thou art needed."

Repeat this going counter clockwise, and changing the Lord to Lady when appropriate as well as the direction and kind of elemental. After the invocation is done, extinguish the point candles by pinching them out. When the Servant of the God has once again returned to the east, he pierces the globe with his wand and going counter clockwise, draws the globe back into his wand. When he has completed the circuit and the wand is full, he points it at the mirror and sends the energy back to the Daga through the mirror. The Servant of God goes and stands in the south before the altar, raised his wand aloft and says:

"The rite is ended."

The candles are then extinguished by snuffing the candles with the thumb and forefinger, starting with the south candle, then the God candle, and finally the Goddess candle.

A Note Concerning the Wand

There should be a note concerning the use of the wand rather than the dirk in casting the globe. First, the dirk began to be used as a magical tool during the Middle Ages. The bolline is an actual tool that is older than the use of the dirk but it is not specifically a magical tool, but a practical tool.

The wand came into use during the time of the warrior cults, which makes it a much more ancient magical tool than the dirk. Originally the globes were cast with the wand, which is the more ancient practice. The difference between casting the globe with the wand rather than the dirk is this: the wand channels the power of the Gods and creates a holy place. It will repel unholy energy directed at it because of the high vibrations which this entails. The dirk creates a sacred space, which is different in that something holy is from the Gods themselves, while sacred means something used in service of the Gods. In repelling negative energy, the dirk will be more useful in casting a globe as it will create an impenetrable magical barrier across which no negativity can pass.

It is for this reason during the difficult times of the past that this practice was instituted, as the dirk is of martial origin. The wand however, is a tool of request and channelling the power of the Gods. This is a return to the elder ways and the creation of a holy temple rather than a sacred temple in this work. Casting the globe with the wand is the more ancient practice, and I wish to return to this as it has almost been forgotten.

However, it should also be remembered that an unholy object carried into a holy globe will disperse the globe, therefore it is of vital importance for the success of the workings that everything be consecrated before the globe is cast, and nothing unholy be brought into the globe by anyone. Also, no unholy or negative works of magic may be done in a holy space, without the dispersal of the globe. If an unholy work is done in a holy globe, the globe will disperse as holy energy will not remain in an unholy place or around unholy actions. A holy globe requires more care in the maintenance and erection of it, but in many respects, it is worth it.

A sacred globe has numerous uses and benefits as well. If you are in need of a protective globe, then the globe cast with the dirk is better. If you are working with any kind of martial energy, such as the destruction of cancer or AIDS in an individual, a sacred globe is used rather than a holy globe. Generally, a sacred globe will stand what a holy globe will not, such as non-sacred objects and is more difficult to disperse.

FULL MOON CEREMONY

Concerning the Descent

The Descents of the Goddess and God are not frivolous or meaningless rituals. The effects are quite real. For anyone in this system, this ceremony is important for a number of reasons, the main one being direct communication with deity. However, some warnings and discussion are in order before this rite is enacted.

First, it is important that if a gay man attempts the Descent of the Goddess that he be truly gay and totally comfortable with his sexuality. He should also be sexually passive in his preferences with another man. If a heterosexual or sexually active man attempts this rite, the actual descent of a different form of power and energy into him that he is not suited or prepared to handle may cause him permanent damage. This may have been why this knowledge was not made generally available to everyone, as it has its very real dangers to the unheeding. In other words, for anyone other than a woman or a gay sexually passive homosexual, this rite is very dangerous and must not be attempted. The true feminine nature must be inherent and experienced in order to be a suitable vessel for the Goddess.

Therefore be warned, the power of the Goddess cannot be usurped by someone who is unworthy, and the inappropriate person who tries will live to regret it.

Likewise, and for similar reasons, the God should only be invoked by a sexually active (as opposed to passive) homosexual or heterosexual male, or a masculine or assertive woman.

The invocation of the Goddess and God are not necessary for the performance of the rite. They are done when direct communication with deity is desired, at the discretion of the leaders of the rite.

Instructions on the Descending of the Goddess and God

The Gods taught them further saying that when the group was made of only men, that the one who portrayed the Servant of the Goddess would wear a veil upon his face, or his hood down so low that his face could not be seen. He would not deny his male gender, but rather he would invoke Bride in such a way as She would know that he himself enjoyed the passive passion of a female. The Moon Bowl would be placed at his feet. He would also wear an apron in the shape of a heart. Before he made the Charge of the Goddess to Descend he would say unto Her, while all the others knelt:

Invocation to the Goddess

"O Thou Gracious Goddess of my clan
Before I give You the Charge to Descend
I tell You I am of male gender,

*But my sexual desires are as Yours.
I humbly ask You, if it be to Your liking,
Descend and enter into me
That I shall give true worship this night as You.
If You desire not to enter into me,
I summon You, come and stand beside me
And guide my every move that I shall give
True worship unto You as Your Servant."*

The Servant of the Goddess then gives the Charge to Descend standing with his wand in this left hand, his arms straight out to his sides and his feet spread apart to create the form of a star, facing east.

Charge to the Goddess to Descend

*"O Thou Gracious Goddess Bride,
Mother of us all, I summon You.
By Life and by love I call to You.
By bud and root, by feather and beak,
By scale and fin, and by fur and paw
I summon You.
Come enter into me or stand beside me,
For I am One with You,
And as I speak so must it be."*

The person on whom the Goddess is Descending should visualize a silver shaft of light descending from the Moon and filling him until he glows. The person should feel the Goddess move into him from this light. All others watch to see if the Goddess descends into or stands beside him. She will come. The Servant of the Goddess brings his arms together and raises his wand and points it at the moon. He draws down power from the moon and starting at the right side of the kneeling wizards, points his wand at each one so that power flows from Bride to them. This is done by visualizing a shaft of moonlight coming down and filling the wand with its light, then visualizing this light going into each member as they are passed.

For the same group situation as above, a group composed only of gay men, the Invocation to the God is performed in this manner. The Sun Bowl is placed at his feet. All remain kneeling except the Servant of God, while he gives this invocation:

Invocation to the God
"O Thou Gentle God of my clan,
Before I give You the Charge to Descend,
I tell You I am of male gender
But I choose as my life mate, another man
I humbly ask You, if it be to Your liking
Descend and enter into me that
I shall give true worship this night as You.
If You desire not to enter into me,
I summon You, come stand beside me
And guide my every move that I shall give
True worship until You as Your Servant."

With his wand in his left hand, he assumes the God position. The legs are together and hands crossed over his breast, right over left. He then gives the Charge to Descend while facing east.

Charge to the God to Descend
"O Gentle God, Angus Og,
Father of us all, I Summon You.
By life and by love I call to You,

Through the Fires

By trunk and branch, by hair and horn,
By tooth and claw, and by flukes and tails,
I summon You.
Come enter into me or stand beside me,
For I am One with You,
And as I speak, so must be it."

The person on whom the God is descending should visualize a golden shaft of light falling from the sun and filling him until he glows with it. The person should feel the God move into him through this light. All others watch to see if the God descends into him or comes and stands beside him. He will come. He draws down power from the Sun and starting at the right side of the kneeling wizards, he points his wand at each one so that power flows from Angus Og to them. This is accomplished with the same visualization as pulling down the power of the Moon by the Servant of the Goddess, only the Sun is used.

This is done in the same way for gay women, except instead she chooses instead of another male, another female. The Invocation and Charge are therefore slightly altered to fit this. If she is the sexually dominant one of the two, then she shall give the Charge to Descend as the Servant of the God. She will also wear her dirk directly in front, hanging down low from the cingulum. This symbolizes the male genitalia as the heart shaped apron symbolizes the female genitalia.

For heterosexual groups with a woman calling the Goddess and a man calling the God, the Charges to Descend are the only invocations necessary. The phrase, "or stand beside me," may also be dropped from the Charge with a heterosexual group.

After power has been passed to each wizard, the Servant of the Goddess recites the Charge of the Goddess, saying:

"Hear now the words of the Goddess Bride, Guiding Light of the Wizards."

Through the Fires

*"When the Moon is full and bright,
Gather then within my sight,
In my sacred, secret place,
And call upon My name.
There sing My song
And dance My dance;
Bring Me love
And win My trance."*

*"Keep pure your ideals, reach towards them – and let nothing turn you aside.
Be free in your mind, body and spirit.*

*"Seek My blessings; I am the Secret Door to the Land of Youth and the Cup of the Wine of Life.
I am the Medium of Rejuvenation, the Holy Vessel of Rebirth and Immortality.
I am the mother bear, the grandmother owl and the daughter cat.
I am the temptress hare.
I fly as the falcon and run as the deer.
I give the gift of joy unto the heart.
I give the knowledge of spiritual eternal,
And beyond Death I give peace and freedom, and fulfill the promise of return to your kin.*

*"Nothing do I demand; for behold, I am the Mother of All and My love is poured out upon The Earth.
Find me in the beauty of the Green Earth, the White Moon among the Stars, the Mysteries of the Waters and Heart's Desire.*

Through the Fires

"Let your soul come to me, for I am the Soul of Nature, Who creates the Universe.
From Me all things come and unto Me all things return,
and before Me, let your divine self be enfolded in the rapture of the infinite.

"Let My worship be within the heart that sings, for all acts of love and pleasure are My Rituals.
Therefore, let there be beauty and strength, power and compassion, honor and humility, and mirth and reverence within you.

"And you who seek for Me, know that seeking and yearning shall not avail you unless you Know the Mystery:
That if that which you seek you do not find within, you will never find it.
Know this: I have been with you from the beginning, and am that which is attained at the end of desire"

After this is done, the Servant of the God recites the Charge of the God saying:

"Hear ye the words of the God Angus Og, Counselor of the Wizards.
"By the clean, straight, and unbroken green-leaved tree and forgotten Way long abandoned, gather there all who would learn My mysteries, for I am He who gathers and He who releases all things. I am Lord of the Stars, the Sun and the Earth, of lonely and unremembered hidden forest glades, waiting patiently for My children to return. Look for Me there, I have never left.

"Look within your hearts, you shall find Me there also. I am the Will that you draw upon, I am the support that you may rest your worn strength upon and I will not fail. I am the Hero and the Mischief Maker. I am your longing to be free, and your need to be held.

"For you I have sacrificed Myself. I die, but I am returned and renewed. I precede you always and follow after. So it is that finally we merge and become One.

"Hear the call and the echoes, there am I. See the eagle float, there am I. See the elk stand tall, there am I. See the bull paw and snort, there am I. When I approach you and you close your eyes at the end of time, I shall gently bear you to renewal."

At this point, the wizards go one by one before the altar. They state their requests before the Gods and before the assembled wizards. These are the things that they wish energy directed towards.

Each wizard shall have no more than three requests.

For each request a tiny pinch of incense is placed in the thurible by the wizard. If a wizard has a personal request that he does not wish to speak aloud, he may say only that he has an unspoken request. Three cones of power are then done, and absolutely no more than this. A group meditation is afterwards performed. It is at this time that personal messages may come from the Gods to the individual. These may be discussed after the meditation, or you can just go on to the next procedure.

A small offering of flowers is then placed upon the altar for the Gods by each wizard. If the time of the year does not permit flowers, then something of nature such as a pine cone or bit of holly is also appropriate. The fertility act is done symbolically by the Servants of the Gods. The wine and cakes are thus consecrated and eaten. The Gods ascend after which the wizards exit the globe. This is done by the Servants going into their respective postures, and visualizing the God and Goddess energy returning to the Stars.

The Servants take the globe up, and the rite is ended.

Fertility Act

The Servant of the God holds a chalice filled with wine. The Servant of the Goddess holds the wand above the chalice, point down, saying:

> "As the Goddess Bride so as this chalice.
> "As the God Angus Og so as this wand."

She then lowers the wand into the chalice, and sends power down through it into the wine to consecrate it.

The Servant of God then says:

> "In this manner, by this union, is change initiated,
> And creation made manifest, and consecrated.
> Thus I consecrate this wine to be the essence of the Goddess."

The Servant of the God sets the chalice down and picks up the pentacle with the cakes upon it. The Servant of the Goddess holds the wand over the pentacle, saying:

> "As the Goddess Bride gives Her blessing,
> So the God Angus Og sends it."

The Servant of the Goddess sends power down through the wand to consecrate the cakes.

The Servant of the God then says:

> "In this manner, by this agreement
> Is joy created, and enlightenment made possible.
> Thus I consecrate these cakes to be the essence of the God."

All partake of cakes and wine.

The fertility act is the way it is, as the female holds sway over the male body through sexual desire, as the male holds sway over the female for the same reason. Whether it is gay or not, usually the partners have a preference in their dominance or submission in the sexual act. The only difference in this sense is that gay people in their sexual acts cannot conceive children.

Alternate Consecration

The cakes and wine are part of a Mystery not necessarily founded in a heterosexual concept. The dirk penetrates the chalice not always for the strict concept of fertilization for offspring. It does bring about fertility of spirit also as any union of opposites does, as the dirk represents personal will while the chalice represents not only love and fertility, but dissolution as well.

Thus, when the dirk is put into the chalice, personal will is dissolved by love and fused then to the wand, which represents divine will. When the dirk and the wand are linked in this way through the love represented by the chalice, it becomes the sacred arrow. It is this arrow which is sent from the Bow of the Goddess by the Arm of the God which pierces the pentacle or material manifestation to the vision and experience of deity in all things. Therefore, the act known as the fertility act is in essence correct but misunderstood if you think that it means only the childbearing or heterosexual metaphor. It is the beginning of spiritual fertility and illumination which is the real focus of this ceremony.

This ritual from this point of view has to do with the process of spiritual illumination, not the sex act itself although this is often all that is remembered. If you are uncomfortable with the heterosexual imagery involved in the previous ceremony of the consecration of cakes and wine, perhaps this ceremony which is non-sexist but metaphorical to spiritual illumination is the one that is better for you.

Spiritual Fertility Act

The Servant of the God holds the chalice filled with wine. The Servant of the Goddess holds the dirk above the chalice, point down, saying:

"As the representation of the power of love and dissolution, so be this chalice.
"As the representation of personal will, so be this the dirk. I conjure the power of evolution into this wine to assist us on our journey to the realization of deity."

He/She then lowers the dirk into the chalice and sends power down through it into the wine to consecrate it.

The Servant of God then says:

"In this manner of evolution is the personal will dissolved to make it more fit for a higher purpose and Union with the divine will of the wand. Thus begins the power and purpose of the sacred arrow."

The Servant of God sets the chalice down and picks up the wand. The Servant of the Goddess sets the dirk down and holds up the pentacle with the cakes upon it.

The Servant of the God then says:

"As the representation of divine will so be this wand. As the representation of the earthed mentality, so be this pentacle. I conjure the power of transformation into these cakes to assist us on our journey to the realization of deity."

The Servant of the God sends down power through the wand to consecrate the cakes.

The Servant of the Goddess then says:

"In this manner of transformation is the divine will joined with personal will, and flung from the bow of the Goddess by the arm of the God, into the realization of deity in All through our present earth bound mentality. Thus is Union accomplished."

As the wine is given to the group to drink the Servant of the Goddess says:

"Partake now of the evolutionary essence of the Goddess."

As the cakes are given to the group to eat the Servant of God says:

"Partake now of the transformational essence of the God."

Instructions on the Descending of Vroiko and Gaith

The Charge to Vroiko and Gaith is optional during the full Moon ceremony, but if direct communion or communication is desired especially with Them, follow these instructions. Fill an earthenware or silver bowl with salt water and place a bronze or golden coin in the bottom of it. Place this at the feet of the person doing the Charge to Vroiko and the person doing the Charge to Gaith. The person should stand with the feet slightly apart, and the hands covering the genital area. Have the wand in the left hand. For a heterosexual man or woman, repeat the Invocation prior to the Charge to Descend. A gay man or woman does not need to do the Invocation before the Charge.

Through the Fires

Invocation to Vroiko and Gaith
"O Thou gentle Guardian of my Clan,
Before I give You the Charge to Descend,
I tell you I am of (male/female) gender
But I choose as my life mate a (female/male).
I humbly ask You, if it be to Your liking
Descend and enter into me that
I shall give true worship this night as You.
If You desire not to enter into me,
I summon You, come stand beside me
And guide my every move that I shall give
True worship unto You as Your Servant."

Charge to Vroiko to Descend
"O Gentle and Gracious Gay God/dess Vroiko,
Flower of love, I summon You.
By life and by love I call to You.
By sensuous touch and salty taste, by stirring sight
And groaning sound,
By flowing lust and musky smell, by thick hair
And hard horn, I summon You.
Come, enter into me or stand beside me,
For I am One with You
And as I speak, so must it be."

Visualize a violet shaft of light in the form of a flower descending from the Daga filling the person giving the Charge with this light until he/she is glowing violet. The person should feel the words and power of Vroiko flowing through him/her with this light.

Through the Fires

Charge to Gaith to Descend

"O Wild and Bold Gay God Gaith,
Unrestrained Gale of the World, I summon You.
By life and by love I call to You.
By freedom demanding and daring deed,
By courage profound and faith enduring.
By enormous strength and singing true,
By thick hair and hard horn, I summon You,
Come, enter into me or stand beside me,
For I am One with You
And as I speak, so must it be."

Visualize a violet shaft of light in the form of a wind descending from the Daga filling the person giving the Charge with this light until he/she is glowing violet. The person should feel the words and power of Gaith flow like the wind through him/her with this light.

These Gods ascend by the Servants going into their postures of Invocation, and visualizing the Gods energy returning to the Stars.

RITES

Yule – Dec 21 (the Winter Solstice)
(Done at midnight)

The Servant of the Goddess says:

"The days are dark and cold, and the Sun gives little warmth. Snechta and Reothadh have made Their homes here, blanketing all the world with glittering snow and sparkling frost, and made our world go to sleep."

The group says:

"But we long for the warmth of a long summer's day. We long for the green grasses, rushes, and laughing brooks. We miss the new born fawns and stumbling colts. But most of all we miss our Bride and worry about Angus Og. Will He live? Has the Daga saved Him? Shall we too fall asleep forever beneath Snechta's white blanket of snow? Tell us, O please tell us."

The Servant of the Goddess says:

"I have heard it whispered upon the wind, and sighs passed among the branches of the trees, that Midhir has regretted His deed. He will relinquish to Angus Og what is rightfully His. He has even asked for Angus Og's life to be spared. Can it be true? Even if it is, can Angus Og be saved? He was wounded sorely, and I am afraid. Let us pray to Bride for intercession with the Daga."

(Bride enters) Bride says:

"Beloved children. I have heard your prayers as well as Midhir's. I have gone before the Daga and asked for Angus Og's life, and it has been granted. Angus Og will live. But take an evergreen tree, to symbolize Angus Og's life enduring, and put light about it to help give My Angus Og His strength. Adorn it brightly, as you would My Angus Og.

Feast and make merry, this is My wish, for sorely would I have missed Angus Og if He were not healed. Great is My joy that He shall stay with Us and grow. Even though I must nurse Him as a little child until He is well and strong, no more wonderful work could I be given to be with the One I love. Be happy with Me."

The Servant of the Goddess says:

"We shall do as our Lady bids. Great is our joy, our feast, and our love. For a moment however, let us give thanks to the Daga Who has granted us our wishes. Then to our feast let us go."

Bride's Day – February 1

The Servant of the Goddess says:

"Today is the day of our Lady Bride. We honor Her especially today, to thank Her for sending Angus Og. We have washed our homes, cleaned our fields and made all things clean for Her arrival."

The group says:

"O yes, Servant, today is the day of our Lady. We would speak with Her for news of Her Lover, to know how He fares. It has been so cold for so long, we need to know it will not always be so."

(Bride arrives) Bride says:

"No, it shall not always be thus, My children, it will not always be so cold. As the sun comes out in the morning, so shall we return from the darkness and coldness to warmth and life."

The Servant of the Goddess says:

"Beautiful Bride, You grace us with Your presence. Thank you for coming to be with us. Tell us, please, is there news of Angus Og?"

Bride says:

"He has been sorely ill, even nigh to death, and I am concerned for Him."

The Group says:

"What can we do to help?"

Bride says:

"Light a candle, a fire or a bonfire, to give warmth and strength to my Angus Og. He needs it, and your love, thus you could please Me greatly."

The Servant of the Goddess says:

"We shall do so Lady, and we wish You strength and courage in your time of pain and waiting."

(At this time, each group member lights their candle from the God and Goddess candle and forms a circle around the altar.)

Bride says:

"Thank you, my children, and now I must return to Angus Og's side to care for Him in His time of need."

The Servant of the Goddess says:

"Thank you for coming to us, Gentle Goddess, may You always return to us."

(Bride leaves)

The Servant of the Goddess says:

"We shall pray for Angus Og's recovery, and His return to us. Now let us go to feast, to celebrate the coming of Bride and the hope She brings."

(All go to the feast)

Ostara's Day – March 21

The Group says:

"O Servant of the Goddess, it seems as if it has been cold for so very long. We miss our Lord and Lady, is there news of Them?"

The Servant of the Goddess says:

"I have heard the winter's ice cracking and crashing, creaking of the return of Angus Og. It is as if Snechta is being called away to the north by Midhir. Let us invoke the Goddess Bride for news of Angus Og."

All say:

"Bride, Bride, Bride, please hear our call and come to us."

(Ostara enters) Ostara says:

"I am Ostara. I come to announce the return of our Lady Bride and Her gentle Lord Angus Og."

The Servant of the Goddess says:

"O beautiful Ostara, Goddess of Spring and new life. You are most welcome, and Your news as well."

Ostara says:

"I have spread Their path with the flowers of Spring to welcome Them. Midhir has fled to the north. All hail the Goddess Bride and Her Lover, Angus Og."

(Bride and Angus Og enter) Bride says:

"Well met, My children, We are glad you are here to welcome Us."

Angus Og says:

"Beloved children, thank you for honoring this sacred day."

The Servant of the Goddess says:

"We are most pleased You have returned to us out of the darkness. You are most welcome in our hearts and our homes. Joyous we are that you have recovered from Your wound."

Bride says:

"Through the grace of the Daga We have returned. Be joyous with Us. Feast, drink, and dance in honor of this day. We shall be with you now."

(Bride and Angus Og leave)

The Servant of the Goddess says:

"For this joyous news, we shall decorate Your sacred symbol the egg, to do You honor, Ostara. Hail to Bride and Angus Og!"

All say:

"Hail to Bride and Angus Og. Our thanks to Ostara."

(All leave to go to the feast)

Cruinda's Day – May 1

A pottery vessel is chosen before the ritual starts, and a seed is planted in it. Each person may bring their own, or perhaps there can be just one for the whole group.

The whole group tamps the soil down and takes part in the planting either on an individual level or on a group level. If there is only one plant planted it is passed from person to person each full moon.

The Servant of the Goddess says:

"We gather on this day to honor the Goddess Cruinda. Have you planted your seeds in Her sweet breast, and danced your planting dances?"

The Group says:

"Yes, we have planted our seeds in our beloved Cruinda and asked Her to make them grow with our dances."

The Servant of the God says:

"Then surely what you have asked of Her shall come to pass, for She is a generous Goddess and full of love for Her children."

The Group says:

"Indeed, She has been most generous with us. Let us invoke Her that we may thank Her."

All say:

"Cruinda, Cruinda, Cruinda!"

(Cruinda enters) Cruinda says:

"Bless you all, My children, and thank you for remembering Me on My ancient day."

The Servant of the Goddess says:

"Our thanks to You, our beloved Cruinda, for honoring us with Your presence."

Cruinda says:
"Beloved children, know that I shall try to keep you well and safe. But you must also do likewise for Me. Put not poisons in Me, for they shall come to you again in your mother's milk. This is not my wish. Do not destroy my face, my beauty, as even a Goddess may have some vanity, does not every mother wish to appear beautiful for her loved ones? What you see for Me

shall come to you, for if you see My death, you see your own, and if much damage is done, your inheritance shall be impoverished, as well as your inheritors. Do you love your children?

"Remember the law of Kavaro and be generous as I have taught you by My actions, not greedy or unloving. That is not the way of the Gods, nor what We have shown you. I love you, My children. Love and honor Me too in your words and actions, and you shall always prosper. This is my promise. So be it."

(Cruinda withdraws)

The Servant of God says:

"Let us remember the words of Cruinda in our daily lives."

The Servant of the Goddess says:

"And let us now choose the Queen and King of May to preside over our feast!"

(Lots are cast for the Queen and King of May. The group exits the globe and goes to the feast)

Angus Og's Day – June 21 (the Summer Solstice)

The Servant of the Goddess says:

"Rejoice, my children. Today is the renewed handfasting of Bride and Angus Og. Long have They been Lovers, and wish once again to renew Their sacred vows one to the other."

The Group says:

"This is truly a day of joy, for Angus Og has now fully recovered from His wound, and all the world is light and bright with His presence here."

The Servant of the Goddess says:

"Quiet, we must be, my children, for soon the ancient ceremony of the Gods begins. Look, here comes Angus Og the Golden. Strong His arms, broad His chest, and beautiful His face. Truly, He is the epitome of masculine perfection."

(Angus Og enters)

The Servant of the God says:

"And here arrives the Silvery Bride. Radiant with a glowing light, Her beauty fills the days and nights. Soft the eyes, gentle the hands, surely it is Love's command that all should bow to Her. If ever joy could find a place, it must be in Her matchless grace. Peerless form, peerless face, clothed in floating chiffon and lace, comes our Gracious Lady."

(Bride enter. Angus Og and Bride walk together to the altar. There in front of the altar, clasp hands, smile at one another, kiss lightly, and walk out again, in silence, holding hands)

The Servant of the Goddess says:

"So the ancient rite is done among the Gods. Are there any here who wish to follow Their example?"

(If there is, perform the handfasting or marriage ceremony, whichever is appropriate. This has been so decided beforehand.)

The Servant of the Goddess says:

"Let us now go to the marriage feast of our Lord and Lady, and celebrate this day of joy in Their honor."

Through the Fires

(All retire to the feast)

Fogamur's Day – August 1

The Servant of the Goddess says:

"The days are sweet and indolent with the perfumes of the hay and grasses. The sun shines warm and friendly upon the naked boys and men splashing in the cool pools formed by a giggling brook. The women lay languidly letting the sun warm them and dry their long hair."

The Group says:

"Ah Servant, it is a beautiful time of the year. Let us savour each special moment forever."

The Servant of the Goddess says:

"Yes truly, we are blessed, as our harvest is carefully being stored away, to protect us from the cold and dark rule of Midhir."

The Group says:

"Who do we have to thank for this special time? Have Bride and Angus Og sent us a special envoy this day?"

The Servant of the Goddess says:

"Then let us call Her and thank Her. We would know of Her."

All say:

"Fogamur, Fogamur, Fogamur!"

(Fogamur enters) Fogamur says:

"I have come, My children. Fare you well?"

All say:

"Yes Lady, we are well because of You."

Fogamur says:

"Happy I am to hear it. Happy I am to see you all here. Long have I slept in silence. It is pure happiness to once more hear My children."

The Servant of the Goddess says:

"Golden Fogamur, we have called You to thank You for the bountiful harvests. We are well stocked with corn and dried fruits and nuts to see us well through the winter."

Fogamur says:

"Thank you, My children. It is a joy to be appreciated, and grateful I am to you for it. Come then, the Gods are at feast and We would ask you to join Us. We celebrate your return, as you do Ours. So feast with Us and let Us all know joy this day."

The Servant of the Goddess says:

"We shall do as You ask. To our feast now we go as You go to Yours."

All say:

"Thank you, Fogamur, thank you!"

(All go to the feast.)

Elanti's Day – September 21

The Servant of the Goddess says:

"Today is the day when we must ask gentle Elanti and brave Torko for a boon. A hard boon it is for Them, too."

Group says:

"What must we ask of these wonderful Gods? Why must we cause Them pain?"

The Servant of the Goddess says:

"Because we must ask Them for the lives of some of Their charges, or our children shall go hungry, and we may starve and die. Let us call Them and ask Them for this favor."

All say:

"Torko! Elanti! Torko! Elanti!"

(Torko and Elanti enter) Torko says:

"We have come and We are here."

The Servant of the Goddess says:

"O Elanti and Torko, we have a boon to ask."

Torko says:

"What is this boon?"

The Servant of the Goddess says:

"We request that You relinquish to us a few of Your charges so that we do not starve in the times of Snechta and Reothadh."

Elanti says:

"What you ask is very, very hard for Us. These are Our children as yours are to you!"

Torko says:

"But We understand the Law of Return, and We understand that you do not take them from Us forever. But Our hearts are sore at Your request, even though We understand it."

Elanti says:

"For Our time of parting that We must pay, you must also pay. Not one of Our Charges shall be taken without first a prayer to Us for permission, and not one without great need. To do otherwise is to create great disharmony for All."

Torko says:

"To show respect for Our children and Kavaro, every part shall be used. We give you strings for your bows, skins for you to wear, food to eat, needles of bone and sinew to sew."

Elanti says:

"If you do swear these things for Us, to show respect and love, We shall grant you your boon"

All say:

"We do so swear."

Torko says:

"Then it shall be as you desire. Remember, they are Our charges, and they are dear to Us. Take not one life without need or thought."

The Servant of the Goddess says:

"It shall be done."

(The Gods withdraw)

The Servant of the Goddess says:

"Let us to our feast go now. The Gods have granted our request, and we shall survive the winter. Blessed be Torko and Elanti!"

All say:

"Blessed be Torko and Elanti, and Bride and Angus Og too."

(All go to the feast)

Samhain

The Samhain rite is actually more of a play than a liturgy. It really depends on how many people are there to perform this ceremony. If there are not enough people to perform it, then the story of Angus Og and Bride is read and stopped at the point where Manannan bears Them away over or under the sea by the Servant of the God.

The play goes like this. A young person plays the role of Bride. She wanders about the globe, smelling a white rose. Behind Her walks a man, dressed in dark clothing and stag horns carrying a spear. Off to the side is another man gazing off into the distance towards the west, where the setting of the sun would be. He wears bull horns, and bright or light-colored clothing. As the man playing Midhir comes close to Bride, making movements as if to embrace Her from behind, the man playing Angus Og moves towards Them and pushes the man playing Midhir back from the person playing Bride. No words are spoken during this entire play. It is totally silent. A mock fight ensues, and the man playing Angus

Og is knocked (gently) to the ground. Then the man playing Midhir takes His spear, and with a flourish places it to Angus Og's chest over his heart. The man playing Angus Og falls back, and the person playing Bride rushes to Angus Og's side and kneels by Him. The man playing Midhir and Angus Og look at each other, Angus Og's eyes expressing pain, and the man playing Midhir expressing consternation, pain and shame. Finally, Midhir moves away and hangs His head in shame, covering His face with His hands.

While Midhir is not looking, Angus Og is helped to His feet by Bride, and the two move away. After a moment, Midhir with a face of determination moves after Them, and then the stage area is empty. The Servant of the God steps forward.

The Servant of the God says:

"Thus goes the ancient story. Bride bears Angus Og away with the dreadful wound, and together They flee to the Evergreen Isle. They go before us so when we find ourselves at this point ourselves, we should not be afraid. We shall call to Them to guide us when Midhir also comes for each of us. It is a time of sorrow and of endings."

The Servant of the Goddess says:

"Tonight the veil between the worlds is thin, and our ancestors and friends who have passed come over to greet us and to let us know all is well. Let them feast with us, and remember them with joy."

All go to the feast. A plate of food is left for the ancestors with a burning red candle beside it. The next day, let the remnants be left as an offering to the forest creatures."

TRADITIONS

Yule

The traditional things to be done at Yule is first cleaning the house. This is preparing for the new year. The first man to cross the threshold at Yule usually brought gifts. Sometimes this was just coal and salt to symbolize fire and food. A feast is prepared and drinks exchanged. Guising, or dressing in costumes was also done. This was cross dressing, as men wearing women's' clothes, old people wearing children's clothes, children wearing clothes of old people, animals, whatever.

Boar was the traditional dish, garnished with rosemary. There were also feasts of capons and geese, a Yule pie, sirloin of beef, followed by tarts, creams, and traditional plum porridge. There was hot spiced claret. There was gilded gingerbread cut into fantastic shapes of dragons, horses, demons etc.

A bonfire was also traditional. The men would do a circle dance around the fire and then eat, drink, and party. Many times, the men were masked or blackened their faces and danced with bells sewn onto their clothing. Sword dances were also a traditional thing to do at this time. The morning was ushered in with a boisterous carnival. There was a ceremonious cutting of mistletoe as the juice of the berry represented the semen of the God. Evergreens were brought in and decorated. If you lived near the sea, the seaweeds were brought in and used as decorations. Rowan was hung above the lintels. There was also the Yule log, which was decorated with ribbons, petitions tied onto it, garlanded, and then set alight. It was usually of oak. There was music of bells and bones played.

There was also charity given to the poor.

The carrying of a bull's hide was traditional as well as singing for drinks and for food.

Bride's Day

There was a festival. There was dancing, feasting, an icon of Bride was made, and she was invited into the home. Divination was practiced freely.

Ostara's Day

Offerings were made to the Goddess of Spring, Ostara. There were offerings of mead, ale, or gruel to the sea, in hopes that the fruit of the sea (seaweed) which was used as fertilizer would come in plenty to the land. This was done at night. Maidens danced around a phallic figure, singing. Ostara eggs were given, Her cult object, and they were eaten or rolled down a hill. They also adorned the feast tables. Buns were baked, the round figure of the moon, and crossed to symbolize the four quarters. Chicken pie was also eaten.

Cruinda's Day

This day celebrates the entry of summer. Blessings were invoked on the herdsmen and hunters. Beltane fires were kindled on the hills. Only sacred woods were used, and usually there were nine kinds. Each bonfire was built in two sections with a narrow passage between and around it was cut a circular trench which was symbolic of the sun of sufficient circumference to hold the assembled multitude. Everyone watched for sunrise as the Beltane fire was kindled at dawn. The need fire, or the fire used to start the bonfire was caused by friction. People walked three times around the fire in a clockwise direction and when the fire had died down, people were sprinkled with the sacred ashes. There was much singing and dancing around the fire. Blessings were invoked upon each other. Dancing in the seasons is of great antiquity.

Butter, cheese, eggs and milk were placed in hollow stones to propitiate the foxes, wolves, eagles, falcons, and storms to spare the livestock. Libations were also poured upon the earth. Cakes with nine square knobs, each dedicated to a particular deity were eaten. No metal was allowed to touch the cakes being cooked.

Charm stones for healing were especially potent at this time of year. People washed their faces with the May dew to acquire beauty. There were also pilgrimages to magic wells at this time.

Robin With A Hood was accompanied by 12 companions, who went about. They all wore green, the fairies' color. Pipes and drums were used. Maid Marian went with them, a cross-dressed man with a blackened face. This represented of course, Cruinda.

A May pole was erected and danced around. A May queen and king were elected to preside over the festivities. Orgiastic rites were held to help the fertility of the earth, as sympathetic magic.

Angus Og's Day

This is the festival for lovers, fire, roses, and omens. It was the custom to row in flower bedecked boats, so it also has associations with water. Stone circles were used for sun worship at both Cruinda's day and on Angus Og's day. Handfastings were performed. Blazing wheels or cheeses were rolled down hills to represent the sun.

St. John's Wort was burned in the midsummer fires. The fire was circled with great solemnity for on this day the nights begin to become longer. Riddles were asked.

The dew also had healing properties on this day.

Fogamur's Day

This was a great season also of handfasting, and of divorce. Great fairs were held, and also feasts. Handfastings were performed at the fairs. Scones, oatcakes, eggs, smoked ham, and dried meat were eaten. After the feast toasts were made, songs sung, riddles asked, and fortunes told. On this day there was not much dancing. Pipes were used for the music.

If by the end of the year the couple had not decided to take their wedding vows or to renew their handfasting vows, they returned to the fair. They walked into the center of the assembled people, stood back to back, one facing north and the other south, and walked out of the group a divorced couple, free to enter into a new alliance.

There was much competition, shot-put, tossing the caber, wrestling, running and jumping, and hammer throwing. There was dancing competitions and singing competitions. And finally, there is the crowning of the Bard for the best poems.

Elanti's Day

There was much horse racing. Men gave women knives and purses, and the women gave fine garters of diverse colors and a bunch of carrots to the men. The carrots represented phallic symbols. The ancient stones were ridden around three times without saddles. A man dressed in white with a white horse leads the cavalcade. The procession went around the graves of their ancestors.

A huge oatcake was made in the form of the quadrant of a circle. Sheep milk was used to make it. All of the cakes made were blessed. Lamb is the traditional food.

The fire should be of oak, rowan, bramble, and others.

Gifts were given to the poor. The old taught the young the old customs on this day. Athletics were performed as well as racing. A dance is held in the evening and if there has been betting, the winner is not allowed to keep his winnings but must all be spent.

A dance is performed called the Carlin of the Mill Dust. A man carries a magic rod in his right hand. The dance is intricate and the man holds the wand over his own head and that of the woman. When he touches the woman with it, she falls down as if dead at his feet. He bemoans his dead carlin, dancing and gesticulating around the body. He then lifts up her left hand, looking into the palm, breathes upon it, and touches it with the wand. Immediately, the limp hand becomes alive and moves side to side and up and down. The man rejoices and dances around the figure on the floor. He does the same to the right hand, and to the left and right foot. The limbs move but the body is inert. The man kneels over the woman and breathes into her mouth, and touches her heart with his wand. The woman springs to live and spring up, confronting the man. Then the two dance as vigorously as in the first part.

Samhain

There are fires lit for propitiation and purification. This is a celebration of Harvest Home, and the day marks the end of summer. November was the season of the earth's decay as well as the sun's. Thus, the day became a remembrance of the dead. Offerings were made to the ancestral spirits, and food and drink is set out for them.

Meetings of the wizards were held beside the lonely moor or the sea shore. Masks and clothes of animal spirits were used. Orgiastic rites were performed to halt the power of death and for life affirmations.

Beltane (Cruinda's Day) fires were kindled at dawn but Samhain fires were kindled at dusk. Bonfires were also lit on small islands in the rivers. Ale was thrown into the sea to propitiate the sea god.

A fair is traditional. Ritual cakes were baked. Ginger bread was traditional food.

Tricks were played to represent the tricks played by the spirits. Hazelnuts were gathered for divination. Hazel was the magic tree that wizards love, being the source and symbol of wisdom, while the apple was the talisman that admitted a favored mortal to the otherworld, and gave him the power to foretell the future. There were two main apple rites, ordeal by water and ordeal by fire.

The act of going through water to obtain the apples is in all probability the survival of a druidic rite symbolizing the passing through water to Avalon, or Apple Land, the Land of Immortals. Ordeal by water was apple ducking, with a master keeping the apples in motion with a druidic wand. If after three attempts he fails, he goes to the end of the line to try again later. If he gets an apple, it is his to eat or more often to be used in rotes of divination.

Ordeal by fire was to take a small rod of wood, suspend it horizontally from the ceiling by a cord, and when fairly balanced, fix a lighted candle (originally a fir candle was used) at one end and an apple on the opposite point. Then set the rod whirling around. Each of the company in turn leaps and tries to bite the apple without singing his hair. He is not permitted to touch the apple with his hands.

Music

In the old symbolism the drum represents the element of earth, the flute air, the harp fire, and the bell was water. Men played the flute as this represented the God, women played the drums as this represented the Goddess, and a youth played the harp. The group wore bells sewn into their clothing although after the persecutions started, this was dropped for obvious reasons. Bells can be heard for a long distance. It would be nice to reinstate this beautiful custom of wearing small beautiful sounding bells upon the ritual clothing, especially for the dances.

Dance

There were several kinds of dances. The ring dance or circle dance is the one most known. This could be used for a cone of power or just to dance the seasons in. All the people held hands in a circle around the altar. All moved in a clockwise direction with a hop skip hop. If it was for a cone of power, at the end, everyone broke from the person next to them and pointed their hands at the mirror and directed the energy raised into it. If it was for fun or ritual, it might have broken into the following dance.

The following dance usually took place after the circle dance. The Servant of the God or Goddess breaks hands from the person next to them, and then leads the group inward in a spiral and then crosses under someone and spirals out in a counter clockwise manner so that there are two circles going, each in opposite directions. Another following dance is when one of the Servants breaks the circle dance, all release hands and all go across the countryside, each person imitating an animal. At the end the group returns to the site of the feast.

The leaping dance was where everyone joined hands like in the circle dance and jumped over an object. This could have been a broom which is a symbol of male and female copulation, a fertility symbol to make themselves more fertile, or over anything that they wished to partake the nature of or to show how high they wished something to grow.

Actually, the old dances may be closer to you than you think. When it becomes dangerous to perform the circle dances the old people tried to think of a way to save them. They thought of the thing most opposite a circle dance, and came up with the name square dance. Nothing is more contrary to the circle than the square so this is what they began calling them to save them from destruction. If you are interested in investigating the remaining magickal folk dances, square dances are the remnants still being performed and it is there you might look.

Ritual Tips

The performance of ritual should affect the people involved all in a certain way, depending on the ritual. Rituals should be dynamic and beautiful.

If a person must read what they are supposed to say from a piece of paper or the proper voice projection is missing, it sabotages the effects you wish to achieve. It becomes an absolutely necessity for people to memorize their lines as though in a play.

Plays come from religious drama, which was one of the reasons that the Protestants denounced them so vociferously. It should be understood that drama came from the Old Religions as it was a useful tool to involve everyone and get everyone's attention focused on one area. Much drama today also contains magical techniques if studied. A good dramatist controls the audience's excitement, anger, sorrow, and joy. To focus many minds on these emotions at the same time creates a very powerful vortex of energy and can be used in a magical sense to create some very real results. Because of this some audience participation yields the best results, hence we have the liturgy.

Just as there are terrible plays however, there can be terrible rituals no matter how sincerely done. A good ritual can be like a good play as well, keeping your attention and enthusiasm. Studying drama is a good way to learn how to perform a successful ritual. If you have mastered your metaphysical training as well as your dramatic talents, you have a good basis for working with other people on a ritual level.

The magical personality and the magical voice are both aspects of drama and of the art of illusion or glamour. A good ritual needs as much effort put into it as a good play, but audience participation is encouraged versus putting your attention entirely on someone else. It is easier to build energy and release it if the audience is involved. If you think about it you will notice that you forget your own ego identification in a good play and relate to the character. This is the goal of the eight-fold path, which leads to the center of your own being, and this is why ritual is included in this category. This is also one of the ways that compassion is learned. It is in such a state of mind that magic can and does occur. If you have to verbally demand someone's attention, the ritual is basically ineffective and you are doing a lousy job. If the person who is watching is simply so preoccupied with their own problems that a ritual will be ineffective for them, they should excuse themselves as they will distract others.

If you are going to play one of the Gods for a ritual, you would use the magical personality to effect this change in your personality. You meditate on the qualities of the God and see yourself as this God and invoke the God into yourself before you start, with a simple personal prayer. Masks can be useful for this as well. The masks are actually more for the actor than for the audience as they cause subtle psychological changes that enable the actor to actually perform a religious drama better.

Magical Personality and Illusion

The magical personality is formed in this way. You think of all the traits that you would like or that you will need for a specific occasion. If you want to be more forceful, you visualize yourself as having this trait. You also visualize how you would like to look as you have these traits. A new name is created for this person you would like to be, appear as, and be known by.

Stand in front of a full-length mirror and see this person you have created standing in front of you. Visualize yourself as this person almost as an overlay on top of your own features.

This is a useful exercise for dealing with people on a magical level, creating a self-confidence you might not otherwise have had. If you wish to look beautiful that is fine, create this overlay if that is your wish. It is a good idea to attach this persona to a particular piece of jewelry or clothing so that it does not begin to overtake your own personal identity. If you do not it can cause an identity crisis which is totally unnecessary and unhealthy at best. In other words, when you put on a particular brooch or ring your magical personality is keyed to this object and at no other time. Marilyn Monroe was able to create a magical identity from some of the stories that I have read about her, as she could turn her persona on and off. This is exactly what I am talking about and she seems to have been an expert at the technique. It helped to make her a star along with her enormous talent.

Remember that this is something worn and taken off. It is not to be used to create an illusion all the time and knowing when to use it and when not to use it is the mark of the professional and the adept. The experience can teach you about yourself and other people, but lessons like this should be understood in terms of personal transformation, not illusion. This is a wonderful tool for ritual use and it can also be expanded on by wearing masks or face painting. Remember that you are karmically responsible for all of your actions whether you are in your magical personality or not. Make your magical personality responsible in all respects as well as what you want it to do.

The Magical Voice

The magical voice is often studied in drama classes with "Project!" yelled at the actors by the director. To do any kind of ritual in front of others requires a certain dramatic flair. It can take many of the same skills and qualities like the magical personality or the magical voice, but their uses extend far beyond just theatrics.

If you speak to someone, be aware on an energy level of how far your voice extends. Be aware of the energy of your voice, not just the sound of your voice, and see if it is really touching someone. If you want to practice doing this with another person, sit in two chairs facing each other a few feet apart. Speak to each other and mentally see how far your voice goes, say as an audio level monitor on a loud note. See the energy of your voice extend out and draw back. This does not always have to do with how loudly you speak, but with how much energy is put into your voice and then pushed out. If you directly touch someone with the power of your voice they will know it. Irate customers usually do this unconsciously as their attention is usually fully directed at one point, the complaint department employee, who would be wise to use a mental shield to protect themselves from this energy. Some obviously do as an immunity or a shield is built up over a period of time, which can be quite annoying to an angry customer as they are seeking a reaction, not an impermeable shield. If it isn't created, the employee will have a difficult time staying in control of that situation.

If you call to the Guardians, you would visualize an open doorway into that realm, and you would use the power and projection of your voice to reach through that doorway and communicate with these beings, asking them to come forth. The magical voice is essential for good ritual performance but it is also essential for drawing forth the magic from other realms.

CLEANSING

Before any magical or religious ceremony, there should be a ritual cleansing of the body. If someone walks into the Wizards temple unwashed in anything other than a life or death need, there is a profanation of the globe. Usually the cleansing is done either with herbs such as hyssop, which is purifying, or with aromatic bath salts. Since bath salts are easier to use, that is what I shall go into a little bit here. Salt baths have a tendency to draw toxins out of the body, so they are good for you. A tablespoon of aromatic salts in a bath before a ceremony is all that is needed. You might also enjoy candle light and incense to get you in the mood as you let yourself relax in the tub.

Purification Bath Salt
1 cup salt
5 drops sandalwood oil

Mix the drops of sandalwood oil into the salt well and use a tablespoon of this in your bath. A pure sandalwood oil such as is used in aromatherapy is best, others should be avoided. If you find yourself allergic to this, although this should not be a great problem for most people, just use plain salt.

GENERAL GUIDELINES FOR A WORSHIP CEREMONY

Announce the intentions of the rite or rites before you begin.

Have a ceremonial cleaning of the persons involved and objects used. If objects have been cleansed and consecrated before, this second part is not necessary.

Create a sacred space to hold the energy in that is raised, otherwise it may dissipate too quickly to be of much use.

Either have the people already in the sacred space and have it created around them, or bring them in at this point. If you have very little experience, it is better to create the sacred space with them in it, although that can be awkward depending on the amount of space you have to work in.

Do your sacred ceremony.

Raise energy. This may be a part of your ceremony or it may not be. Raising energy would be done at this point.

Direct the energy towards a target goal and send it.

A group meditation can now be performed.

Eating of a sacred feast inside the sacred area helps to bond the people and to earth the energy raised. This is so that people are not uncomfortable later.

Deconsecrate your sacred space.

Declare the ceremony over.

Go to a more general feast. The sacred feast is usually a token eating of a small cookie and a small drink.

This is a general outline of how a ceremony should be structured. Perhaps you may not raise power because you simply wish to honor someone, so changes are permissible depending on what type of ceremony you are performing.

Dos and Don'ts

Do not bring profane items into a sacred space. Perhaps you have picked up the area to be used in your ceremony. It is a good idea to pick up trash, but it is not necessarily a good idea to bring it into a holy place. The intent of most ceremonies is to expand the essence of the sacred space to purify the area around, not bring in objects to pollute the core of purity which you hope to expand from.

If profane objects are brought in, let them be brought in for destruction to symbolize the triumph of cleanliness.

Never set a profane object on the altar or on the focus point of your sacred space. At best, place the profane objects beside the point, but do not let them touch it before the dissolution of the sacred space.

The rite should be prepared beforehand to avoid loss of impetus and/or energy. If materials need to be drawn or written upon, it should be done prior to the entrance of a sacred space. The creation of a sacred space should be done with a specific object in mind.

The requests that people desire should be drawn in symbols, rather than in words. These should then be dissolved in the sacred space through one of the four elements. The incense should be burning to send these desires to the Gods.

Chapter Five: The Eight-Fold Path

Most Old Religion traditions have what is called the eight-fold path. These eight paths are often called the Paths to the Center. Now what is meant by that is that each path or technique has the tendency to make you more aware of your own true being. Different traditions have different eight ways of doing this, but it seems consistently to be eight ways per tradition.

Basic Principles

Each person has certain basic ideas of who or what they think they are. For example, you may think of yourself as Joe, with black hair and blue eyes. You're a professional in a certain field and behave in a certain manner. You like burritos, dancing on a Saturday night, and a myriad of other things that you define yourself by. All of the ways that we see ourselves defined by is what is basically called our ego. If practiced, each one of the paths or techniques cause us to forget those definitions for a moment and experience undefined awareness. In magickal and spiritual training this is very important. Let us take the path of Spells and Rites for example, although the basic principles are the same for the other seven.

If a spell or a rite is effective it will cause a psychological change. It will subtly, or not so subtly, change the point you are focusing on, but more importantly it will change the point you focus from.

Let's say you are going to do a healing for your friend Bill, who (Goddess Forbid!) just broke his toe. First, with the concepts of natural healing magic in mind you would find the appropriately colored candle (a green one would be perfect), as well as an appropriate incense, and perhaps a picture of Bill if you have one. You also need to make up a small rhyme to the effect that Bill's toe will heal quickly and cause him pain no more.

How about, "Bill's toe will hurt no more, heal quickly and be like before." Eat your hearts out, all you poetry lovers.

Now you light your candle, incense or what have you, and you sit and calm yourself for a moment. At this point you move your point of focus away from your concepts of who and what you normally perceive yourself to be. Once you have done that you start to sing your rhyme. If you put your consciousness into this state you'll find that the internal dialogue stops and thinking is difficult because most of your energy is going into simply being aware on this level. That is why it should be in rhyme as an altered state of consciousness can make it difficult to function in the mundane world.

Actually, what must eventually be achieved is maintaining a dual awareness with clarity, to be able to function quite well in both the mundane state of awareness and an altered one. But back to the rhyme. The words must almost say themselves without much effort on your part. What these words in rhyme do is call your attention to certain concepts, like 'Bill's toe, heal quickly – be healed now,' although you won't be thinking in words as much as being aware of concepts. That is the important thing to be learned from this. Just as concepts are defined ideas, you put your awareness in an undefined state of being. Right at this point then, you are touching a "Universal Awareness." If this state of consciousness is deepened through practice and repetition one begins to experience the awareness of divinity.

This is a valid path to "cosmic consciousness" and feeling a sense of being finished with your work, you snap back into normal awareness. At this point, it is best to leave what you have been doing and go out and take a walk, or do something else for this reason; once you have effectively achieved this state of altered awareness, it is fairly easy to go back into it. If you're thinking about what you have just put out there, it is easy to unconsciously slip back into that undefined state of awareness without particularly being aware of it. Consequently, you might much tip or change, with very little effort, the concepts which you just worked so hard to put out there.

The Purpose of Spells

This is why spells are important to the Wizard's Way. They are training tools for the consciousness to begin to start breaking the limiting ego focus and start to experience divinity directly. This is also why you don't want to be fooling around with something negative because you can start to draw negative, or non-aligned energy patterns towards you (or in you) and it ends up being self-destructive. This is one of the dangers in this particular path and it is a real one. So, the next time someone really angers you just remember that karma is there to take care of the situation and you don't need to react to their unkindness or meanness.

Remember, if you react you are no longer in control of your own responses or the situation. If you just react without thought from emotions, someone else is controlling you and it is perilous for you to do that if you have started on this path. These altered states of awareness can become very easy to slip into if you have lost awareness of yourself, which can happen very easily with strong emotion. I know that this can be very difficult at times but I never said that this didn't take discipline and self-control (self-control, not control by states, authority figures, or other people). It takes tremendous discipline, but if you persevere, you can find your life enriched tremendously and come closer to your own being of divinity. Underneath it all, we all do want that very much although we may not want to take the responsibility for all of the work that it takes. We must always stay centered, no matter what.

Again, all eight paths cause you to start to break the ego focus and the Paths to the Center are the techniques to the center of your own awareness, your own being, your own all-pervading consciousness. But remember, if you get caught up in the outcome of the work, not that you shouldn't enjoy it, but if all you get out of it is the final "side effects", you've missed the point and you'll probably stay at the beginner's point of "doing spells" for a long, long time. There is much more beyond this. Don't misunderstand; spells are important, they are a wonderful tool if they can cause that change of awareness just by doing them correctly. In the end you must be able to manipulate your awareness without the aid of spells to truly progress. Don't get caught up in the trap of the first sign post. There are other traps to come after, but recognize them for what they are. These are tools to be used, mastered, and passed on to another for their development. It is only a tool however, and our goal is to touch divinity, not get lost in paranormal side shows. That is not spirituality; it is the delight of a limited ego focus which cannot see beyond to a great goal or a greater existence.

THE EIGHT-FOLD PATH

These are the traditional paths used in the Wizard's Way to develop one's power in this system. Not all are used now, but others are still very important.

One – Trance

This is a form of self-hypnosis. It is a strong aid in any form of scrying, divination, or magic. It is helpful in creating a oneness with the God or Goddess of one's choice. It is helpful in getting around the limitation of one's ego.

Two – Drugs

Artificially induced trance. Among the old traditions drugs were alcohol, fly agaric mushrooms, mistletoe berry, aconite and henbane. These are all poisonous, as any substance which creates an altered state of awareness is toxic to the body. All drugs are dangerous, particularly to someone in a weakened state and therefore are not recommended. They can also open psychic paths that lead to psychic experiences when the person using them is the least able to cope with them. This path is no longer used. The persons who taught this path in this tradition were wiped out during the persecutions, so there is no one left to teach it.

Three – Dance

This varies according to the Wizard's tradition. In many old groups this consisted of the joining of hands and running in a circle until they were exhausted. This might in some respects be compared to the whirling dervishes of Rumi. Strong or exhaustive movement can lead to altered states of awareness, and this is undertaken by people in good physical condition, as any dancer can tell you. This is a good path to use in combination with others, as it can be very beautiful. The dance of the seven veils referred to the unveiling of the beauty of the pristine soul, or undefined state of awareness. Each veil represented a planetary aspect, a state of consciousness, or a phase of existence that obscures the soul from pure realization. This is a dance of illumination, which was later corrupted by prurient minds.

Four – Rites and Spells

This is the one most used these days besides meditation. If a spell or rite is done effectively, it creates an altered state of awareness which if properly focussed upon, leads one closer to deity and away from ego focus. If one focuses upon the effects of the spell only; the path is misunderstood. This is, besides drugs, one of the most misunderstood and abused paths. Properly done, it creates great beauty for the practitioner and the observer.

Five – Sex

Some groups and individuals use sex for magical purposes. The Great Rite refers to the sex act, actual or symbolic. It is a valid path but it is best done in private. Basically, one concentrates on what one desires while copulating or masturbating. At the moment of orgasm, an altered state of awareness is achieved, giving access to the subconscious and therefore access to the superconscious. Some sigil magic is also based upon this and is usually quite effective. This is what tantric sex is all about; although, unfortunately, I have never seen any books on gay tantric sex. Perhaps that is an area that can be explored by others as it is valid. It is not stressed in this tradition as it seems more of a private matter to be followed, as are any of the paths. It can be a path open for the abuse of others and some traditions have been given a very bad name they did not necessarily deserve because of a lack of responsibility by perhaps one or two people. It is unwise to open this system up to that possible abuse on a religious level as it is just not in keeping with the times or the ethics of the system. It is recommended therefore, only on a private level and never in the religious rites or ceremonies.

Six – Music

The drum or flute, particularly if played in a repetitious manner can induce altered states of consciousness, as can singing or chanting. There still exist singing wizards who use the mastery of their voices to do their powerful magic. This is a very beautiful and magical path and is recommended particularly in combination with others. Shamanic drumming or singing is part of this path as it is the singing of invocations to the Gods. This can be done with a dance invocation as well. There is much to be explored on this path and it can be most rewarding.

Seven – The Cords

This is a path that is no longer used because of its danger. Flaxen yarn was tied with holy stones at intervals and wrapped around pulse points to limit blood flow to certain parts of the brain. If done incorrectly, it can cause permanent brain damage. The knowledge of this has survived, but it is not used. I have seen pictures or diagrams of how it was done, but have never tried it and have no intention of trying it. It is not recommended.

Eight – Meditation

This is the path most recommended. It can be very easy, but it does require discipline to master. You should meditate between 15 to 20 minutes a day. This clears out psychic blockages and helps to restore balance and perspective to your life. If meditation is done properly, the internal dialogue stops and the pure awareness of being is experienced. This is a wonderful way to remove ego limitations and should become a powerful and consistent part of anyone's life who truly wishes to master this tradition.

Priesthood Spirituality

The spiritual path of the priest is generally achieved through meditation and ritual. The shaman's path is usually through music, dance, and especially trance.

This book is mainly concerned with the path of the priesthood and this particular path will be discussed here. In a typical myth or story of spiritual illumination in a priesthood structure, one finds common points relating to psychological function.

Usually there are 7 to 12 doors, portals, stations, or stops which the hero or the heroine must traverse. The hero or heroine is actually each one of us and represents our own psychological transformations as we seek spiritual illumination. This form or structure can be traced through a number of myths, sometimes hidden in historical happenings or contexts, or stories of the gods and goddesses, or even heroes like Gilgamesh. Each of these doors, portals, stations, or stops represents a giving away of something.

It is symbolic of us giving away limiting definitions of our own ego or self-conceptions which we use to define ourselves on a path back to the realization of undifferentiated deity. This must be a willing trip as no one is forced to undergo this type of psychological journey or expansion against their will. It is a spiritual path, not a forced conclusion. In other words, if you do not wish to progress along these lines you will not. Thus, you don't hear the hero or heroine doing much to stop the progression of events. Indeed, they are heroic because it takes such courage for them to go on. These heroic journeys should be regarded more as a psychological function rather than a physical happening. Having identification or sympathy for the individual undergoing them can be a mistake, as in the end that individual is you and the path can be lost through feeling sorry for another individual in this context because it takes the emphasis from your own evolvement. Finally, the progression will lead to their liberation in states of awareness, as the stories are allegories of psychological transformation.

There is usually a whipping which is symbolic of the individual's intent to stick to his or her personal limitations by not permitting, cooperating with or accepting the divine in all things. This is what we all go through when we place personal will above divine intent and do not permit the realization of the universal, but stick to the definitions of dichotomy. This can relate to the feminine not accepting the masculine, or vice versa, in a person's psyche; it may be not accepting social structure; mind or body; it may not be permitting the unity of the inside and outside of yourself. Any dichotomy in any form must be stepped beyond or personal pain results. It can be not accepting life or death. In the end, the pain causes the realization that we are masculine and feminine, we are individual and social structure, we are life and death in process.

After this there comes an acceptance of what has been rejected, and a submission or permission granted on our own psychological levels to accept the dichotomy within ourselves and unify them into a working principle in our own beings.

After this point comes the moment of transformation when the temple veils are torn and the barriers between the divine and the human are ripped apart and the human psyche steps beyond differentiation into the realization of the Unity. The divine is no longer 'out there' or 'behind the veil', it is manifest in the human psyche and realized. It is permitted by man or woman, it is permitted by the psyche as there is always free will and the human is transformed into the divine. It is the union of god and man, goddess and woman, of deity with itself.

In a shamanistic sense, the person may be interred, returning again to Mother Earth, with a hymen created by sealing the entrance to create a virgin birth by the emergence of the person from the Great Mother. This is usually attended to by women as this is part of the women's mysteries.

After the integration of the psyche and the discarding of the differentiated ego, the person becomes realized in a spiritual sense, through the unification of masculine and feminine, inside and outside, mind and body, self and social structure or whatever level is achieved or desired.

STAR ASPECTS OF BRIDE AND ANGUS OG

Bride and Angus Og, besides representing the lunar and solar consciousness, are also perceived as the Star Goddess and Star God. In the Old Religion theology there is a lunar, solar, and stellar level of consciousness with the stellar mentality being the highest.

The reason for the star crystal over the heart area of Bride is that to achieve this high a mentality, the mind is centered in the heart area. The wand with the star on the tip with the golden corn stalks entwined around it refers to the human spine with the stellar mentality achieved with the Kundalini energy raised up it to the top-most area. The wand has usually been perceived as a phallic symbol, which it can be, but this has a deeper meaning with Bride's wand and crystal. The corn stalks entwined around the wand refer to the lunar and solar mentalities and energies, similar to the Hindu concept of the ida and pingala currents running up around the spine, or like the serpents on the caduceus of Mercury, Messenger of the Gods in the Roman myths.

However, the wand itself would refer to the *sushuma*, or the center of these two and is based upon the union or third path of energy, which is considered bisexual or gay which leads to the stellar mentality. Because of these three mentalities the ancient Europeans perceived that instead of the seven chakras of the Hindu system that there were three, similar to the Chinese Taoists, and it was in reference to these three energy points that much of the theology of the Old Religion came to be based. In many respects much of the lost lore of the European traditions seems to have been preserved in some of the oriental Taoist traditions as there are certainly many similarities. This is one of the reasons that Angus Og's shirt has dragons, which represented the old Kundalini serpent power, and griffins embroidered upon it. There is more to it than that, but this is an aspect of it. The two are associated with more than fertility in mind. Since the sun and moon mentalities are represented by the pingala and ida currents, this represents a dualistic mentality, but these are joined in the highest magic and mentality, which is neither masculine or feminine, but both combined; which is why bisexuality or gayness was considered the highest mentality of all and which lie within the bounds of the Star Gods.

Through the Fires

As the wand represents all three levels of consciousness, it also represents the channelling power of deity similar to the caduceus. The star mentality, safely done, is the highest aim of the Wizard. Working with these kinds of energies are very dangerous and since there are so very few people left in the old systems to teach this kind of power, it almost becomes necessary to follow the meditations and works which have survived in forms of Taoist meditations. I recommend the Tao exercises much more than the Hindu yogas. In certain respects then, Bride corresponds to the Hindu Shakti, and Angus Og corresponds to the Hindu Shiva, but in a western form, or the yin and yang joined together in the circle becoming one.

CONCERNING THE UNION OF THE SEXES

In most spiritual mythic systems, such as the myth of Merlin, etc., the power of the masculine or the power of the feminine is surrendered to each other in order to fulfill destiny. It is of course, in this system as well. The Goddess and God can be symbolic of many things such as the spirit of spring, the spirit of winter, the soul, the mind, or even opposite poles of electricity. Thus, it is in this system as well as on most any spiritual path towards union with deity, the two must be merged into one. This is usually a struggle as neither the masculine nor the feminine wish to submit to the other. Therefore, there is usually a conflict on a mystic level just as there is a conflict on a psychological level.

The Fear of Gays

What is it that heterosexual, monotheistic people have feared or objected to in a gay man? I think personally, that when they come into contact with the Gay Spirit, or the Gay God, which manifests through gay people, they are truly frightened by its strength and power. Most gay people themselves are unaware of it. What they innately sense from the

Gay God is the lack of limitations and boundaries, and the people most intimidated by this are the ones most terrified of freedom. Possibly it is the insecurity of their own sense of identity or persuasion. It seems that straights, and many gay men themselves, are afraid of and don't wish to acknowledge the feminine aspects of their own beings. Yet in the final word this is what is balanced. In order to progress to a true state of spiritual realization, the masculine and feminine traits in our own psychologies must be united – for both men and women. We must have the strength to be gentle and the courage to be compassionate. Therein lies one of the keys to true spiritual realizations and actions.

Since the feminine in our culture has been degraded and discriminated against, is there any wonder that men who have feminine characteristics should be degraded and discriminated against? Only the restoration of the feminine to a place of honor will stop the discrimination and degradation of gay people.

On a sociological level the cultures that honored the feminine also honored gay men because they had feminine characteristics. Consequently, in order to attain a closer union with deity, the feminine aspects of our own being as well as the masculine, must be acknowledged and accepted.

On a sociological level gay people, if they are smart, will promote goddess worship or the veneration of the feminine (and I do not mean the Mary cult), as in the end the sociological implications will be the end of discrimination against the feminine (i.e. gay people as well).

Balance

However, it should be remembered that the masculine and the feminine achieve union, not the dominance of the male over the female, or the female over the male. This just leads to reverse discrimination. The Wizard's Way is a path of balance so consequently in this tradition neither the man nor the woman should have total dominance on a cult level over the other, but should be in harmony and balance. If this is not done, tyranny will often result followed by disintegration of the group of people working together. Remember respect is earned, not given, and as a spiritual teacher you can only guide people on their path of development, not command them or tell them what to do with their lives. There are as many personal paths to deity as there are people. Acceptance of their total selves is necessary.

In a certain sense such a union creates a fear of loss of your identity. Remember fear is not only a guardian but a guide, and it does not mean that you must indulge in any physical activities. What we are talking about is psychological integration, not dressing up in drag, but if dressing up helps you, why not? My point is that it takes discipline to achieve this kind of balance within yourself and there is more to it than wearing a piece of clothing.

What is inside is reflected outside, and I don't want to give people the excuse not to do whatever they need to do to obtain balance, but in the end, it is a psychological transformation that is important, not what people wear. What it does mean is stepping into the unknown and in some cases giving up things known for things unknown. In giving up a limitation you gain more freedom. People love their cages but if you step beyond your insecurity new horizons open. That does not mean being irresponsible, but courageous.

In the case of the sense of loss of a certain identity, you will find that after the step you will have understanding of how you were but you will also have realizations of how you are. Nothing is really lost but smallness and limitation. For those people who are afraid of recognizing the feminine or masculine in themselves, remember to put balance foremost in your mind always and take the step on a personal level to these realizations. It is unlikely you will ever regret keeping balance in mind. Remember that it is wise to yield sometimes simply for the sake of yielding.

THE EXPANSION OF AWARENESS

How does one begin the expansion of awareness? There are many ways, but here is one of the easiest.

Be aware of where the center of awareness is in your physical body. There is usually one area from which your thoughts originate. For most people nowadays, it is the head. Be very aware of yourself, and place the center of your awareness in your right hand. Cause your thoughts and perceptions to originate from there. After you have done this, move your perceptions to your left hand, then your right foot or your left foot. Learn to move your center of awareness around in your body. In the end, this makes you more aware of yourself, and gives you practice in altered awareness, and the moving of it.

After you have become competent with this, visualize lavender light around you for protection just in case.

The "Antlers"

Now imagine that you have deer antlers growing out of the top of your head. Being imaginary, these are elastic. Cause these imaginary horns to extend and touch an inanimate object near you. It is important that you focus solely on the sense of touch at this point. As you touch this with your antlers, extend your awareness through the horns and become aware of the texture and feel of the object. Be aware of how cold it is, or how warm. Be aware of how smooth or rough. After you have done this till your impressions are quite strong, get up and touch the object and see how your impressions compare with the actual touch and sensation. You may be right or you may be wrong, but practice does make a difference and soon you'll be amazed at the accuracy of your impressions. You will find that after a while you'll need to check very little, as you will be close to right about 100% of the time. You must always keep your eyes open as you do this exercise, so that you will be able to use this anywhere, any time.

Dangers and Etiquette

It is wise when you are beginning this technique to avoid touching people with your "antlers". There are several reasons for this. One is that it is an invasion of someone's personal privacy. Let's face it, nobody likes to be groped and if you happen to run into a disguised adept, you are most likely to get a slap you will not soon forget.

The second is that you may receive emotional impressions that you may not realize are not your own. To touch someone suicidal or self-destructive at this point in your evolution is truly perilous as you may start to assume this behavior yourself. So, for heaven's sake, stick to inanimate objects! It is wise.

The Next Steps

What you may try after you have mastered this part of the technique is to touch an object and see the object from a very close perspective. By that I mean touch maybe 1/8 inch in all and in your mind expand this view to fill your whole field of mental perception. Be aware of the small scrapes and indentations or whatever texture the object has on a magnified level. It is best to have the object still in visual range at this point but far enough away not to be able to perceive the fine detail that you will sense in your mind. If you have used your "antlers" correctly and moved your awareness you will literally feel the object with your mind from this perspective.

It is best, as you have probably figured out by now, to practice this while you are alone. If you can't find privacy then what you need to do is to touch the object with your antlers, memorize the impression in a flash, and then continue on doing what you were while on a mental level examining your textural impressions. Thus, you can function in public and not appear to be a total idiot gazing off into space. That type of behavior is to be avoided at all costs.

Perhaps you might practice reaching out and touching say, a lamp post in the street ahead of you as you walk down the sidewalk. Casually touch it as you walk by it running your hand over it. Again, memorize this quick impression and keep on walking. Don't stand around and examine the object in public, this can attract an unacceptable level of attention.

Memorizing an impression and continuing with a normal conversation can lead to a dual awareness, which in the end is essential if you ever hope to be really good at this. Most people can learn to chew gum and walk at the same time, for some it just takes longer.

The next step in this progression is to find an old tree, one fairly straight and healthy with no deformities or knots. Cancerous, distorted, or twisted trees are traditionally considered unsuitable to work with. This is because there are legends of the Gods imprisoning evil spirits within these trees and the twisted spirits caused the trees also to become deformed. It has been my experience that coming into touch with these cancerous trees is an unpleasant experience. So avoid them, do not form a rapport with them and do not hold your rites near them as they are considered a bad influence.

Reach over to the tree with your "antlers" and touch the tree. Feel its bark and texture. Now reach inside of the tree and touch the very life force of the tree. As you touch the awareness of this being, you will generally find a sense of peace and tranquillity pervading your emotions. This in most cases appears to be their nature and you will know you are successful if you are aware of this happening.

Quieting the Internal Dialogue

One of the most important things necessary to do this is to stop your mind's internal dialogue. If you really pay serious attention to something, the internal dialogue will stop. If you listen intently to a piece of music you really like, you will notice that the internal dialogue stops, even if just for a moment.

A good way to practice is to listen for your own heart beat when it is quiet around you. To get it to work however, you must really listen and not just pay attention to see if you've failed. It may take some work but with intense focus applied, it can be done with any of the five senses. When this has happened in the past (and it has happened to everyone), people have been so entranced by the object that they never noticed their internal dialogue had stopped. And when their enchantment is over they don't even recognize what they have done. You must learn to recognize, extend, and walk in your own enchantments.

When you touch the awareness of trees your internal dialogue should stop as you will be concentrating so intensely on your perceptions. After you have touched the life force with your "antlers" and have become aware of it, speak to it mentally and say who you are. As strange as it may seem, in any social situation this is usually the correct thing to do. You may be aware of a gentle force of attention being returned towards yourself and you may start to get visual or emotional images back. Communication at this level tends toward the universal language of concepts. Concepts are undefined ideas. Take the concept of a car. There would be no thought of color, shape, make, or model of the vehicle. It would simply be the undefined idea of a vehicle, without even a visual image to go by. These ideas can be translated into most any language, although that may not be necessary as concepts are usually understood with more clarity than language. Concepts are "pre-language"; it is the primal way of thinking or realizing.

Asking Questions

At this point you might ask a question of this awareness you have contacted. After a moment you will usually get a response. The trick to this type of communication is to ask and then listen, and by that I mean stopping the internal dialogue and waiting in silence. If you maintain your internal silence, you most likely will get an intelligible response and a conversation will ensue.

I might add that some trees are friendly and some are not. If one doesn't respond, well perhaps another will. They are each as different as you or I. First, lean against the tree keeping your eyes open. Remember throughout all of these exercises you should always keep your eyes open. Ask permission of the tree to enter it. Each being has a specific vibration or tone. What you might do as you are experiencing your rapport with the tree is to listen for its specific tone or vibration. Become aware of the tone or frequency out of which you operate and change it to match that of the tree. Communication will then become much easier. Ask the tree you are working with for a message. Ask it then for a healing, a name, and a teaching. Finally ask it for a gift. Stretch yourself up to the top of the tree and look out through its leaves. Look to see if there are any other trees around you as you are looking out from the tree's perspective. See if you can sense any communications coming from the trees that you are perceiving at a distance. Extend yourself down then into the trees roots and feel the connectedness with the earth. Let all of your emotional blockages and fears drain down through the roots of the tree and sink into the earth to be lost forever.

After you have established a good rapport with this being, what you might do, providing you feel competent, is to take one antler and touch one tree. Take your other antler and touch another tree and go into them both simultaneously. Be aware of them both at the same time. This may cause a feeling of disorientation but that's alright, you'll be perfectly fine. You might also feel a sense of fear. That's alright too, perhaps even better.

The Value of Fear

Remember on this level your fear is a guardian but it is also a guide. When you start to feel like you are losing yourself, this is a threat to your ego and to the safety of who and what you think you are. To blend with the Universal, you must step beyond your own ego and conceptions of yourself. No true magic or any true realization of deity will ever be gained unless you do. So even if you are afraid, go ahead and try it anyway. Nothing is gained without a price, and the price of your freedom is the courage to step out of your cage and beyond your limitations. Remember, what goes around comes around and it is not yet time to work with people. You're not ready yet even though you think you might be. Only a fool would not listen.

When you have achieved a deep rapport with these two trees, you might extend out to even more. In the end, the trees themselves might show you some of their realizations and magic. The greatest teachers are not always in our species. We are one sentient tribe among a great many. We however, have lost the power of common speech and so the doors of fairy land have closed to us. Perhaps it would be better to say that we have closed those doors ourselves through our lack of perception. Here then is one of the keys to the rest of the world.

After you have worked with trees, try flowers and plants. Each being has its story to tell. Try extending and touching a single blade of grass in the lawn. Listen for the tone or sound to which it vibrates. It is usually very high and crystalline. Extend your awareness even more and listen to the sound of the whole lawn, or to the sounds of all the grass together. While being aware of this, extend your antlers deeper and become aware of the tone of the earth beneath you. Add this to the sounds you are perceiving from the grass. Next reach out and touch any tree, bush, or vegetation near you, hearing their tones as well. Let yourself become immersed in the harmonies of the life around you. Let your own being vibrate to this and merge with the melodies.

The Use of Western Ego

This is a Western way to perceive and communicate, to achieve harmony and be at peace, realizing deity as well. In the West we don't destroy our egos and our conceptions of what we are or how we are to act in society, we just stop identifying with old conceptions while continuing to live peacefully and happily in our social structure. Other people must have their own realizations, and if you tell them what you have found they may just believe you. This is error. Belief in this sense is a useless thing. It prevents you from searching for the truth of realization by substituting something which may or may not be real. If you believe something, you don't really know for sure. What you believe may just be an illusion but it will prevent you from seeking further.

Any system which says you must believe what it says unquestioningly is not dealing with the truth. If it is dealing with the truth, then how do you know? What we seek is knowledge, not belief; realization, not obedience; harmony, not dissonance. By learning the inner harmonies of nature and life, you will eventually be able to work with people. In achieving true harmony with all nature, you must perhaps change some things in your life. Herein is courage required.

Powerful Sofa Sorcerers

Many of the things I am talking about here do not come through intellectual knowledge. There are a lot of intellectual armchair sorcerers out there looking through their volumes of lore, muttering spells, and thinking they are powerful. They have missed the point – the lore and spells were to expand their awareness. They have focussed upon the tools of awareness expansion instead of expansion itself. They have collected hammers and never built the house.

What I am speaking of comes through direct experience and no reading about it will give you what you need except on an ego level which, in the end, is accepting defeat. So, get out there and work with this.

Listening With The "Antlers"

Now when you touch an object and focus on its vibration using your "antlers", you will perceive a tone if you listen for it, as we have been doing. This is a combination of your sense of touch and your ability to perceive vibration. This is how the art of hearing is achieved at this level. Everyone has a special sense that they use more than others. Experiment to find the one you use the most, but do not use all of your five senses at this level.

After a period of experimentation with this, you will be able to perceive tones, sensations, visual images, and so on because these will all be expressions of one thing, and that is the core essence of the object. Indeed, at a certain point this is what should be focussed on, experiencing the very essence of the object that you touch which expresses itself in physical form, sight, sound, taste, touch, and smell.

Touching the Essence

When you touch the very essence of something and perceive it properly, you will recognize it in its many-aspected form, as well as know its essence accurately. This can and should be done as it leads to the breaking of the identification with the ego, the limited focus of our own being, to the expanded focus of deity. But how do we touch the essence of something? When you extend your "antlers" to touch something, once you have really learned how to do this well and accurately, you focus so intently on the object that you step beyond sight, sound, touch, smell, and taste to a space without time or limitation and move into an experience of the undefined essence of the object. You forget yourself as you are and the diverse reflections of the object and you touch the very being-ness of the object. Then you can perceive on a deeper level the essence of its existence. That perception you can translate into sensory form.

Attempt to see this as a gradual expansion of your senses and do not rush it. These things sometimes come gradually especially if you don't have someone to help you touch these states of awareness, but it can be done on your own.

To achieve an undefined state of awareness and maintain it is a great step on the way to the realization of deity, which is a major goal on a spiritual path. Religion, if it is uncorrupted, can be an allegory of the path to achieve realization, which is why it is important not to take religion too literally.

Deity is not to be found in laws, ceremonies, or rituals, but a metaphorical map to it may be. To get too caught up in religion is to be caught up in a path that never reaches the goal to which it purportedly leads! What will lead to deity are realizations about yourself and your own being, and religion can help. After all, all Gods and Goddesses, yourself and the earth, space and the stars, even eternity are all aspects of one thing. To touch the true essence of one thing is to touch all things, and all things touch you. Thus, is compassion learned, and pity discarded; wisdom learned, and ignorance left behind.

To touch the essence of all things, even your own being, this is the fountain head of all creation. It is of special interest to people with artistic and creative pursuits, be what they may. When you have touched the very being-ness of an object and experienced the state of awareness which has no limitation you have just started the work. We now must start on the last step: to let yourself expand so much with your "antlers" that you cease to exist on an individual level but flash into total union with deity.

What is required in this type of meditation is expanding your consciousness until you cease to exist, as you are on a psychological level, and merge or shift into the mind of infinity. If you hold the concept of the totality in your mind and expand into it, you will achieve realization. One of the side effects of this attainment is personal emotional peace, a state that can also be very helpful in spiritual attainment. Sometimes, when the transition point in awareness comes, the ego – which is of course, threatened by this challenge to its conceptions of itself – generates tremendous fear in order to maintain itself. It can be controlled only by having complete peace within.

Repressing Emotions

I am not speaking here about the repression of emotion. To repress the emotions is harmful for the individual and life must be experienced fully, in any case. Therefore, to ground your emotions and release your fear and pain is essential to spiritual advancement. A good meditation to use to achieve this involves taking a stone or finding one on the earth. Slowly let your fears and pain, your hopes and expectations flow through the stone into the earth. Slowly attain the serenity of the stone. Eventually after you have released your pain and fear you will attain peace of spirit in the immediate now. Maintain this meditation throughout the day, especially at times of emotional stress. This will give you a serene point of focus, and will help you to see things clearly and realistically. This is a useful aid in the ultimate expansion of awareness which is the ultimate goal from which, on the Wizard's Way, you must never deviate.

THE PATH OF THE RED GOD, THE GREEN GOD, AND THE RAINBOW

This book is mainly concerned with the path of the Red God. The Red God path is the path of animals, vitality expressed vibrantly, actively, and sexually. There is another path and that is the path of the Green God. The path of the Green God is the path of plants, of vitality expressed in a gentle subtle manner, with growth, patience, durability, and persistence.

The Servant of the God should master the path of the Red God, while the Servant of the Goddess should be a master of the path of the Green God. In the path of the Red God, your extensions of awareness are seen as "antlers," while in the path of the Green God, the extensions of awareness are seen as tendrils of plants. Each will bring slightly different sensations or perceptions, yet are very similar. For those on the path of the Green God, which should be considered as fairly well balanced but slightly leaning towards the "feminine" (I use the term in a conceptual and energy sense), replace the word "antlers" with "tendrils" and see your extensions as the runners of a plant, like a grape vine. The path of the Red God is balanced as well, but leaning towards the "masculine" (and I use the term in the same way as I did the feminine) so "antlers" are correct and appropriate.

You must search within yourself to find which way is best for you. As Elanti is the patron of the path of the Red God, Vroiko is the patron of the Green God.

The Green God

The path of the Green God offers a different way of approaching this system of magic. First, you might surround yourself with lavender light, and then send your tendrils up over your head. You might also send tendrils up and let them grow wider, so that you become the trunk of a tree. As your tendrils reach up, cause the tips and branches to expand out like leaves. Vibrate the leaves faster and faster until they are vibrating at another level of consciousness. Slowly move your center of awareness up into the tendrils and let your awareness gradually begin to vibrate more quickly as it ascends. Raise yourself to higher levels of awareness in this manner. Perhaps you might like to just stand in the soft sunlight, and draw in energy from the leaves you have created. What an energy boost it can give! Perhaps you might feel the birds of Angus Og alight in the branches you have created, and sing you a song or give a message. If you wish a closer tie to Dionysus, perhaps you might see your tendrils as grape leaves, and taste your own fruits in the grapes that appear. (If they're a little sour, you might take a look at yourself!) Or seeing the Star of Bride descend and enter into the tree trunk, the area of your heart. Let the light spread out into you until you are totally permeated with its brilliance. Experiment with your tendrils, as long as you do not invade someone else's space. (There is surely enough to try without doing that.)

The Rainbow

There are a number of interesting aspects of the "antler" technique, which I am sure you are finding out. There is another one that is also particularly useful in contacting deity and achieving higher states of awareness. This is to visualize "rainbows" emanating from you in the place of "antlers" or "tendrils". This also has a different feel and gives access to a more refined perception of sense.

This technique falls under the auspices of Bogha Frois, and it is to Her you call for greater access and understanding. This technique is more related to the contacting of deity rather than to the perception of things on a material plane around you.

Visualize the deity that you would like to contact and send your "rainbow" and touch your visualization of the deity with them. This gives greater contact and communion with the deity of your choice. There is more to the technique than this, but you should investigate the Rainbow Bridge yourself.

NATURE SPIRITS

The Wizard's Way focuses on work with nature spirits. This is most appropriate in our day and age. Much of the existing material written about nature spirits comes from people who are working with cultivated gardens and that is wonderful, but the Wizard's Way focuses more on work done in the forest or an undisturbed area of land. In learning to use the "antlers", it is the contact with these beings and awareness that creates the experience of healing and beauty. Making contact with nature spirits is a rewarding and genuinely mystical experience.

This is accomplished by finding a very old tree, several hundred years old if possible, and making contact with it and asking it to instruct you about perspective, balance, energy and consciousness. This prepares you to ask it to introduce you to the other nature spirits in the surrounding area. This is why many of the old wizards lived off in the forest even in legend. They were not lonely, as they had lots of company among the forest animals and the nature spirits of the plants and trees. Only people who had limited communication abilities would have thought of it as lonely. If you are as lonely as many gay people in isolated areas are, this gives you an opportunity to fill in at least some of the gaps so that it will not be so bad.

We focus particularly upon trees, but we also make contact with the awarenesses of all things. Generally, a forest or an untouched piece of land has a different feel, or quality, as it exists in a more pristine state of consciousness. It is sharper and clearer and helps you to be that way as well. Once the land is changed, even landscaped, the awareness is dulled or seems to have a lack of edge. It therefore becomes vitally important that areas of the earth be totally untouched or the pristine consciousness of the land itself will become muddied, and this inhibits personal growth on this path or any other. It becomes not only destruction of the land but impoverishment of the soul.

Forming a Bond

Once you have found a favorite tree, it is good to visit with it to form a bond at least twice a week. The communication will probably become clearer as time goes by. You may also notice that sometimes the awareness of the tree may move about into the surrounding area. This is similar to our astral projection and is the cause of the legends of the dryads. As the ancients learned, some consciousnesses of trees are very powerful and are not to be taken for granted. If you study tree lore, you will find that the veneration of the tree was universal, and the consciousness experienced by the ancients was held justly in awe. There are also some nature spirits which take care of and guard a particular area of the forest. These are beings full of love and care for their charges, and you will find some quite angry at the annihilation of their friends by the thoughtless destructiveness of man.

Some may ask you to leave the area, and if they do, abide by their wishes. No doubt there have been times when you have walked into a certain part of the forest and have gotten a very uncomfortable feeling, or even a feeling of fright. You have probably invaded the realm of a nature spirit which does not want you there, or you are sensing an animal in your vicinity which may not have your best interests at heart. These beings can be very influential as you can tell if you have experienced this. Nature spirits are to be respected. They are not inferior to you, they are different from you. Their right to exist is just as valid as your own.

If you have created a rapport with the trees and have come to know the nature spirits and to touch their wisdom in an untouched area, your trips to the forest become a truly magical experience. Eventually you are likely to experience some form on manifestation or vision if you are persistent and are truly sincere. These beings are so full of love and serenity that you may be amazed, and they may teach you abilities that no one has written about or knows about, save the ancient wizards of old.

Sometimes it is good to write down your meditations with them, you might wish to take a small note book along with you when you go on your trips. Often the conversations you may have are quite pertinent for others as well. I am not going to write a lot about what I have encountered here, but I am going to encourage you to go out and have your own experiences. That is where true validity lies. The nature spirits will teach you personal balance, and how to be in harmony with the environment around you. They are a precious gift of the Gods.

Saving Nature Spirits

In this day with the destruction of our natural environment, each of us faces the destruction of a special tree or plant that is meaningful to us. One of the ways to save the spirit of a particular tree, if it is possible, is to get a cutting from it before it is cut down, then propagate it asexually. This is not difficult to master with some study, and a number of good gardening books are available that talk about how to take cuttings and let them grow. After taking the cutting, inform the tree spirit what is going to be done and ask it to go into the cutting you have just taken in hopes that the cutting will thrive. This is a way to save an ancient intelligence, and a very old spirit will then start to manifest in a very young tree. So, if you have a favorite tree slated for destruction, get a cutting and at least try to save the spirit of the being that you have come to love.

NUMEN

There is a "belief" in the Old Religion that all natural things have their own form of the life force. When your perceptions begin to sharpen and you acquire the ability to extend your awareness out to other things, this idea will be verified by your own experience. Animals certainly have their own awareness and life force – as do plants and trees. Eventually one finds that this also holds true even for the very stones of the earth. It was the old way that the spirits or awarenesses of all things should be respected, as all things hold their own kind of power.

If all of the trees are cut down, there is nothing to purify the air we breathe. Beyond this however, that power extends beyond this into the purification of the energy fields around them. This is one of the reasons that the forest can be so calming and healing. These powers are wise, and are to be studied by the wizards of this system, but it should be a personal matter. All things contain life and consciousness and we must hold life sacred and the balance of life and nature paramount; we must respect the earth and all of the creatures on it. If a life must be taken for survival, it is honored. If a tree is cut down, it is left a token of respect and another planted to grow and take its place. To take life without respect, honor, or thought is the closest thing to evil in this system. It is severely out of balance with the natural laws of life and honor, and therefore out of balance with us. If continued long enough it will cause disruption in the systems around the perpetrators, and karma will begin to accrue. Be warned.

It was the old way to respect and replace what was taken, thus ensuring our harmonious existence in the scheme and net of life. It is time to realize the wisdom of returning to this way of behaving. In fact, it is glaringly apparent to all but the most blind and selfish among us. This may mean bringing thankfulness into each moment of your life. It may mean being aware constantly of the bounty of the earth, and of divinity. This was the old way. Spirituality was an ever-present awareness, a way of thinking that permeated the life of the people. It takes so little time to be grateful, and to resent the small amount of time that it takes is ingratitude at its worst.

It is hard to teach this mentality these days when so little is appreciated, but at least it should be pondered. Each action shall bring a reaction, and so nothing is done thoughtlessly. Each moment is a moment of thankfulness to divinity, and this thought is held constantly in mind. It makes life a way of spirituality instead of a way of survival or of acquiring more for reasons of insecurity. If you let your heart rest in gratitude, you shall be provided for. Let this thought rest in your heart.

Transformation and Evolution

The path of the Goddess is the path of evolution. The way of the God is transformation. How does this apply to the theology of the Old Religion? One should remember that myth is the history of the soul in process, and that on one level the story of the Goddess represents our own soul on its journey towards Union and enlightenment.

If one refers to the myth of the Descent of the Goddess, we see Her progress through the seven guardians in an evolution. The God is however there already at the end of Her journey. When the God and Goddess finally embrace, there is union and therefore transformation as the psyche becomes whole, and transcends limitation. The Goddess permits this transformation to happen after Her own evolutionary process.

Since the God concerns transformation, He is the Guardian of the Gates of Death. He also is the Guardian of the Gates of Birth, as both of these are transformational experiences. The Goddess is the life in between.

Enlightenment

On a psychological level, the God also represents the flash of illumination into true reality. The path of the Goddess is the discipline and effort involved in any path towards this ultimate realization. Without the effort and discipline, realization is often impossible. To have a flash of illumination without frame work often causes a disorienting, harmful reaction creating not a Union, but a breakage of the mind, in essence a break with reality. Therefore, it is necessary for both to go hand in hand, as effort and discipline that does not lead to transformation is pointless.

The God has always been associated with death, but in our modern culture, it should also be stressed that He is also a God of Life. Angus Og is the God of Life, the Guardian of the Gates of Birth, as Midhir is the Guardian of the Gates of Death. In truth, they represent the two aspects of the same transformational force.

In ancient symbology, the God dies, the Goddess does not. She continues because of Her evolutional nature. Transformation is not something She does. Transformation is the process of the God. The God represents final illumination and therefore teaches the Goddess about this, as She teaches Him the evolutionary process He must follow to reach this safely.

He has already gone through this transformational process and therefore is a friendly face "on the other side", both in the process of illumination and of death itself. Indeed, illumination is both death and rebirth on an instantaneous level, symbolized by the death of the sun at Yule, and His instantaneous rebirth.

Since the powerful transformation of the God resides in all of us, His rebirth in us is celebrated every Yule. That is why we acknowledge the rebirth and transformation of the God within by giving each other presents on this day. It is acknowledging the God in each of us, just as in the Orient we bow to each other with the prayer gesture of two hands pressed together.

On our Yule tree, the shining spheres represented the path and the powers of the moon, and depending on their other colors, the other planets, evolving and teaching us. The shining star that at one time shone at the top of the tree, represented the illumination of the God, as the tree itself represented the eternal life of true realization, and the lights represented the strength and energy put forward to achieve that spark and star of illumination, finally at the top. These small candles represented the small realizations necessary to gain the ultimate awareness of the nature of our own beings and divinity.

It is not my intention to go into the God mythos. That can be traced in other places, but it is easy to see why He was venerated and even held in affection, as "the one who had gone before us into the darkness" to save us from our own fear of transformation.

It is on the four days that mark the beginning of each season that special reverence should be given to the God, for it is on these days that He manifests His transformational powers.

CULTURE, SOCIETY AND THE GODS

In speaking of the transforming powers of the God, it would be wise to consider the religions of a masculine god where the feminine is forgotten. Without the evolutionary process of the Goddess giving us a framework that involves the holistic perspective of life and the earth and society, the transformative process becomes destructive. It disastrously disorients and breaks proper perspectives of reality. Because of our separation from the evolutionary spirituality of the Goddess, in most modern relations, a disorientation has occurred and a break has taken place on a personal, social, cultural and environmental level; often we fail to recognize the reality that we are directly affected by our environment and society. This, unchanged, will lead to our eventual destruction and possible elimination as a species, along with many others. This is "madness" in its true form. It is suicide. All we need to do is look around us and see another area of wilderness destroyed by industry, or to look at the discriminatory processes which still exist in our culture, to know this is true. Unless the process of stabilization and reintegration reoccurs on all of these levels, the subject stays insane. Unless the evolutionary aspect of the Goddess is restored to its proper place on all of these levels, it is in the end, self-destructive.

THE RETURN OF BALANCE

It is interesting to note that the environmental movement, the women's movement, the gay rights movement (being linked to the women's movement through its demands for respect for the feminine) and equal rights movements all arose about the same time. This is a definite attempt to bring balance and justice to an unbalanced, greedy, abusive system and way of thought. It is based upon a solely transformational religious system, which has introduced caste and justified its discrimination. It is the Goddess energy reasserting itself in order to bring a wholesome balance to an unbalanced system before it is too late. The Goddess is arising through these movements.

However, to ignore the transformational powers of the God and to focus solely on the evolutionary process of the Goddess eventually leads to a slow stagnation on these levels as well. Eventually, as in any stagnant, unbalanced culture, without transformation, abuses begin to occur. This is on all levels, not only culturally.

Consequently, it is necessary to have a slow evolution and change together. Think what America would be without the transformational Revolutionary War, yet also consider that our government was based upon years of thinking about and studying the evolution of forms of governments. In retrospect, both are needed for the best advancement of life on all levels.

The Old Religion, if properly understood, is based upon an integrated, evolutionary, and transformational psychology. The rites should be transformative on a psychological level. If they are not, they are ineffective, and the rite remains only a ceremony with no real value. The workings throughout the year, following the seasonal festivals, leads to a slow evolution in the awareness of the proper priorities of life and systems which surround us, both environmental and societal.

The meditations which are necessary for progress are central to the discovery and merging of our disowned selves, from the feminine and masculine, child, or adult aspects, all the way to the divine principle. If the religious system that one follows does not contain these processes, it is an unbalanced and/or ineffective religious system.

RELINQUISHMENT

Much of the world's sorrow comes from holding onto things that it is time to gracefully relinquish. Whether that is material possessions, social prestige, or relationships, much grief and loss comes from looking towards the past rather than the future.

An essential step towards wisdom and enlightenment is permitting something that is important to you to leave in peace. That does not mean that certain things are not worth striving and working for, but that wisdom is needed to discern what should be pursued and what should be left alone. In many cases rather than trying to get back a certain thing, say a stolen car, it is better to invoke deity for compensation or something better rather than for revenge or the return of the item. This is true for most other matters as well.

If you look towards the past too much, and that which is lost, you are living your life as though you were driving a car forward while looking out of the rear-view mirror. In the end you create another loss as this type of behavior is self-destructive and usually harmful to others as well.

Self-love — love in general — is an essential ingredient on the path towards self-awareness. If you really love yourself and those around you, you will not hurt yourself or them by self-destructive behavior. Love yourself enough not to hurt yourself and learn to accept the vicissitudes of life with grace and flexibility. If you invoke deity for balance and compensation, something greater than what you have lost will be sent to you.

Past Lives

Religion places a great deal of emphasis upon what happens after death. Much of what they have to say must be taken on faith. After all, how can you possibly know about death unless you have experienced it, and once you do it is rare to come back and talk about it. This is only true in a system with a linear time focus, not one with a circular time concept, where your past becomes your future, and vice versa. In this case the focus, instead of on the future, should be to reverse the time line and focus upon the past. In the old theology, if your past is your future, then if you go back in time and consciousness you will confront your future. This is where the examination and experience of past lives is valuable. It is important to remember them yourself, not simply be told of them. This can become just another useless belief system subject to abuse and manipulation. If you remember it by yourself, it takes away the fear of the unknown, and releases you from the chains of a false dogma used for social control. This is where realizations come in handy, and where a belief system will try to block your investigations. If a spiritual system is valid, it will encourage you to investigate other paths. If a belief system is invalid, it will do everything that it can to keep you from exploring alternatives as it will feel threatened, with good reason. If you simply believe the manipulative stories of church and state instead of finding out for yourself, you will always be an expendable puppet.

Beliefs generally are used to allay personal fears in place of the serenity of sure knowledge. Beliefs are a substitute for the truth, and keep you from the search for the truth of reality on a personal level. If you do not know something, say so, and then begin your search for the truth; it is better than belief. Knowledge takes away the fear of the unknown, and releases you from the fears, pain, and manipulation used by conscienceless controllers. Therefore, an exercise for going into past lives is included for your personal release from fear. It is in the Meditation Section.

Chapter Six: Making Your Own Magic

It is best if you can to make your own spell of magic. No one else is going to have exactly the right words or intent for what you want. It is best then to get the right twist on your workings by tailoring the work yourself. Imagine this as a suit. You can probably buy one off the rack, and it may be OK, or you can have it tailored and get an exact fit. This is the value of doing your own work, in addition to the creation of something beautiful yourself.

There are some obstacles to this process. The first is the lack of self-confidence, that what you make will not work. If you place your confidence outside of yourself, you are likely to search through volumes and volumes of spells and lore to try to find exactly what it is that you want. This wastes a lot of valuable time and may get you nowhere anyway, because nobody has ever published something that fits your exact situation. I cannot help you trust yourself, you must do that yourself. Another obstacle is not knowing what is needed to make a spell that will work effectively. There are a number of components necessary to make an effective work of magic.

Step 1

The first component is that you need to have a very clear idea of what it is that you want. It is best if you have a very clear visualization of this in your mind. The clearer this is, the more effective the work will be.

Step 2

Gather to yourself all of the objects that will help you bring this type of consciousness into the working that you are doing. If you are doing a money spell for example, you would use a green candle, as this is the color of our money. Pine might be a good one, but it really depends on the associations that you have in mind. Candles, oils, incenses, and other tools fall into this category, and this is their usefulness.

The next step is to take these objects and directly associate them in your mind with exactly what it is that you want. Step 2 is what determines what the object will be that you write your goal upon, which was decided upon in Step 1.

Step 3

Now you must decide on the words that will most directly state your intent, and how you hope to achieve it. It is at this point that you might write your own personal invocation to the God that you are asking help from. Also do something symbolic with the objects that you are using to represent the goal. For example, you might move a green candle close to a large silver dollar until it rests on top of it as you chant an invocation to the deity whose help you are requesting. This is the symbolic achievement of your goal, while you do this work, to bring the end product into manifestation. It is the process that the mind must go through in order to achieve this goal. It is necessary to go into an undefined state of mind at this point, which can be achieved by meditating to the point of excluding the limitations of self or the surroundings, or by chanting, singing, or any one of the eight-fold paths.

Step 4

It is important at this point that you feel the work is completed or fixed. This can be done symbolically by crying a loud "Ha!" or by clapping your hands or making some definite gesture. What is important is that you quickly leave an altered state of awareness after achieving the peak awareness and concentration on what it is that you want. The longer you can achieve this peak awareness and focus of concentration, the better the work will be. However, it is important that this concept be fixed and completed in your mind, and symbolic acts help to do this. If you feel incomplete or unfinished, you should do it again until you do feel that it is finished. If the spell does not give you this feeling, it is an ineffective spell.

Step 5

This is the point where your symbolic object should be dissolved to step into the Universal Energy. It can be dissolved through one of the four elements, usually with a prayer of thanks to the God that you have called upon and has assisted you. You should then leave the area, and not go back for several hours to clear your mind of the whole process. If you don't you could muck up your own working as you may linger in an altered state of awareness and muddle the very process you were hoping to achieve.

ELEMENT OF SPELLS

Candles

Candles may be used to represent the person or situation you want, or want to change. The color of the candle should be appropriate to the work you have at hand. You may anoint the candle with an appropriate oil, or inscribe the candle with a name or situation, or both. Sometimes candles are notched if you wish to do something over a period of time. They are burned a little bit each day as this may be appropriate to the work you are designing, particularly if you wish things to move slowly in what it is that you wish. Other times you may move the candle about in a symbolic manner towards a symbolic goal (possibly another candle).

Incense

The appropriate incense should be used that will correspond to what it is that you want. The sense of smell is a very powerful stimulant. It is the sense of smell which has the longest memory of any of the five senses. A whiff of lavender can take you vividly back 50 years, and stir memories long forgotten. Thus, incense is very important. It also symbolically carries your prayers to the Gods, and this is why you find incense used in most every religion in the world. The Buddhists, Catholics, Muslims, etc, (to only name a few) use incense. This pervasive use shows just how important and effective its use is. Incense conditions the mind towards what it is that you want. Do not leave incense out of your working unless you are absolutely forced to. The more associations your mind has, the better the work may be. Smell and scent are very powerful, primeval influences. You may wish to use a planetary incense which is associated to your desire if you can find nothing specific towards what it is that you want.

Oils

Oils are very useful in spells. If you charge an oil with energy, what you anoint with that oil will also become charged. If you have created a sacred oil, you sanctify the work in a religious sense. If you charge the oil with a planetary or God energy, you will consecrate the object to that influence. You may wish to study these correspondences to get a better idea of what it is that you should be charging your oils with. Since oils hold an energy charge better than most any substance, they are very useful in this sense. To anoint a candle, rub the oil from each end towards the middle of the candle. Do this three times from each end. This puts the energy that you want into the candle. Oils are used to add power to the object and to the working. Use these if they are available, or perhaps make your own.

Herbs

Herbs are fun things to add to your workings. They are the living vessels of spirit, and they still carry the remainder of this essence after they are dried. Many plants have particular associations to the Gods you wish to invoke, or to the planetary influences. If you wish to charge a candle with herbs, you may hollow out the base and put in an appropriate herb, or use a certain herb in your incenses. You can also make your own candles and put herbs that you want in them. This is also a very nice and pleasing way to charge them. Herbs are usually aromatic, and so this has a two-fold quality: the herbs symbolically represent something and their scent may be used to stimulate the mind towards what it is that you want. Herbs can be buried or burned, and thus easily returned to the elements. Herbs can also be used to make a potion that may be useful in your working, or to help charge an oil that you are making for the specific purpose of the work, or for a general use you may want to use all of the time. A side effect is that you may learn how to use them medicinally and for pleasures other than spell casting. *The Holistic Herbal* is a good medicinal Herbal, and *Wylundt's Book of Incense* also teaches about how to use herbs to make incenses.

Condensers

Condensers are used much in the same way that oils are, but condensers are liquids which do not have an oil base. They therefore can be used to charge an object, but will evaporate and leave no trace, which might be more to your liking or your intent. In certain respects, a potion could be considered a condenser, but a condenser might also be something that you would never consider ingesting. It might just be something that you would pour out onto the ground in order to fix a spell, or anoint something on which you wish no trace left except magically. Condensers are basically used the same way as oils, so they can be more diverse, as well as mixing with other liquids without separating.

Amulets, Talismans

All of these carry a magical element. I was taught that an amulet was a natural object like a holed stone which had inherent natural magical qualities. A talisman was something which was specifically created and charged for a magical purpose. Definitions of these two vary, but that is how I shall use them in my discussion with them. Amulets, talismans, or charms may be something you carry to remind you of what it is you are focusing on that you want to bring into your life, or they may have something inherent within them that you wish to bring into your life. A cowrie shell represents the feminine principle, so you might wish to carry one to bring that energy into your arena of life or your spell, while a bit of antler represents the masculine principle, so you might wish to carry that if you wish to call that energy into your life. Herbs again fall into this area, but in a subcategory. Whatever object you may wish to use in this sense can be turned into a talisman if properly charged. You may want to carry the oil anointed coin that you used in your money spell to draw money to you, or to carry that vibration around with you and draw it to yourself.

Word Magic

Usually when you are doing a magical working you use a chant or song. Anything done repetitiously lulls the conscious mind asleep and gives you deeper access to the subconscious. This is why so many shamanic songs are monotonous. Keep your words simple and easy to repeat. This is why so many magic spells are done in rhyme, because a rhyme will say itself after a while with very little conscious attention. This permits the person doing the work to focus his attention upon the rest of the working. If you do go deeply into an altered state of awareness, you will find yourself forgetting any complicated wording, so it is essential to have something which will in the end "say itself". Another way to do this is to simplify what it is into a few words which you can repeat over and over, such as "I want a car." This is not a rhyme, but it will work equally well as long as you can say it without much thought and it is exactly what you want. This part of the work should contain an invocation to the deity that you want to help you. This is achieved through emotional rapport, and is important to the working. Each working should be dedicated to a specific deity as this is a spiritual path we are working with, not just simply manifesting something through meditation upon it. Remember that spells are learning devices to teach us how to make contact with deity.

SELF-RESPONSIBILITY

Where you are at, right now, at this moment in your life, is the culmination of every decision you have ever made. Most appropriately in a section on spells, in this chapter we will seriously consider the issue of self-responsibility. For only when you are willing to accept without question this reality, can you consider walking the Wizard's Way.

Perhaps you feel that someone else made the decisions that have put you where you are. But you, of course, accepted that other person's decision, which is a decision in its own right. You are responsible for your actions whether you take responsibility or not. If you step off of a cliff, you are going to fall no matter how many times you say you didn't do it. In the end, by taking Self-Responsibility, you take control of your life.

If you don't like where you are at, you must change the way you think, as all else follows.

In our culture we are taught never to take self-responsibility. We believe in church and state to "take care of" us. If you follow gay history at all, you will find that they most certainly have – to our detriment.

Leaving responsibility to someone else is the greatest mistake each of us can make. Ultimately, it is the choice between self-preservation or self-destruction.

Taking Responsibility

Along with taking responsibility for your life now, you should also be taking responsibility for your past. If you are unhappy, you have put yourself in that situation. If you are angry, you got there by yourself. If you wish to take your anger and aggression out on someone else using this path, then you are making a mistake. As the wise Malcolm Mills pointed out, if you are going to do something negative against someone, then you consider yourself a victim, and victims never make real masters. If you are interested in doing something negative to someone else, what you are really saying is that you are inept in managing your own life. This type of person is always a failure not only in magic, but in life. Since people on a negative path seem unable to make the changes necessary to take charge of themselves, they remain impotent of any real evolution in spirituality or power. If you are not in charge of yourself, who is? Leave the dark magic intentions to the incompetent. Hurt people end up hurting people, usually you find that if someone has hurt you, they are already hurt. Left to their own devices they usually end up cursing themselves unless they find a way to change. As James Hillman wisely commented, if you are still being hurt by an event that happened to you at twelve, it is the thought that is hurting you now.

Magical Attacks

Another issue we must consider here regards paranoia about magical attacks. If you have met someone who has some metaphysical training, and you feel like they are putting a "spell" on you, this is an example of an alleged psychic or magical attack. Magical attacks do happen, but most of the ones I have seen are the ones that people put upon themselves through their own fears and imaginations. Frequently, this is a form of emotional masturbation, the person deriving excitement from the titillating idea of being important enough to be the target of psychic attacks. People can jump on a bandwagon and start screaming psychic attack against someone totally innocent, and how can the person prove that he didn't? People like to believe the negative more often than the positive. If you use this tactic of slandering people, you will most likely end up having it used against you. Ordinary disagreements or discourtesies can be taken to slanderous and ridiculous lengths. If someone leaves something for you to find, then he is taking psychological advantage of you, and you make yourself the victim if you buy into it. To stand outside of the situation and watch it, it seems ludicrous that people buy into this. From inside it, it may not seem so funny. Seek balance in your life, not paranoia.

Spiritual Growth

You cannot expect someone else to take responsibility for your spiritual growth. If you put an outside authority in control of these matters, you are surrendering your self-responsibility. You should remember that even I am only an older brother trying to give you the tools to help yourself, not an authority figure "out there" to whom you surrender again your responsibility for growth. You get out of something what you put into it, so if you don't practice and strive for perfection yourself, there really isn't much I can do anyway. Each of us must have our own realizations about life and love. The most I can do is to try and guide you down a road but you are the one who must walk it.

Your own realizations are more important than those of anyone around you because they affect you the most. So, take your life into your own hands, face it and live it. It is up to you, after all.

Reflections

As we go through life we become reflections of everything around us. As children, our self-esteem develops in the mirror of our parents. As young adults we reflect the times and environment we grew up in. Some of us who have had traumatic childhood experiences continue to reflect this for years. We reflect the sorrow, pain, and joy around us. In a sense we are a giant mirror for all of the input sent at us. We reflect life, influences, change.

Only by meditation on an unchanging, immortal, energy like deity can the internal core of the psyche stabilize and cease to reflect the people and events around us. It is only by stopping our reactions to things that we become stable and still. Instead of reflecting everything around us, we become a light.

If we only reflect the thoughts of how we think deity wants us to be, then we are not illuminated by the light of deity flowing through us. If you create something in your life, make sure that it is just not a reflection of something someone told you that you would want, but something that is correct and integral for your own being.

Similarly, society in general is a reflection of our selves. When we look at something like war, we realize how ill or unstable we are on a personal level. The war is not outside ourselves, it is a reflection of what is inside of us. This lets us know that there is a basic problem with how we by agreement have set up a sociological, psychological construct reflecting ourselves, our inner psyches. If we consider personal violence unacceptable, then why do we accept it on a cultural or national level? Is it perhaps that because, underneath it all, we do consider violence acceptable? If we find war in this context acceptable, then both the context and ourselves need to be changed from angry and violated, to constructive, creative, and peaceful.

In the ancient days of the clan there was no war. In the beginning times war was unthinkable among the clans of people. It was a paradise-like place and war was not permitted or even contemplated.

In war, with the destruction of our reflections, we commit the ultimate aggression upon ourselves. If we are secure within ourselves we do not need to posture for other people.

The One True Spell

Many people are looking for the One True Spell. It is a spell which will make them all powerful, move mountains with a whisper and destroy annoying people with a gesture.

This is what is generally behind someone collecting spell after spell after spell until volumes upon volumes are created. If this grows from a genuine desire to collect folk traditions it can be beautiful, but generally it is a side track taking away from the true work of personal and psychological development.

The One True Spell does not exist in the general understanding of spells. If it exists anywhere it is the development of your own awareness, not in a formula written down by an ancient sorcerer. If he did write something down, it was probably just to lead you to yourself.

If through the working of one of the eight-fold paths you achieve unlimited awareness, then you can achieve the One True Spell. It is achieved through the active effort of meditation, not through the searching of old volumes of lore. Look for it inside of yourself, for if you do not find it there, you will find it nowhere.

Honoring Your Words

Honoring your words is very important in the Old Religion. There are two main reasons for this. One is that it keeps the discord within the clan at a minimum. There are few things more disruptive than an oath breaker or liar. To dishonor your oath dishonors the person to whom you have sworn the oath. The other has to do with developing the power of your own magic. If you give your word to someone and then intentionally break it, you send a very negative message to the deepest levels of yourself. Even if the person you have let down is willing to let go of your offense, you yourself still remember it. When you say the words "so be it" to seal a magical statement, inside you know that it is not really so. If you break your word, you break your power. It is really as simple as that.

Consequently, you sabotage your magic-working. Knowing for sure, without a doubt, that something will come to be is essential for anything magical to work, the inner certainty that if you say so, it must come to be as your word is never broken.

If you doubt your own integrity, then your magic will fail. It therefore becomes imperative to live your life with total integrity all of the time, as a slip up may not harm anyone else, but may do a great deal of damage to yourself on the psychological and magical levels. In this sense, your magic must be lived, not only taken out for a spell. In fact, if it is not lived, then you have nothing to take out to make a spell work later. This principle will flow over into your daily life; it must if you are to be successful in assuming your power.

I know a number of Wizards from whom it is very difficult to get a commitment. They usually qualify their words with "I'll try" of "if I can," as saying "I will" means they will. In this sense, it is better not to make a commitment at all than to make one without following through.

To be a successful Wizard on all levels is to live your life at all times with integrity.

How To Do It

There are several factors which do come into play when we look at how a spell will be done. Let us make an analogy to a trip to a vacation spot in a car.

First of all, you need a goal. You must desire a specific end. How much you desire to go will depend on whether you actually do go or just stay at home. Obviously, the desire to go must be strong or the goal will not manifest either in your magic working or in your achieving your goal of going to a particular spot for a vacation.

Secondly, you need to do some self-examination to see where you are at. To take the vacation you need to know where you are at so you know whether to go north, south, east or west to get to your desired location. To work your magic, you need to examine your real attitudes about the goal of your spell. If underneath you feel you do not deserve what you are asking for, subconsciously you may sabotage the achievement of your goal. Perhaps you need to work on self-esteem and look closely at your motivations because if you are unclear about this, you will only sabotage your spell as you are already sabotaging your life. If you sincerely believe you deserve what you are asking for, then you must hold the concept in your mind that this will come to you. This is one of the key steps in making the process work. Visualization becomes important in this step as you start to see yourself already in the situation of achieving your goal. This leads you to the sure anticipation of the goal, the trip and vacation.

Third, you get a map out and see how you are going to get where you are going. This is the place for the altered states of consciousness in spell working. It is the vehicle to get to your desired goal. It is sometimes best if you can consciously put yourself in situations to help it along. If you are seeking a new work situation for example, it is wise to be putting in applications to where you want to go. There are also times when it is best just to sit back because you have no idea from where what you are looking for will manifest.

Now what else do you need? One last thing, silence. It is wise not to talk about a magical working. It seems to be the fuel that the spell needs to operate, along with the oils of your desires and anticipation. If people find out that you are working spells, most often they will draw away as they are afraid of being manipulated or harmed. Speaking of spells can lose you friends as well as cause emotional turmoil which detracts from the energy of the anticipation of your goal. If you talk about your spell, nine times out of ten it will fail. It is just how it works.

You will not be successful in magic if any of the above qualities or actions are missing as these are fundamental tools for any magical working.

Objectified Prayer

A spell should be recognized as an objectified prayer. In many ways rituals are the same thing. Therefore, each spell should be dedicated to a God or Goddess of your choice that is appropriate to the working. Generally, the spell will symbolize what you want or an obstacle to be overcome. At the end of the spell the request must be sent to the Gods either by the dissolution of the object that you have made your request upon, or by destroying the object which represents the obstacle, so that psychologically it no longer stands in your way. After this you thank the Gods for the assistance that they have sent.

The Small Pebble

Put on a protective oil and visualize lavender light around yourself before you do this work. Set up your altar with the God and Goddess candles, and the four elements in their proper quadrants. In the middle, set a small bowl or plate with a small pebble in it. It is best to go outside and pick up one yourself. Any pebble will do. Light the candles and incense on your altar. Sit quietly for a while, humming softly, breathing and humming while both inhaling and exhaling. When you are relaxed, stop humming and extend your antlers out and touch the pebble. Feel all around it, feel its texture and the sensation of hot and cold. Feel the pits or smoothness or sharpness of it. After you have thoroughly explored it, move your antlers into the pebble itself, and become aware of how it is constructed internally. Explore each molecule, and how it is put together.

Now send your total awareness down through your antlers, and put it into the pebble. See your physical body standing over it, and become one with the material in the stone, almost as if it were another body. When you have achieved this, concentrate on what you want. If you want wealth, put this idea of having wealth now into the fabric and molecules of this rock. See it being imbedded into each atom of the pebble and then see it becoming a part of the stone as if your desires were written into the very stone itself, never to be changed. When this is accomplished, withdraw your awareness back into your own body, and sever the connection by totally withdrawing your antlers. Thank the Goddess and God, and leave the area.

When you come back in a couple of hours, take the pebble and if, for example, you did a work for money, put the pebble in your wallet or purse. If it was for love, you might put it in a small locket and wear it close to your heart. In other words, place the stone where it would be most appropriate according to your wish. Be careful what you wish for, you might get it.

If you are working on something you want only to have influence on for a limited time, you should see the effect you have put into it slowly fading away, and the rock returning to its former situation. It is done.

The Pyramid

Make a piece of paper into a square, equal on all four sides. In the center draw a symbol of the God and Goddess. Bend one corner over, and on the top draw a symbol or objectified concept of yourself. This can either be a stick figure, an abstract symbol, or an elaborate picture. That's not so important as what it symbolizes or represents, and that is you.

On the second corner, fold it over as well and draw symbolically what it is that you want.

On the third folded-over corner, draw in symbols how it is to be accomplished that what you want shall come to be.

On the fourth folded-over corner, draw what it is you want, resting in your possession.

Now take a small piece of tape and join the top together so that the paper becomes a small pyramid with the symbols of the Goddess and God inside, and the pictures on the flaps are on the outside of the pyramid where you can see them.

Set up your altar with the Goddess and God candles, and the four elements in their proper quadrants. Also have a small cauldron available or, failing that, a small plate with sand in the bottom.

Light the candles and incense and put the pyramid you have made in the center of the four elements. Start humming in a constant mid tone, without variation. Do this for about five minutes, both on the inhale and on the exhale. After you have done this, while still relaxed, point your finger at each symbol you have drawn, letting the basic meaning of the picture come into your mind. Go in the sequence of the way that you drew them. When you reach the fourth side and have let the meaning come into your mind, exhale quickly and visualize a flash of light leaving the centre of the pyramid, and going directly out of the top and on into the sky.

Thank the God and Goddess for their help, and then light the paper pyramid in the Goddess candle and put it in your cauldron or on your plate to be totally burned up. It is done.

The Cone of Power

A cone of power may be raised in many ways. This is usually done through dances and songs. Most importantly, it is done through going into an altered state of awareness and letting the energy of the Gods flow through you.

Since the altar is in the centre of the globe, it is proper to stand in a circle around it. All of the wizards involved take hold of the person next to them. At the same time on a psychic or mental level they all interlock their antlers (or tendrils as the case may be). This works to help form a gestalt, or a group mind which is more powerful than working alone. Traditionally, the strength of the working goes up on a logarithmic scale instead of a linear one. The Servant of the God or Goddess begins the chanting of the names of the God or Goddess that you wish to channel into your working. It can be Bride or Angus Og or anything that you wish.

Meditate upon the God or Goddess that you are asking for assistance. Think upon the all-pervading energy of the God and feel it begin to flow into you, slowly filling you to the brim. When it feels right, sing the name faster and faster until the leader of the chant decides that it has reached its peak. At that point, he releases the hands of those around him and claps as a signal for others to release those hands that they are holding. All point their hands at the mirror in the centre of the altar, and let the energy flow out of them and into the mirror. Of course, all must agree on this work of magic, or it cannot be done. If you are doing this by yourself, stand at the south point of the altar facing north, and do the same. It is done.

A Healing Work

Set up your altar as before. Draw a picture of the person or animal or plant for which you wish to do a healing. Sprinkle some dust on it, recognizing that the basic nature of all is health, and that the dust represents illness. Light some incense so that your prayers may ascend with the smoke to the Gods, and set the soiled picture before you, and feel yourself expanding and assuming their features. When you feel a certain solidity to this image, inhale deeply and blow the dust off of the picture you have drawn, while in your mind, blowing away the illness or dirt from a person with the breath of your God or Goddess. When you have finished and the dirt is gone, leave the area. It is done.

Clairvoyance

To attain the air of clairvoyance, take a picture frame of any size you wish, and put inside a blank piece of paper, unlined and white. Consecrate this to the Gods. Place this on the wall where you can gaze at it comfortably as you lay in bed, or hang it on the ceiling above your head so that you can gaze at it in a totally relaxed position.

Keep looking at the blank paper enclosed by the frame, but not staring hard. Gazing in a relaxed manner is preferred, as you will get more results working this way than with great intensity. Remember, you are letting visual images come out of your subconscious mind, and if you keep your conscious mind in direct focus, you are stopping or inhibiting the process, not helping it. In a sense this is conscious intentional dreaming with your eyes open. If you relax and keep your eyes open, and your relaxed awareness directed towards the picture frame, after a while you will notice a movement in the frame of the picture. Don't move your eyes, as what you noticed will immediately disappear. This phenomenon will start with the peripheral vision, and spread from that peripheral vision to the centre of your eye, not the other way around, so it takes a little discipline not to look directly at what is catching your attention. Just keep a relaxed mindset, not moving your eyes, and the movement will increase, and move more towards your center of focus. When this happens, soon you will see a whole picture. Write these things down later, and don't fall asleep. This is the easiest way I know to practice the art of scrying, and I have had greater success with it than any other method. Try it! It can be a lot of fun.

Cord Magic

Use embroidery thread for this work. You may braid or entwine two or more threads together to complete the symbolization of concepts you require. Tie nine knots in this in an evenly spaced sequence while you are meditating on the union of concepts represented by the threads. Tie the ends together to form a circle.

One thread should represent you and your life. The other threads should be what you want to draw or bind to you. This should be for goals, not people. You can get into trouble by manipulating people, so avoid it. It usually backfires.

Through the Fires

Now hold the thread in front of you, and hold in your mind the concept of the thought (not the words of the thought) of what it is you want. Now visualize yourself and the string expanding, growing as large as the house, the city, the state, the continent, the earth, the solar system, the galaxy, and beyond until your awareness of yourself ceases to be. Your mind will seem to go blank for just a moment, but hold your intent never the less. If you fail to hold it at this moment, what you desire will not manifest. When you come back to normal awareness, take the string and burn it in the fire. Thank the Gods, and get up and leave the place.

White	Purity, reflective, Spiritual light
Red	Sexual forces, life and vitality forces, anger
Light Blue	Spirituality, peace, peaceful unions
Dark Blue	Depression, "the blues"
Yellow	Intellect, compelling, mind, will
Green	Fertility, love, money, healing, nature magic
Brown	Earth related, physical, neutral or grounded energy
Black	The Void, negative, destructive, drawing, absorbing
Purple	Wealth in earthly matters, gay, ruling, highly spiritual, royalty
Gold	Solar magic, compelling or drawing
Silver	Moon magic, enchanting

Empathic Emotions

The most common form of psychic perception is that of clairsentience, or the experiencing of other people's emotions. Many people are empathic, or sense the emotions of other people quite easily. This can be quite confusing as you may be depressed or out of sorts for no good reason. If you are naturally very empathic, it can be very difficult to distinguish your own emotions from other peoples, and this can cause erratic behavior and anguish.

To gain control over this natural ability one must begin to be able to distinguish between one's own feelings and those coming in from other sources. The best way to do this is to visualize a steel pole going vertically down through the center of your body and continuing down to the center of the earth. Mentally grab onto this metal pole and hold it tightly, letting all of your stress flow down the pole to the earth. As you find this core of stability within yourself and ease the emotional stress, you should concentrate on remaining securely in place. What you will begin to notice after you have thus centered yourself, is the alien or outside quality of some of the emotions that you will begin to experience. Once you begin to know that some of these emotions are coming from others, you will be able to control them and "disown" them and recognize them as being from other people.

When someone of particularly strong emotions affects you, visualize a wall of glass or a strong barrier in between the two of you. You will notice that this has a tendency to dampen a lot of the emotional assault flowing through to you. The more you wish to dampen this flood, the more you mentally begin to opaque the glass, or visualize a mirror around you and begin to simply reflect it away. This technique is not to be used all of the time. Centering with the steel pole however might be beneficially used a great deal. The more you practice with this technique, the better you will become at it and feel more in control of your own life.

This particular type of talent is a great gift. It is the tool of the counsellor, or the person most able to understand how someone else is feeling and advise them. If you are thrown off center by someone's intensity of feeling, then you will be unable to give wise counsel. By being aware of the intensity of other people's feelings, while coming from a point of personal stability you will be able to influence others to become stable as well, instead of being pulled off center by their intensity.

You can also place your emotions into the future and see how you would feel in a future situation, to know whether it will be good or bad for you.

Natural Magic

Although there are magical works as listed above, it should be remembered that here we are mainly concerned with natural magic. This book really tries to concern itself very little with ritual magic, not because it is not effective, but because it simply is not the focus.

Natural magic is the use of the natural world around you to effect change in your life and environment. When rituals are used, it is to focus on a point of the natural world around us. It should be pointed out that I am not saying this is a complex or sophisticated system. In most ways it is a very simple system, but then simplicity is often best. Working and communicating with the trees is a form of natural magic. You can gain a lot of energy by leaning your back against a tree, laying on a large stone, or dangling your feet into a running stream. These are all sources of natural energy that can be drawn upon to refresh and recharge your energy. This is natural magic. Visualize the blue of the sky in your mind and see how it affects your emotions and thoughts. Now try red, then yellow, finally green. Did each one make you feel slightly different? Did each one give you access to a mental state and emotional feel? This is natural magic. Does the sound of the rain on the roof give you a comforting feeling? Does the wind's howl make you uneasy? This is how natural magic works. Does the smell of cinnamon, or roses, or garbage affect you? If you think about it, it does. Knowing how this affects you and how it affects the people around you is a valuable tool. When you wish to do a bit of magic to change your environment, you utilize these tools to form a certain mind set and also to draw upon the inherent energy of the life force around you that permits itself to be used. Then using one of the paths of the eight-fold path, you alter your consciousness, your goals become easier to access because of the cues of the natural magic around you. You do your work and then go back into your normal state of awareness.

It was said that one of the old Wizards could just watch a leaf drop from a tree, go into an altered state of awareness and state that when the leaf touched the earth, that the work would be grounded into manifestation, and it would come to be. This is a mastery of natural magic and it is what we are aiming for. Don't underestimate natural magic, it is a path of beauty and is very powerful.

DISSOLVING OBJECTS BY THE ELEMENTS

After a work is completed, the object or energy of the object generally should be dissolved in one of the four elements in order to send the request to the Gods. This has the effect of merging the energy of the work into the universal energy of the totality.

Fire

The first way to do this is through the combustion of the element of fire. You burn the object in an open flame and its smoke takes your prayer to the heavens.

Water

The second way to do this is through the element of water. If the material is liquid, pour it into running water, if possible. It is through the process of evaporation (and mixture) that the request is carried aloft.

Earth

The third way is through the element of earth. You bury the object in the soil and it dissolves through the means of decomposition. This is carried to the earth goddess.

Air

The fourth way is through the element of air. The object is tossed into the winds or is permitted to evaporate, and through this means the prayer is then carried aloft to the Gods.

Any one of these four ways will work to create the dissolution of the object in order to send your request to the Gods.

SIGIL MAKING

A sigil is a symbol which represents something in an abbreviated form. The kind of sigil making which we shall concern ourselves with is made by taking something recognizable as being a symbol of what you want. It is made unrecognizable to the conscious mind, but retains an impact on the subconscious. Write out your desire on a piece of paper. Remove each letter which occurs more than once. Transpose these letters over each other, or work them into lines of another letter. The fewer lines, the better. You may have so many words that you may need to make a couple of sigils. Enclose these in a circle to indicate that they represent a complete thought. Make the symbols you come up with as abstract as you can so that they are meaningless on a conscious level. This is done as the subconscious has a direct link to the superconscious, and manifestation is made easier by directly affecting the subconscious mind. To be more effective, most of your magical symbols especially in the areas of the goals or desire should be sigilized.

SMOKE SPELL

Take a stick of incense and light it. Enter a meditative state, and when you have gone into a light altered state of consciousness, take the stick of incense and write your desire into the air in the form of your sigils. Visualize glowing lavender lines following your stick of incense, and burning themselves into the consciousness of the universe. Meditate on writing your sigils into the mind of deity. When you are finished, enclose the sigils in your circle with a clockwise wave of your incense. Pierce the earth with the stick of incense to symbolically ground your desire into the earth plane. It is done.

POWER

There are two kinds of power. One is raised such as we have already discussed, and the other we are going to touch upon is drawing power. Simply speaking, raised power is energy you generate with your own self such as a cone of power. Drawing power is power drawn from an elemental, deity, or object and then used for your desire. Drawing power is accomplished through rapport with nature. Through this rapport you come to know the beings you wish to invoke to aid you.

ELEMENTAL WORKINGS

The Elementals are the beings which inhabit the four elements. They are easily offended so you must be very courteous to them, but if treated respectfully they will accomplish a great deal for you.

Through the Fires

Place your altar or table due North, and lay out the Kings of the tarot, one to each side of the altar. Always be sure to lay all four of the Kings out, as the elementals are sensitive and easily slighted, and leaving out one of the cards would be an offense to the one who identified with the card.

The King of Pentacles represents the King of the Gnomes, whose element is earth. This card should be placed at the North point of the altar. His kingdom deals with material matters such as money or jobs.

The King of Wands represents the King of the Sylphs, whose element is air, and should be placed at the East point of the altar. His kingdom deals with intellectual matters, such as ideas or concepts.

The King of Swords represents the King of the Salamanders, whose element is fire. This card should be placed at the south point of the altar. His kingdom deals with matter of energy, such as drive for getting a project finished, or healing energy.

The last is the King of Cups, which represents the King of the Merpeople, whose element is water. This card should be placed at the west point of the altar. His kingdom deals with emotional matters, such as love or desire.

These four cards represent the four elements. The Emperor and Empress are also set out at the top of the altar to represent Bride and Angus Og. The Emperor card is set out upon the top right, and the Empress card is set out upon the top left. Pick out a card which represents the person or situation you are going to work on, and pick out another card which represents your end desire. Place this card over the first one, and put both in the center of the table as a center of focus.

Candles should be anointed and incense should be burned, the kind depending upon which Elemental King whose help you wish to ask. All of the Elementals like a lot of ritual. When invoking them, chant your request in a sing-song manner. Be sincere and do not call on them for frivolous purposes. They do require our respect. Call to them something like this:

"Lord of Air, Lord of Space, send me your sylphs. I need their help. Let me see them, feel them, I need their help."

Then state your desire, also singing it.

Fire Elementals are the most sensitive, and the Earth Elementals have been the most taken for granted, which never should be done. When you are done with your ritual, thank them profusely. They will be faithful if you praise and appreciate them. You can use them to send messages to other people, or anything that you don't want to bother the Gods and Goddesses about. You can even use them to find something for you.

Elemental Correspondences

The correct colored candle to use to invoke the Air Sylphs is pale lavender, pale blue, or pale pink. For the Water Merpeople or Undines blue, green, or lavender is used. For the Earth Gnomes use brown, or deep green. If you are invoking the Gnomes for money matters or treasures, use silver or gold candles. To invoke the Fire Salamanders, use a red, yellow, or orange candle.

To charge and anoint the candles, use oil of heliotrope for the Fire Salamanders. Use oil of lilac for Air Sylphs. Use oil of frankincense or myrrh for Water Merpeople. Use oil of patchouli for Earth Gnomes. The correct incenses to use for the Air Sylphs are lavender, frangipani, honeysuckle, or lilac. For Fire Salamanders use musk, dragon's blood, or sandalwood. For Water Merpeople use Irish moss, or ambergris. For the Earth Gnomes use patchouli or pine.

Elemental objects which are good to also have on hand for their associations, are olivine (peridot) for fire, shells for water, salt or dirt for earth, and a feather for air.

The Elemental Beings respond to love and that is how they must be approached. If you happen to see sparks or lights out of the corners of your eyes, then they are letting you know they are close. They can be wonderful friends.

Tarot Altar

If you are doing magical workings with the tarot, or perhaps if you are in circumstances where you would like to set up an altar of the Old Religion but cannot easily, then the tarot altar is for you.

Take out the Emperor and the Empress cards, along with the Ace of Wands, Swords, Clubs, and Pentacles. The altar is oriented towards the north. Place the Ace of Pentacles to the North of your altar set up to represent the element of Earth. To the East place the Ace of Wands to represent Air. To the South place the Ace of Swords to represent Fire, and to the West place the Ace of Cups to represent Water. To the top right place the Emperor to represent the God, and to the top left place the Empress to represent the Goddess.

This sets up a fairly well-balanced area for you to work in. A protective globe can be created to keep you focused on your work as well as protect you from outside psychic distractions. This is the basic set up and it can be used for a number of things.

Tarot Portal

The tarot is an old set of symbols which can access certain layers of the subconscious. The symbols of the I Ching, runes, or geomantic figures can also act in the same way. Through these tools enormous access can be found for hidden potentials within yourself, and also abilities which can be considered "paranormal".

The way that this is accomplished is to take a tarot card, or a card with one of these other figures on it, and place it in the very center of your tarot altar. Sit and look at it very carefully. Memorize each detail. Quietly sit in a place where you will not be disturbed and visualize the card in your mind as a door. Clearly see in your mind each detail of the card. If you visualize the card "doorway" long enough, it will swing open. Go through this doorway in your mind. You will find the inner meaning of the card. If you do tarot readings or other kinds of readings for people, this will greatly increase your accuracy. It will also teach you about your own consciousness, and the nature of reality. I recommend the Albano-Waite tarot deck for this kind of exercise.

Animal cards can also be used for work with totems. Care should be used when this is done as if the identification with the animal becomes too great, it can be like a self-hypnosis and you may for a time actually believe you are physically the animal. This can lead to problems with the neighbor's dogs much less the neighbor himself. So, as you can see, this is better as a light- to medium-depth meditation.

You can make cards for whatever you wish. Scenes of a beautiful tropical island can be useful as a place of meditation for relaxation. Access to places of mystical significance can be gained through a drawing or a photograph. You may also wish to create your own magical sigils to work with and to create your own meditation guides that are unique to you alone. The possibilities are endless.

If you can draw or find a picture of certain Gods or Goddess, this can also be used to contact Them. If you cannot do that, you might make a sigil of a particular God or Goddess you would like to be in contact with, and put that on your own card to use as a doorway to access Them.

Chapter Seven: The Ancestral Altar

The ancestral altar is set up in your home in honor of the ancestors who gave you form. It is also to invoke their benevolent aid in times of pain and stress.

In ancient Italy, and in other countries, small altars, with offerings of grain and food, were set up near the entrance of the house for the guardian spirits of the home and family. This was similar to the banshees of Ireland, so the guardians of the families extended into the far West. The fairies and spirits of the dead were often confused, as some saw the dead go to Tirnanog, or the fairy land, after death, and of course, offerings such as milk were left out for the fairies every evening. To not do so would have been to court disaster, it was thought. Hence, the guardian spirit of your personal family is propitiated, as well as the ancestral spirits of your own family or genetic line.

Set up a small shelf somewhere in an obscure corner of your home. On it have a few small bowls, one in which you put some grain like wheat, corn, or rice, and another for a small glass of water or milk or wine. It is proper to burn a bit of incense every day as you sit before it and do a meditation on deity and for the welfare of all your families, past and present. On occasion, burn a candle in their honor. As you do so, you will find that the energy around this ancestral altar will increase. Asking to learn your ancient ancestral wisdom and power is a good thing. Seek only the benevolent ancestors, and you will start to find your life changing for the better.

ANCESTRAL INVOCATION

After your ancestral altar is set up, you may use this invocation.

"O Guardians of Ancestors of the blood family of _____, come, attend me here. Recognize and accept this offering of grain and milk I give you. Come, most reverend ancestors, give me your protection, your guidance and your love from the Unseen Realms of Bliss. Guide me into truth and happiness, and teach me our ancient family magic, and pass on to me our ancient family powers and Guides to use for my evolution, and that of others. So be it."

PERSONAL ALTAR

Many wizards have a small personal altar set up somewhere in the privacy of their homes or bedrooms. This, like the ancestral altar, is optional or the two may be combined.

Usually the altar used to perform the high days and full moon ceremonies is set up and then taken down right after the ceremony. The personal altar is never taken down, but remains there constantly for the spiritual support of the person who maintains it. It is always kept clear and never neglected as this is a sign of devotion to the Gods, but it is a personal devotion which others will not see. A personal altar has usually the same elements as a ritual altar, but since it is a personal altar it does not have to be maintained for magic. You may have upon it whatever you wish that will bring you into personal balance and proximity to the peace and joy of divinity.

TEACHING

The manner in which the Old Religion was taught among the hereditary pagan families was the grandfather taught the granddaughter and the grandmother taught the grandson. There was an oral transmission of the information from male to female and vice versa, but also from age to youth. If one of the grandparents passed away, the other grandparent took over the training of all of the grandchildren. If both were gone, then it was up to the parents. This could be changed to save the tradition, so to make a hard and fast rule that same gender teachers cannot teach is foolish, discriminatory, and paranoid.

The paranoid fear of some traditions that same gender teachers of students would lead into homosexuality is an embarrassing remnant of the Christian bigotry, and was uncommon among the elder systems. It was most uncommon for a sexual relationship to occur between a grandparent and grandchild, so fears along those lines seem silly. In many cases, it was the grandmother who passed on secret female teachings to the granddaughter, so obviously there were same gender teachings there. There seems to be little fear of lesbianism in these cases. Besides that, why is homosexuality to be avoided in the Old Religion anyway? Anyone who studies the old European cultures before the advent of Christianity finds that homosexuality was honored and respected. Read Caesar's account of the Celts sexuality during his trips into the Celtic countries.

The graceful surrendering of the wisdom of age to the youth was beneficial, as usually the older folk had more time to spend with the children while the parents were out working the fields, nor did they have to be such disciplinarians. Therefore, the understanding between the grandparents and grandchildren was deeper, and the teachings more easily passed on.

It is therefore the Old Religion understanding that the elderly are to be treated with care and respect. They are the keepers of the wisdom of life, and of the Old Ways. They are not cast aside, but are cared for and looked after for their wisdom and understanding of life. All Wizards are thoughtful and caring of the old.

It is also understood that sometimes it is in the best interest of all if there are same gender teachers, as there are some matters that women understand between themselves, and sometimes the same for men. Opposite gender teachings can be good to release the inherent fear and discrimination that sometimes exists between the sexes if there is little or no contact between them otherwise. If was a beautiful and old way of teaching about life. It would be nice if it could be preserved.

Teachers

If you can, find a teacher whose family line has carried down the Old Religion. There are very few of these people left, but they do exist and they need to be listened to. In most cases they do not let their teachings go out of the family, but in cases where there are few family members left (if any) then sometimes it is done so that the memory of the Old Gods can survive. It is better to let the system go out of the family than to let it end, as it can bring as much hope and joy to others as it has brought to the elder keepers. It was not always confined to just the family, but to the clan and sometimes others. It is true that there are few people sincere enough to dedicate the rest of their lives towards one specific tradition, but they do exist.

It should be understood that if someone teaches you a hereditary system, it is entrusted to you to carry on, not just to dabble and then skip off to another system. A number of the old systems will have difficulty lasting past this current generation not only in America but in Europe as well, and it is a tragedy of incredible proportions. To have lasted so long, only for our generation to drop the ball on our heritage now is cause for real sorrow. It is an irreparable loss if the states of consciousness that have been carefully passed down and nurtured from ancient times are lost now, much less the lore and ritual. Granted, new rituals may work all right, but there is the energy of the "well-worn path" which may make something work easier and better. It is wise to learn of the old heritage not only for yourself, but for all people. The sacred trusts have been carried so far forward that it is important not to let them falter now. As we discard the elderly in our society so we have discarded their wisdom. In our arrogance is folly. Therefore, seek the old ways of the hereditary wizards if you can find them, and you will find your life enriched.

The Fall of the Matriarchies

There must be a question of why the matriarchies were so violently suppressed. In short, the matriarchies were abusive to the male. If you go back to the hunter gatherer civilizations before the nature of procreation was understood, the Moon was considered to be the fertilizing force in the world. If a woman wished to get pregnant, it was thought that if Moon light touched her, she would have children. Where did this leave the male? Not in a very good position. The male was then superfluous to the tribe. Even after the nature of procreation was understood by the women the knowledge was kept from men because it would have undermined their social control of the tribe. Women were thought to magically give birth from themselves alone and so were honored above men as the maintainers and renewers of the tribe. It was the death penalty for any woman in those times to reveal to men that they had anything to do with procreation, as both the woman who told and the man who heard would be put to death.

To think that this emphasis on social control would not have led to abuses would be folly. It has been passed down in the old lore that the most ancient matriarchal tribes practiced male sacrifice. This came down as ritual regicide in later times, although earlier a man might be executed by being thrown down into a pit or having his throat slashed. In the earliest times this was voluntary as these men's spirits became the intercessors for the tribe to the Gods, after which they were reborn info the tribe again through the beneficence of the Mother of the Clan. It became an obvious fact, particularly in later times, that not all were willingly sacrificed for this practice.

In much later times yet, pigs were made to take the place of men after the patriarchies began to gain more influence. To dehumanize someone male by calling them the name of this ancient sacrificial animal is a chilling reminder of women's past, and what they were capable of. It is a reminder to men of what the matriarchies did to them. This serves no purpose.

The utter fall of the matriarchies came when the men rose up and killed every woman in the tribe, keeping only the very young female children alive to be trained as they wished and for the continuance of the tribe. The abuse must have been very intense for this type of reaction to occur. Not everyone wanted to end up having a knife slash their throat or be thrown down into a pit to have their bones broken and starve to death just because of their genitalia.

This reinstitution of the matriarchies as they were is really no longer a possibility as both men and women are unlikely to accept it. As this is now the case, the discrimination of the feminine must end as the abuses of the past to the extent that they were are unlikely to be repeated. To think that women's lives have not been sacrificed unnecessarily for the patriarchy would be folly, as men's lives had been under the matriarchy. Neither was or is right and to continue to do so is not to learn the lessons of the past, because the pendulum does swing both ways, and it must be brought to a rest by compassion, sanity, and civilization. Co-rule or total lack of discrimination for both genders with mutual respect is the only way to avoid both the abuses of the patriarchy and the matriarchy. It is the idea that if one is oppressed, we are all oppressed. Whether the rule is patriarchal or matriarchal there will be abuse to the opposite gender. Co-rule is the only way to stop the discrimination, abuse, and murder of one gender by another.

Chapter Eight: Animal Guides

The Egotism of Being Human

In our culture, which reflects our religious views, is an egotism in respect to being a human being. This is a problem. First of all, in the web of life the ancient Mother doesn't play favorites. She loves all the children of life equally. In the more ancient sense, all other beings, plant or animal, were considered equal but just different from us. We belonged to one tribe of living beings and the cats or birds belonged to another tribe, a different tribe. Remnants of this are seen when a plant is harvested, or with an animal when it participates in the giveaway, an offering is made to their spirits. It donates its body for the continuance of other life, but its spirit is honored as an equal.

A more correct view is not domination of, but harmony with nature. The animals of the earth should be considered equal, but of other tribes whose specialities are different from our own. In some other things they are better skilled than we are. Thus, it is good if we take ourselves out of our separate category and realize that we are not above nature but part of it. We are no more, no less than any other living creature.

Respect should be shown to the other tribes if we wish nature to show respect for us. If you attempt to dominate nature or exploit it, you yourself on a cultural, personal, and societal level will be dominated and exploited. This also pertains to you if you idly permit it to happen. You should realize that awareness resides not only in your own form but in all other living beings, and should be respected if you wish yourself to be respected.

THE ROLE OF THE ANIMAL GUIDE, OR FAMILIAR

Many people in the Old Religion were persecuted and murdered for holding the natural rights of all beings in honor. The Old Religion had a tendency to form deep bonds with the creatures around them even to the point of establishing a mutual form of communication. It is our own thoughts of "that creature can't talk" that has lost for us the ability to speak the languages of other creatures. The magic has not faded from the world, only our ability to perceive it. In order to overcome this cultural handicap, it is wise to choose a fellow creature, such as a cat or a dog, and really observe them, not as a cat or a dog, but as a small human being. Just like gay people, most animals have been treated very badly, with total disregard and disrespect. For true communication with any being, those negative attitudes that are taken for granted must be dropped.

You will need to observe the expressions in their eyes for these are the windows to the soul. Animals communicate a great deal through the expressions in their eyes. Their love or hate can be observed in their expressions. If listened to carefully, their meaningless cries can be understood through mood tones and finally, you may be able to understand a few words that will start to filter through. Cats do seem better in this regard than dogs if worked with. Once you begin to understand the "speech" of the other tribes, it does not set you apart so much. Once you begin to have one creature open the doors of communication, there is no longer a master/slave relationship, but a communication of two understanding hearts. Physical size does not determine the greatness or smallness of the heart.

ANIMAL TELEPATHY

Another aspect of communication is animal telepathy. As odd as it sounds, animals do communicate through telepathy. This is done through emotions and visualization. Spoken language is not really used in this form of communication. Visualize very strongly what you want when you are focusing on your familiar. If it is not exactly what the familiar wants to hear, you may very well end up ignored, but what else is new in life? Anyway, cats and dogs are particularly telepathic, and you can communicate very well through this means should you learn the knack of it and have a familiar that will cooperate with you. It is good to train them from when they are very young in this, but it can also be done with an older animal as trust and love is established. I have done both, so don't let that stop you from adopting an older pet for a familiar.

The creation of understanding is the true role of the animal guide and it is a fairly heavy responsibility, and that is to help guide us to the right relationship to the other tribes with whom we live. Once you do have communication, doors of magic open and new worlds are revealed.

OTHER USES OF AN ANIMAL GUIDE

What are the other uses of an animal guide? There are several. Once the mental jump of achieving equality is achieved, there is the gentle mental opening of your guide so that you can see through the eyes of the creature. If you choose a bird, you can enjoy the mental experience of flight, or whatever is the experience that your friend would wish to share with you. The familiar is also a doorway to your totem spirit, and the totem spirit can be invoked through them. When this awareness arrives, you had better have treated your familiar quite well as you are calling upon a real power that you can make your ally only through love. The expansion of awareness along these lines is fundamental to the understanding of the Old Religion and the achieving of harmony with the universe. Sometimes we do need to learn that there are other priorities than our own.

Another reason is for psychic protection. If there is negative energy directly aimed at you physically, usually the familiar will sense it before you do as their psychic senses are usually sharper. The familiar will warn you and give you a chance to raise your protections. Indeed, if the link is strong enough, the familiar may sacrifice its own life to save yours from a strong enough attack.

Another reason is that familiars can also give energy. For instance, the stroking of a cat's fur stimulates static electricity, but also psychic energy. That is one of the reasons that there are a number of old spells involving the combining of the hair.

Of course, the most important reason is for the love and companionship. Following a way of wisdom can often be quite a lonely path and often it sets you aside from many other people. A familiar or an animal guide then becomes something truly wondrous and needed for emotional stability and companionship.

In the process of breaking the chains of our egos, a sense of stability can be lost. A familiar is a being which anchors us with the feeling of its touch and its constant unconditional love and companionship. They also remind us of the responsibilities we have to others and to ourselves. There are other reasons for having a familiar, but I think it wise to let you discover those reasons on your own. The greatest wisdom is not written in the pages of a book, but in the living and experiencing of life. So, find your familiar and experience what I am really saying. You might try the **Animal Meditation** in **Chapter Eleven** of this book.

Wolf Ways

In ancient times when the wolf was a close member of the clan, it was used for hunting and stalking. They were also used for the protection of the clan. If there was someone who had angered the clan, perhaps by killing a clan member, there was a foray to the home or farm of that person.

An article closely associated to that person was taken and given to the wolves to smell. The rest you can probably figure out.

If a man saw one of the old people running away with a legging or a shirt, it must have been an awful sinking feeling because he was not just losing an article of clothing, he may have been losing his life.

This is one of the beginnings of contagion magic. This fear lasted very late as the Victorian ladies would bury their hair clippings in the back yard to avoid someone doing them harm by taking it.

This was the darker side of the wolf lore and this no longer happens, but it does give an interesting insight into how some of the old magic evolved. It must have seemed magical how the wolf could follow the scent and trace one individual and not another.

Since the wolf clan and the human clans intermingled, and humans imitate so well, it would be interesting to think upon the way we have set up our clan social structure might actually have been drawn partly from the wolf, as the wolf was considered a part of the family and clan with all the same rights. In other words, they were seen as equals who the clan cooperated with and respected as equal tribal members.

The honor with which the wolf was held is seen in the Roman Lupercalia, or feast or the young Wolf God, an ancient remembrance of the time when man and wolf were friends.

Animal Magic

Many of the animals have their own rituals and magic. We have this in common. Certain kinds of animal magic can be very strong and are not to be taken lightly.

Through the Fires

The crane's ritual mating dance was known to be a very powerful magic dance and was imitated by the Old Peoples as they wished to draw upon this powerful magic. These atavistic types of dances can bring in powerful altered states of awareness, abilities, and teachings.

Learn to mimic the rituals of the animal you have chosen in order to learn its magic and gain access to their perceptions and powers. If you have chosen the coyote, go out in the wild and call loudly to the moon. If you have chosen the crane, learn the crane dance, or perhaps you might stalk like a cat if a cat is what you have chosen.

Animal magic rituals can be approached in many ways, but always remember that the animal will always be better at it than you.

Chapter Nine: Groups

It is human to bond together, to see social interaction. This is good as it gives a sense of belonging and community to people who might not otherwise have this. It is also human nature to bond together when confronting the energies of the divine, as concepts so vast can be frightening. Thus, it is common to human history that religious and spiritual groups have been formed, and this is no exception. Like minds will come together, no matter what the subject, but there are some safeguards and ways to set up groups that work better than others. Groups of Wizards should be set up according to the following guidelines.

Leaders

The Servants of the God and Goddess are elected by group vote. This is an honor and a privilege but mainly just a lot of work. Someone who is not willing to put in a lot of effort should not let himself come up for a vote. Before anyone sets himself up in a position of leadership he should study the issue of co-dependency and interpersonal relationships rather thoroughly. Some small basis in transactional analysis is helpful.

Unfortunately teaching or leadership situations can put you in a position where people can expect you to rescue them. This is a dire mistake and should be avoided at all costs. If you study co-dependency thoroughly, you will understand what I am talking about. This should be a requirement for anyone sitting or placed in a position of authority. It is wise therefore, to go to some meetings where these issues are addressed, such as Adult Children of Alcoholics, or Codep. You are absolutely certain to run into these issues and if you are unwilling to research them and address your own relationship to them, perhaps teaching others is the last thing you should be doing. Some good books on the subject are *Codependent No More* by Melody Beattie, *Games People Play* by Eric Berne, and *Scripts People Live* by Claude Steiner. Without examining the sorts of intense personal interaction that these books address, you run the risk of passing your dysfunction on to others.

I would strongly recommend studying dysfunctional family systems. Unfortunately for many gay people, such systems exist quite often. In order to understand the motivations and problems of many people, this should also be mandatory for leaders before they take a position of leadership. Some good books on this issue are *Healing the Shame that Binds You* by John Bradshaw, and *The Self Sabotage Syndrome* by Janet Woititz. If you had problems with members of your immediate family, then you might assign family roles to others in your new group unconsciously, and that might lead to unnecessary misunderstandings and inappropriate reactions. If someone that has a number of co-dependent or dysfunctional family issues wishes to join the group, he should also join a twelve-stop program for his issues to be resolved before starting to study magic intensively. What is inside of us will manifest outside of us particularly when the study of magic is initiated; it is therefore necessary for the well-being of the individual and the group that these issues not be swept under the table, but addressed directly and supportively. Otherwise, disaster may result for the individual and the people around him.

Whether he studies magic, or not, dysfunctional issues inside of a person will manifest in dysfunctional situations around him, but magic will intensify and speed up the process. Unfortunately, people who emotionally self-sabotage usually take others with them. This is to be avoided as it will cause disruption in the group. This is a spiritual system. It is not a way simply to alter one's mood, but to spiritually evolve. If it is used to mood alter only, it corrupts the individual and the system. It is not an escape but a way to confront our issues in the most healing and loving way possible. Twelve step programs are highly recommended in dealing with issues of family dysfunction and emotional pain. Do not use religion or spiritual systems as means of avoiding them.

Unfortunately, magical lodges or groups often can and have become the playgrounds of dysfunctional individuals who are looking for fantasy rather than evolvement. For the emotionally starved adult child, it becomes an arena to gain attention from others; always with disastrous results. Often people drawn to the study of new religious systems are people with troubled backgrounds who have been abused mentally or physically by a religious parent or caregiver. This makes them turn away from the old system as it is difficult for them to associate deity with an abusive caregiver.

As children, the ideas of deities that we possessed were based upon our ideas of our parents. It is these people that granted our wishes and protected us, or should have. The God and Goddess theme is based upon the concept of divine parents, which is why there is not often a gay set of deities set up in this manner. Few people had a gay set of parents initially. If you had an abusive father, and that includes neglect, you may be drawn to a Goddess religion. If your mother was abusive, you may be drawn more to a masculine-aspected religion, or one in which the feminine is very gentle. If you are gay and both parents were abusive, you may look for deity in a Lover Aspect, which is where a set of gay deities may figure in, or you may search for this because it is more personally empowering. Either one of these reasons is valid and should be respected, but generally motivations for coming towards a religious system such as this should be examined. Is one seeking personal power or personal balance? The concepts of personal power should rest in the security of self-knowledge of one's own being, not upon what spell or magic that is known.

If someone does come from a troubled background, that in itself is not insurmountable, but it can become a problem if these issues are not confronted directly by the individuals themselves. As a group leader you must have already dealt with these problems yourself and you must be able to direct people where to go if they have them. Nobody expects you to be a professional psychotherapist, but you should be able to recognize when someone needs help beyond what you can give them. As a leader you become the ear for a lot of troubled people so be prepared both emotionally and with practical resources.

POWER MADNESS

There is also the problem that sometimes someone in a position of leadership goes power mad. Perhaps those people should read the Tao of leadership! Remember, all you potential little Caesars, that the people are there because they want to be, not because they have to be. Power can be tempting, but used in a manner other than with love or care, one will be left with no group to lead. Actually, you cannot really lead people at all, you can only guide them. Think of yourself as a Guardian or Guide of your people, but not in a possessive sense.

Expecting a lot from other people is also a problem as you will often be disappointed. It is much better just to be hopeful and realize that other people may not set the same standards or requirements that you set for yourself. If someone is unwilling to help himself, it is a mistake for you to do it for him. Let him fail until he is tired of it and truly wishes to succeed, at which point he will. Remember you are there to work with people, not have them work for you nor you do all the work yourself either. As a leader you do end up doing much of the work yourself, but if you end up doing it all, it is time to bow out of an irresponsible group.

When the God and Goddess are called down and are in the ritual globe that is when the words of the Servants become law. At that point they may not be disobeyed in the globe and order and discipline will be maintained. There is a time and a place for everything and respect and honor will be paid to the Servants while the Gods are descended, for they become holy receptacles for the God forces. Indeed, it may be perilous not to do so, because if the Gods have truly descended, you are dealing with more than an individual. Be warned. At other times there may be disagreements within the group but at that moment they are not permitted. If some do come up, it is up to the Servant of the God to deal with the matter immediately. If someone cannot get along with the Servants, he is free to start his own group, so there is no reason to stay where he is not happy, or to cause disruption.

If is best to remember that a very happy group is much more productive than a very solemn one.

COUNCIL

A small group of the longest worshipping Wizards are elected to act as the Council by the group. There is always an odd number so that if something comes up which requires a vote, there are no ties. If a person feels that there is a problem with the Servants, it may be presented to the Council. They will in turn take it to the Servants, and the Council may hold nothing back from them. They act in an advisory capacity, and to help others when the Servants are simply too busy to deal with the personal problems that may arise with members. They are also available to answer questions about the Wizard's Way. The group size will vary, and therefore the size of the Council may vary, but usually seven people are enough even for a very large group. These are people who through their experience have become skilled in the Wizard's Way, and can pass on that experience. They should be able to communicate easily with people, as people will come to confide in them. With the exception of the Servants, these conversations are strictly confidential, and if one of the Council members divulges details to others, they are not really worthy of sitting on the Council. A good Council member also keeps his own counsel, or easier said, speaks little and listens much.

GROUP

A group should not contain more than 50 people. If more people than that are arriving, it is time for the group to begin to establish other groups. It is not necessary to let everyone enter into the group who wishes to do so. This is not to enforce exclusivity, but to achieve harmony. If you have a well-functioning group of people and someone comes along who wishes to join, but is felt to have a domineering, adversarial, or abrasive manner, it is not necessary to let the person participate on a group level. This has nothing to do with sexuality, but has a lot to do with personality conflicts. After checking with other groups, you can try to refer such people that may be more open to them as members. You might try to instruct them on how to work in a solitary manner since the tradition itself is closed to no one.

To let a person join a group of the Wizard's Way takes a unanimous vote of the whole group. If someone says no, then the person may not join. This is done by giving each person a white stone and a black stone. A person goes around to the whole group and collects the stone that the person wishes to deposit by holding out a small bag. The person drops the stone without it being seen, and afterwards the tally is counted. The black stone is a negative, and the white stone means yes. If you have a group of 14 people and you collect 14 white stones, then the new person is accepted. It is a secret vote and no other members are to know how any individual voted. Magic is a very personal thing. It sometimes requires people to join minds together. If there is someone who is contrary or who does not wish to do the work, it can foul up the workings of the whole group. These types of situations are to be avoided. A problem in your magic can mean a problem in a situation later, so total group harmony must be maintained in order to achieve maximum effectiveness in the metaphysical workings.

Initiation

No initiations or hazing are permitted in this system. All who wish may enter the system. A working group is however, permitted to be exclusionary. The closest thing to an initiation rite in this system is the Dedication Rite.

Feast

Planning elaborate meals for the feasts involves assigning members particular courses, which in the end is a trial for all concerned. It is much better to just let each person bring whatever they want. Let the feast be as the Gods dictate.

The cookies for the fertility ritual and the wine or mead for the sacramental drink should be either assigned or taken care of personally by the Servant of the Goddess as these are essential ritual items.

Classes

Classes in the Old Religion were generally held on the nights of the crescent moon, or first quarter. The Servant of the Goddess arranges for the location and class material. Generally speaking however, everyone contributes to the classes. For this, members are usually assigned lectures either to research, or to elaborate on something they already know. The best type of learning structure is one in which group members learn from one another. This helps stop people from elevating one person into a demigod position on a personal ego level. Each has his own valid truths and insights. Learn from these.

For example, Tim knows astrology and gives a good class on it, drawing on his own experience. Harold knows nothing about the tarot, but is assigned a lecture on it for the next month. If people have a speciality, it is good to let them have time to elaborate on it in a class environment. If the situation turns into more of a social gathering, the Servant of the God shall redirect the course back into the teaching mode, although the experience should be fun as well. Religion should be a fun experience, not one tied into solemnity, dogma, or too much seriousness. Do not take yourselves too seriously, but do get some work done. In this way, certain people will gain specialities from which the rest of the clan can draw knowledge and use. They can also guide someone who wants to specialize in those areas. A general pooling of knowledge and research is extremely beneficial to all who are involved in it.

Attitudes

Many of the attitudes and ethics of the Old Religion were inherently understood, but in this day and age when the dollar rules all and personal, spiritual, and social integrity is dropped at the sound of a clinking coin, perhaps it is time that these points were brought up and spoken of openly so there is no misunderstanding.

Fees

First of all, the traditions are never sold. No fees are charged for the teaching of this or any other Old Religion system by an ethical teacher. For a Servant of the Gods, this time is donated as a sign of devotion to the Gods. To accept money for the teachings of the God and Goddess is a base form of spiritual prostitution. After acceptance in a group, no fees are charged to another Wizard for the worship of the Gods. No fees are charged by a teacher or Servants of the Gods for performing the rites or for their students' instruction.

Dues and Offerings

Dues can be collected from the participating members depending upon a group vote to pay for the materials used. It is not fair to expect one person to pay for everything if many people participate. This money does not go to any one individual teacher, Servant of the Gods, but to a treasurer of the group, duly elected to look after group funds and is accountable at any time for the full amounts to the group.

A love offering can be left on the altar for the Servants if it is felt that the Servants deserve it, but it cannot be solicited, coerced, or even hinted that the Servant wants your money. To do so is a base violation of ethics and questions the motives and abilities of the Servant.

What Can be Charged For?

Now what can be charged for is the working of a bit of magic, doing psychic readings, or other psychic workings. Group members are never charged for these things. You do not charge clan members, period. People outside of the group may be charged along these lines but never people in the group. This doesn't mean that everyone descends upon one member for freebies. This is about caring about people, not greed.

To give you an example: If someone asks you to do a spell for them, a fee may be charged for this to cover materials and for your time. In many cases the old Wizards supported themselves by their readings and magical workings, not on the religion or spiritual path they taught or worked in. It seems pretty cut-and-dried along these lines.

Perhaps, just like people, the Gods do not wish to be sold; and just like us They would turn away from the greed that would cause such a violation of trust and truth. So be warned, this is not a path to make a great deal of wealth from unless you scam the people who believe in you. Hopefully, the Wizards will have more of a sense of honor and honest shame when it comes to this type of behavior. If there is a question about money, look at the intent of what I have just said. You can twist words and semantics every which way to justify your lack of personal integrity, but the intent is not altered, and that is what should be examined.

Group Funds

These are the rules concerning the funds accumulated by the group.

- A treasurer will be elected by the group.
- Dues may be charged depending upon a group vote, but at a rate of no more than the equally divided cost each person will pay for the consumable items.
- Dues are to be used only for consumable items for the group ritual use. This means things like incense, candles, or ritual mead. When one or more of these items are purchased for group use, the receipt will be presented to the treasurer who will make payment out of the group fund. Whenever possible, let the treasurer or Servants make these purchases.
- The group fund will not be used to purchase food for the feasts.
- If dues are selected by the group, all members will pay dues, with absolutely no exceptions.
- Group funds shall not be used to purchase particular tools, books or magazine subscriptions for the "group use", as this causes problems of ownership at a later date.
- If any other uses of the group funds are desired, it must be discussed with all of the wizards who are members before any action can be taken. Approval must be by unanimous vote.
- The treasurer must be ready to open the accounting books to anyone who asks at any time it is reasonably convenient for him. To not do so indicates a violation of trust, truth, and responsibility which will not be tolerated by the group. If you run into this problem, it will seem wise not to have too much money in this fund.

Laws

For any social system, there must be laws. This is so that everyone is treated in a just manner, and anarchy does not reign. For anyone practicing this system, these are the laws to be followed:

Through the Fires

- Find a place where the full moons and high days may be celebrated.
- Gather together in groups, of not more than 50, to celebrate these days.
- Within the globe the words of the Servants of the Goddess and God are law.
- No one shall charge for performing the rites. Each member of the group shall help maintain it with a small donation to cover the costs of the materials used in the ceremony only; no more.
- All shall bring food for the feast.
- All shall be physically and spiritually washed prior to entrance to the hallowed globe.
- A council of elders shall be elected, of an odd number, to act as intermediaries to the Servants of the God and Goddess if problems should arise. These are also to act in an advisory manner to the Servants of the Goddess and God, but may not command them.
- If there is a problem, present it to the Servants of the God and Goddess to be worked upon.
- All works of magic shall take a unanimous vote by all present.
- The art is a blessing to be used only in earnest and never for vain glory, show, or pride.
- You shall draw upon the power only for good.
- You will not violate the privacy of another with your powers.
- You shall become one with all nature, realizing deity is all things, everywhere, at all times, created by nature.
- There shall be no proselytization, all must come of their own free will.
- Never do anything which shall bring disgrace or dishonor upon the Arts, or anyone practicing this system.
- Any member who does bring dishonor shall be warned three times, then cast out of the group.
- You must heed the call of a wizard in need. No one shall be left in need.
- The globe shall not be violated; no one shall pass through the perimeter of the globe save through a properly prepared doorway.

- There shall be no criticism of another group because of differences. Their existence may not be revealed.
- The Servants of the God and Goddess shall appoint helpers if they need them, but these helpers may not be members of the council.
- A member of one group shall not belong to another.
- There shall be no sex in the globe, except the symbolic great rite.
- The Servants of the Goddess and God shall be elected by group vote. If this cannot be done, it shall be decided by the casting of lots.
- The council shall be elected in the same manner. The Servants of the God and Goddess shall not be members of the council.
- If strife arises, present it to the Servants of the God and Goddess. If there is a problem with the Servants of the Goddess and God, present it to the council who shall keep nothing back from the Servants of the God and Goddess. If the Servants cannot agree among themselves, then the Gods shall decide by the casting of lots.
- Order and discipline must be maintained. It is the responsibility of the Servants of the Goddess and God to do this.
- If someone cannot work with the Servants of the God and Goddess, they and all who wish to go with them may leave to form another group.
- No harm shall ever be done to a child, or to anyone else.

Chapter Ten: Rites of Passage

It is much easier to control children than self-directed, self-sufficient adults. It is therefore expedient for the controllers of a fossilized society to remove the personal rites of passage which would ensure the child's move into an adult psychology. To withhold these rites is a sign of derision from a control structure.

Rites of passage are necessary for a child to enter into a functional adult psychology. When these rites of passage are removed, it leaves the child at a stage during which he is unsure that he is an adult. He may try to prove to himself and others that he is an adult by exploits which he would consider proof of his courage. Many of these exploits may very well be courageous but they can also be ill-conceived, resulting in pain and destruction for the individual and for others.

It is for the good of the tribe that these rites be initiated by adults, since if the child has no other adult to look to, he may well look to his peers of the same age. These other children will give him social approval and fulfill his need to belong, but they lack the fundamental ability to grant entry into an adult, self-determined world. They are unable to give guidance as they simply have not been there themselves to chart the path for another.

The religious institutions may take over some of these rites of passage, but it is usually because they are often involved in directed social control, not in the well-being of the tribe. It is necessary therefore, for rites of passage to be instituted by adults who are genuinely concerned about the growth of the individual in a societal structure. Rites of passage include adulthood rites, marriage rites, divorce rites, funeral rites, puberty rites, or any passage from one type of lifestyle to another or one stage of life to another.

If there is no divorce rite, the individual may hold on emotionally to a failed relationship and not progress on into another better one. Rites of passage involve the relinquishment of the past situation, and give the dividing point for people to find themselves already in the new situation. They are definitive psychological structures creating beginnings and ends of times in a person's life. If a person is unsure of where he stands, it is harder to go on and insecurity can result. Effective rites of passage put these problems to rest and ease the anxiety connected to knowing where you stand in relation to other individuals, and society.

Rites of passage also cause psychological change and that is why on an ancient tribal level, so many of them were arduous. If a rite is so mediocre that there is no psychological change created, it is ineffectual, and should be changed. If it causes physical danger instead of psychological change, it has missed the point as this is treading beyond the well-being of the clan. Rites of passage can also define an individual's role in a clan structure so that the clan's people will relate to the individual in an appropriate manner. Marriage ceremonies fall under this heading as they are not only rites of passage for the person's getting married, but it is a rite also for all the rest of the clan's people, and they should all be there if they can for their own well-being.

Since the rites should pose no physical danger to the person undergoing them, in times past, danger from the spirit world was introduced. For example, for a rite of becoming a man, a boy had to make his tools of magic and ritual and go off alone into the forest and create his own magic globe. He then had to stay awake all night long while the men of the clan dressed and painted themselves like demons, who came and tried to steal the young person's tools as he fell asleep. It is this level of emotional intensity that creates these changes.

RITE OF MANHOOD

This rite is done at puberty. The young man undergoing the rite must go into the forest alone, or another deserted place, on the full moon. He is to take the tools of ritual and magic that he has made, and he shall create his magic globe. The men of the clan shall go to him several times during the night, dressed in strange costume, and seek to find him asleep. If he is asleep, they may take his tools, and then if he wakes and finds them gone, he may try again, only 6 months later. After the person has completed this rite, he is escorted back to the clan gathering by the men of the clan. He is brought before the clan elders or the Servants of the Gods who will perform the following:

The Servant of the Goddess says:

"The time has come for you to relinquish your boyhood to assume your manhood."

The Servant of the God says:

"To do this you must make a willing sacrifice of your dependence and fear. In order to step into the world of men, you must leave the world of childhood, and stand among men, knowing equality, not insecurity, community, not separation. Do you wish the continuance of this rite?"

Youth says:

"I do."

The Servant of the Goddess says:

"Then kneel." (The Servant of the God then snips a piece of hair off and places it in a bowl. Youth stands.)

The Servant of the God says:

"Surrender one of the joys of your youth." (*Youth gives a childhood toy to the Servant of the Goddess.*)

The Servant of the Goddess says:

"Welcome into the clan as a man, and receive the acceptance of the Goddess." (*Servant of the Goddess gently embraces the youth.*) He is given a silver chain to wear about his neck.

The Servant of the God says:

"Welcome into the clan as a man, and receive the acceptance of the God." (*Servant of the God gently embraces the youth.*) He is given a pendant with the Clan symbol upon it to wear upon the chain.

The clan then goes to feast.

Rite of Womanhood

This rite is done at puberty. The young woman undergoing the rite must go into the forest alone, or another deserted place, on the full moon. She is to take the tools of ritual and magic that she has made, and she shall create her magic globe. The women of the clan, dressed in costumes of the Goddess, shall go out to her, one by one, and she shall permit them entry. The older women shall impart the duties, rites, secrets and honors of womanhood within the clan.

After the young woman has completed this rite, she is escorted back to the clan gathering by the men of the clan. She is brought before the clan elders or the Servants of the Gods who will perform the following:

The Servant of the Goddess says:

"The time has come for you to relinquish your girlhood to assume your womanhood."

The Servant of the God says:

"To do this you must make a willing sacrifice of your dependence and fear. In order to step into the world of women, you must leave the world of childhood, and stand among women, knowing equality, not insecurity, community, not separation. Do you wish the continuance of this rite?"

Youth says:

"I do."

The Servant of the Goddess says:

"Then kneel." (The Servant of the God then snips a piece of hair off and places it in a bowl. Youth stands.)

The Servant of the God says:

"Surrender one of the joys of your childhood." (Youth gives a childhood toy to the Servant of the Goddess.)

The Servant of the Goddess says:

"Welcome into the clan as a woman, and receive the acceptance of the Goddess." (Servant of the Goddess gently embraces the youth, now woman.) She is given a silver chain to wear about her neck.

The Servant of the God says:

"Welcome into the clan as a woman, and receive the acceptance of the God." (Servant of the God gently embraces the woman.) She is given a pendant with the Clan symbol upon it to wear upon the chain.

The clan then goes to feast.

Group Dedication Ceremony

The dedication ceremony is not considered an initiation as no vows are taken and no state of awareness or power is passed to the person receiving the ceremony. It is not necessary to perform this ceremony to practice or be part of this tradition. It is only a ceremony based upon a person's desire to express outwardly a personal dedication to the Old Religion and the Old Gods.

The globe is erected and the clan is gathered. The drawing down of the God and Goddess is performed by the Servants. The person wishing the ceremony kneels before them.

The Servant of the Goddess says:

"We are here to perform the dedication rite of _____(name)_____ Is this your will?"

Person says:

"It is."

The Servant of the God says:

"Then arise and stand among us, your brothers."

(Person rises) The Servant of the Goddess dips the first two fingers of her right hand into consecration oil. She then touches the person on the forehead.

The Servant of the Goddess says:

"May all your thoughts be touched by the divine beauty of the God and Goddess."

The Servant of the God dips his fingers in the consecration oil also and touches lightly the person's eyelids.

The Servant of the God says:

"May you see only the grace and beauty of our Gracious Goddess and Gentle God."

The Servant of the Goddess says: (Anointing each ear)

"May you hear only Their harmony and sweetness through all time."

The Servant of the God says: (Anointing the nose)

"May you breathe only of Their divine essence as you walk through life."

The Servant of the Goddess says: (Anointing the lips)

"May you speak only of Their graciousness and love for all of the tribes."

The Servant of the God says: (Anointing the heart)

"May you experience the ecstasy of joy of Union with the Goddess and God within yourself, and express it in all of your actions."

The Servant of the Goddess says:

"Do you accept with this dedication the blessings of the Gods?"

Person says:

"I do, I dedicate my life and being to the service of the God and Goddess and to the manifestation of their beauty."

The Servant of the God says:

"So be it."

At this point, the person gives a new name, which he has chosen earlier, to the Servant of the God. The choosing of this name is a very important thing, for it is how he shall be known to the Gods and also to the brother Wizards in the performance of the rites. It is used at no other time, save in the globe and in the presence of the Gods.

The Servant of the God says:

"I present to you the dedicated wizard, now to be known as _____. So be it. The rite has ended."

Self-Dedication Rite

If you have no group to work with or feel uncomfortable in a group situation, this is also an acceptable way to accomplish the dedication rite. After all, the rite is for the person who wishes it performed, it is not meant for others, so to do it privately is perfectly acceptable.

Set up your altar and create the globe. Kneel before the altar and ask that Bride and Angus Og be present as you perform your dedication rite. Dip the first two fingers of your right hand in a consecration oil, and touch your forehead and say:

"May the blessings of the Gods rest upon me, that all my thoughts are touched by the divine beauty of the God and the Goddess."

Touch your eyelids with consecration oil.

"May the blessings of the Gods rest upon me that I see only the grace and beauty of our Gracious Goddess and Gentle God."

Touch your ears with consecration oil.

"May the blessings of the Gods rest upon me that I hear only their harmony and sweetness through all time."

Touch your nose with consecration oil.

"May the blessings of the Gods rest upon me that I breathe of Their divine essence as I walk through life."

Touch your lips with consecration oil.

"May the blessings of the Gods rest upon me that I speak only of Their graciousness and love for all of the tribes."

Touch your heart with the consecration oil.

"May I experience the ecstasy of the joy of Union with the Gods within myself, and express it in all of my actions."

Place your hands over your chest, thumbs interlocked and say:

"I accept the blessings of the Gods and dedicate my life and being to the service of the God and Goddess, and to the manifestation of Their beauty. I choose the name of _____ for the Gods and Wizards to know me by. So be it."

INSTINCTUAL NEEDS

When the instinctual needs of a gay man or woman begin to arise within them, it can overwhelm them. When this is suppressed, it becomes a dam, which if not drained in expression, will burst forth violently doing devastation to the person who ignores it.

There is a fundamental need to be with others like oneself which is perilous to deny for any reason if you are gay. If the absolute need for gay action is suppressed, there comes an inescapable depression. The depression alone warns us that this is not right because depression is anger turned inwards upon one's self. Anger is a survival mechanism and is very useful, but when turned upon the self it is merely self-destructive and will continue to be so until action is taken either to heal one's self, or to commit an even greater aggression against the self. No man or woman who has experienced the fulfillment of these powerful desires truly wants to go back to the way that they were.

In ancient times there was performed the *hieros gamos,* the sacred marriage. It was required that non-personal sex be practiced. A priest who was considered to be the god incarnate, a phallic object, or a stranger who had to be gone by morning, were used to consummate the rite.

This was done for the realization that sex itself is a divine experience, desire, and need. When gay men have this kind of sex, it is a form of divine marriage, a sacred union with a principle, not even necessarily thought of as with another human being. In its own way, it is a divine union with the masculine principle on an intellectual level.

One can however, be overwhelmed by this experience and this can cause imbalance in one's life. How then does one walk in harmony with overwhelming instinctual needs? It is to be found by having new realizations about the instincts themselves. It is found by realizing that instinctual compulsions are a manifestation of the divine. It is the recognition that the drives within each one of us is divinity manifesting through us. It is the universal life force itself which arises within us and has nothing to do with ego decisions, thoughts or responsibilities. It is simply how deity has decided to reveal itself through us. It should therefore be treated as a thing of splendid beauty and reverence, including religious and spiritual awe.

When these realizations are made, such instincts no longer become the property or responsibility of the ego, or the defined "I", but indeed the ego itself must bow before the power and rightness of the divine force. After recognizing that gay needs and instincts are not created by the ego, but are manifestations of a divine Apollo, Dionysus, Hercules, or Vroiko in each of us, our sexuality as well as others should be honored and celebrated and acknowledged with joyfulness. To not do so offends the Gods.

A gay man who feels restricted by society or other people's opinions is not fully in touch with the divinity or holiness manifesting through himself. He is not whole; he is not complete; and he has not experienced his instinctual depths fully, perhaps taking only a cupful of water from behind the dam, instead of realizing the ecstasy of life itself in the flood that anxiously awaits.

To be complete or whole in oneself involves the recognition and the experience of divine union with one's Self.

THE RITE OF ACKNOWLEDGEMENT

This rite is not needed by all, but it is included for those who do need it. It is the rite and right of acknowledging one's own or another's divine instinctual drives and needs.

The rite is begun with the Wizard standing before the group of people gathered, between the Servant of the God and the Servant of the Goddess. The Servant of the God requests quiet, and the rite is begun.

Through the Fires

The Servant of the Goddess places salt (a few grains) upon the tongue of the Wizard. The Servant speaks, and the Wizard repeats after her:

"I accept the inherently spiritually pure salt upon my tongue, and into myself as I accept my inherently pure drives from the God and Goddess which manifest as _____ (hetero, gay, bi)."

The Servant of the God places a candle that is unlit into the Wizard's hand. The Servant has a lit candle himself, and lights the Wizard's candle.

"I accept the beauty and illumination of fire as I accept the beauty and passion of my own _____ instincts, the God himself flowing through me, for all to see."

The Wizard hands the candle back to the Servant of the God.

The Servant of the Goddess places a chalice of wine into the Wizard's hands.

"I accept the fulfillment of the essence of the Goddess, as I accept the fulfillment of my own needs and desire, recognizing the power of the Gods manifesting through both."

The Wizard drinks some of the wine and returns the chalice to the Servant of the Goddess.

The Servant of the God hands the Wizard a stick of incense.

"I accept the pervading essence of this incense, and I recognize and accept this same expanding essence among my brothers and sisters, making us One."

The Wizard returns the incense to the Servant of the God.

At this point the Wizard should begin a chant, which everyone should join in and follow. All should be standing and one by one come up and hug the Wizard, kissing him upon both cheeks as a symbol of acknowledgement and acceptance. The Wizard shall then sit among his people, while the Servant of the Goddess and God declare the rite to be ended.

MARRIAGE INSTRUCTIONS

A few words appear to need to be said about the marriage rite in relation to gay people in particular. To really understand these rites, we have to look at the cultural context in which these ceremonies first arose.

In our modern times it seems that many gay people do not take the idea of marriage as seriously as heterosexuals because it is not legally possible for them at this time. Although one of the reasons that marriages arose was to determine the legitimate inheritance of properties, it was not the only reason. The fact that there was and is a gay marriage rite proves that people also bonded because they cared for each other outside of the legal dispensation of properties. The marriage rite not only dealt with the dispensation of mutual property, it also informed the tribe through this rite of passage that these two people were to be treated in a correct manner in relation to the tribe and other individuals.

The marriage rite was and is valid for heterosexual and homosexual people because it arose from a time when there was no discrimination against either party. The roots of this rite go back to before the time that procreation was understood, as the myth makes specific reference to, plus the fact that women in this culture were not discriminated against. It was this total lack of discrimination against the feminine that made the idea of gay marriage or heterosexual marriage acceptable.

Because of the culturally and socially degraded status of gay people in our time and culture, gay people often feel they need a little "something extra" to make their rite as valid as a heterosexual's. This truly did not occur to me until someone questioned me about what I was writing, as it didn't seem to apply specifically to gay people. It is specifically applicable to gay people as well as heterosexuals, but because of the lack of discrimination in earlier times, there was no need to do something "special" for gays as it was considered valid equally for all, as all valued themselves equally.

There is also the old concept that the laws of the Gods transcend the laws of the land. You still find this old idea in our modern times, and in this system it is no different. The Old Religion transcends the legal laws of the land. It is the Gods' decree that gay marriages are just as much a valid right as heterosexual marriage. So whether the legal law of the land accepts it or not, it is still a valid marriage in the higher and more valid eyes of the Gods.

THE NATURE OF THESE RITES

The marriage ceremony and the handfasting ceremonies are sacred rites. Any marriage rite should be taken very seriously and meditated upon before entering into it. I highly recommend the handfasting rite first because it is to express love, one for the other, without a permanent obligation. I normally recommend at least a three-month period because if the partner is not what the other person expected, it should show up within about three months, but usually a year and a day has been traditional.

Neither partner should try to dominate the other. They should feel free to talk to each other about what is displeasing, and if possible, the actions, words, or habits should be eliminated. Every good relationship is based upon good communication. It is important that you do not underestimate the other person's strength to hear what you have to say.

What you may consider very harsh may be necessary to save the relationship. This is not saying that tact is not necessary.

Under no circumstances should physical or psychological abuse be tolerated. It then no longer becomes a matter of how much you love the other person, but a matter of how much you love yourself. If you do not love and respect yourself, you simply cannot expect anyone else to do so either. This must begin with you. If what you want changed would make the other person miserable for the rest of his life, then you should try to accept the other as he is.

Marriage can be a trial, but it can also be heaven on earth if both parties try to make it so. One cannot do this alone; it takes the two putting effort into the relationship. The relationship becomes a thing in itself, and effort should be thought of as going into the relationship, not just time or effort spent on another person.

Each party should know that an Old Religion wedding is most sacred and if one cheats on the other, the cheater has broken one of the most sacred Laws of Life, the Law of Love. Love can make a happy or a broken heart. Therefore, the choosing of a marriage partner is a very important step in life.

Usually the Servants will counsel the two before the marriage, speaking to them about the matter of being faithful and of not flirting with others. Marriage is not a prison, but a contract of love on a 50:50 basis. If one becomes bored with the other, which will happen, then they should give each other space, knowing that the other will not break the Law of Love.

In marriage, trust is paramount; it is the only way to be happy. If one partner gives the other reason for doubt, then the one who cannot trust the other will soon feel no love for the other. At this point they should talk it over and release each other and get a divorce. It is also a violation of the Law of Life and Love to refuse freedom to each other. Love does not die on its own, there is a reason and it is usually not being able to trust the marriage partner. Mental or physical abuse is self-evidently also another killer of love.

Gay Homophobia

Something that must also be addressed is homophobia within the gay community. You must be completely comfortable with your own sexuality or else you are certain to run into problems in a relationship. Homophobia is so prevalent and insidious in our culture that it is very difficult not to be affected or influenced by it. This is tragic but true, and if you hold yourself or others in lower esteem because of gayness, then you do everyone a disservice. Some good books on gay relationships are: *Gay Relationships* by Tina Tessina Ph.D., and *Permanent Partners* by Betty Berzon Ph.D.

A relationship in general should not be entered into from a position of need. You should find yourself whole and complete within yourself, finding the partner and relationship complimentary, not something to complete yourself. If you do this, then you will find that when your partner needs to grow, you won't hold him back with your own insecurities and make him frustrated with you. Remember, whatever you focus on is what you create. If you focus upon abandonment, you will create it.

If you are focussing upon past failed relationships, you will recreate them. If you focus upon your insecurities, you will manifest them. You must focus instead upon the fact that the relationship will work and look to the future of joy that you are creating now. When you choose a partner and you find that he is focussing upon insecurities and/or fears of abandonment, you should understand that it will be nearly impossible to maintain the relationship for a long period of time as such people are self-sabotaging as far as relationships go. If this is the case, it is wise not to get into a deep relationship with them until they have cleaned up their own problems.

Often this goes back to childhood and to a dysfunctional family, and our families are where we usually get our basic standards and views of relationships and the world, and the ways that we deal with them. If this is the case, get counseling from a professional on these matters before you make a commitment, as the commitment will be nearly impossible to maintain without great anguish, and that is not what marriage or commitment is all about. If someone has felt emotional abandonment at an early age, he will feel like there is something wrong with him deep inside although he may not be able to put a finger on it.

As adults we know that some people are simply unable to provide love for reasons of their own woundedness; to a child, this sort of detachment is impossible and thus he feels that he must be personally to blame, that he is unlovable. Mommy and Daddy are always perfect; this is a child's innocent logic. Therefore, there must be something wrong with the child; he must be wrong or bad. The person should understand that there is basically nothing wrong with them, it is how they have been treated that has caused them to feel this way. This becomes a problem in relationships because if a person feels this way, his self-esteem has been severely damaged. He will be afraid to expose his true emotions because of the feeling that if he does, the other person will walk away. He has been taught not to like himself, and he feels that if someone sees beneath the facade he presents, he will be abandoned like before, and this is simply too incredibly painful to be borne.

The problem here is that—even if he is truly loved by his partner—when he looks at himself and sees nothing to love, he cannot really believe anyone else could either. In this case he is not dealing with the reality of the situation; he is dealing only with severely damaged self-esteem. This causes major problems for a relationship.

It becomes imperative therefore, before you enter into a commitment with someone, that your own self-esteem be healthy, that you love yourself and think yourself worthwhile. You will always be a beautiful spark of divinity and your self-esteem should be based upon this. It should not be based upon what you do or what you possess. This is confusing being with doing and is a fatal flaw in relationships. If you love yourself and think yourself worthwhile, you will create a positive relationship for yourself.

HANDFASTING CEREMONY

The globe is cast in the usual manner. The Servant of the Goddess and God will recite the following, and the two handfasted will repeat after them:

"I, (person's name), before Angus Og and Bride and all the people who are assembled here to witness this Union of Oneness, do here and now pledge to take (other party's name) to be my spouse for (number of months). I pledge to be true to (other person's name) having no other, wanting no other for as long as this pledge is made. At the end of this pledge, if our love one for the other still lives, we shall become spouse to spouse in the Ceremony of the Marriage Vows."

Now the two will face each other kneeling, and take hands and give the pledge to each other.

"With this ring I make my pledge to you, my love, and by the powers of all that is holy we are joined as One."

Now they may kiss or just drink of the consecrated wine. The Servant of the God will dismiss the Guardians, take up the globe, and go to the Handfasting Feast.

CEREMONY OF THE WEDDING VOWS

The altar will be set up as usual. The globe will be purified and the Guardians called to attend. The Servant of the Goddess will give the Charge to Bride, and the Servant of the God will give the Charge of Angus Og. Since a wedding ceremony is a very sacred and holy rite, all the people, Wizards or non-Wizards, will anoint themselves on a pulse point with a holy oil such as frankincense. All will be robed and the bride to be will have flowers in the hair. This was done in ancient times with flowers that were protective as the inimical powers of old were hostile to fertility, and if the head was protected, the body was as well. This crowning with flowers was usually done at times of great power. The groom will have bay leaves in his hair. The bay leaves should be in a wreath, but if this cannot be, then three bay leaves on the front of the hairline (or where one was) will do. The bride and groom may, if they wish, write their own words to say and then the Servant will declare them spouse to spouse. The Servants of the God and Goddess will find out which is the most comfortable for the bride and groom, the terms husband and wife, or spouse to spouse.

The Servant of the Goddess says:

"We are gathered here today/tonight in the presence of the Gods and people to join in holy wedlock (both person's names)."

The Servant of the God says:

"If there be any present who has just cause to believe this wedding should not take place, let them speak now or forever hold their peace." (Pause for a few moments)

Servant of the Goddess speaks these words to the bride, and the Servant of the God speaks these words to the groom.

"Do you (Name of Person) take this person to be your wedded spouse, according to the laws of the Wizards?"

(Pause for answer)

"Do you promise to love and cherish (Name of other person) for so long as love shall live between the two of you?"

(Pause for answer)

"And if love for (Name of the other person) should die, do you promise to tell him that love for him no longer lives in your heart and be honest in all things, one to the other?"

(Pause for answer)

If it is a ring ceremony, the rings are placed on the wands of the Servant of the Goddess and God. At the correct time, the rings are taken off of the wands and exchanged. Each will say to the other:

"With this ring I thee wed."

The Servant of the God and Goddess together say:

"I now pronounce you spouse and spouse/husband and wife."

All then go to the Wedding Feast.

A Child's Acceptance into the Clan

When a child is born it is a wondrous, magical time and it should be celebrated with great joy by all of the Clan. At a certain point when the parents feel ready for a public viewing of the child, usually after 7 days, then the parents and the child go before the Servant of the Goddess and God. They present the child for all to see.

The Servant of the Goddess says:

"The Goddess blesses this child, formed of Her nature."

The Servant of the God says:

"The God blesses this child, formed of His nature."

    The Servants then give the child a small bouquet of flowers, each flower having a certain symbolic significance of that with which you wish to gift the child in this life, and announce the child's acceptance into the Clan. Circumcision for the male child is strictly forbidden, as any maiming of children, male or female, is not permitted. As an adult, a man may decide for himself to be circumcised, but it shall be done to no one without his permission.

    If a child dies, it goes to the realms of the Gods, no matter what clan or religion it is, and it is gently and lovingly cared for by the Gods themselves until it is time for it once again to try and reincarnate. No child is ever harmed by the Gods or punished for lack of a ritual or ceremony. Some children may be so special that the Gods may wish to hold them themselves, but the small souls are always gently cared for and loved in the Evergreen Isle until the Gods can relinquish them again out of care for their growth. Know then that if you have lost a child, the Gods themselves will care for it with the greatest of love until it is time for you to meet or time for it to be born anew.

THE RITE OF DIVORCE

    The Rite of Divorce is not a holy rite as holy rites are comprised of actions that create a union of some kind, symbolizing union with the totality of deity. Divorces or endings of handfastings do not, as they represent deity falling into matter, or enlightenment lost. Though not holy, they are necessary for the happiness and harmony of the clan. It is a rite of passage, of growth for an individual, and should be respected as such. The Gods are not called down although They observe the rite. This does not mean They are displeased. It is not a crime to be wrong about someone or to grow apart. The two who no longer love each other should come before the Servants at a gathering of the Wizards. Sometimes it is not possible for both to be there as in the case of desertions, so the rite can be carried out for one person alone if the other cannot or will not be there.

The Servant of the Goddess says:

"You have come before the clan. What is your wish?"

Partners say:

"We wish to dissolve this Union."

The Servant of the God says:

"Is there no love left in your Union?"

Partners say:

Situation 1: "No" (for both partners)
Situation 2: One says 'Yes" and one says "No"

The Servant of the Goddess says:

Situation 1: "It would be ill to stay together if there is no love left in this Union. The Union therefore, is dissolved in the sight of the Gods and the Wizards. You are free to be alone now, or free to enter into another Union. So be it."

The Servant of the God says:

Situation 2: "If there is no love left in your partner, it is best to release him. If you do so, an even greater love will be sent to you. A Union is a contract of love, not possession or domination, and this contract is broken. Therefore the Union must be and is dissolved in the sight of the Gods and the Wizards. You are free to be alone or enter into a Union with another. So be it."

Each returns to each other the rings and the possessions brought into the Union by each other. All the rest acquired is split evenly or justly. It is done.

This ceremony is appropriate for both weddings and handfastings.

Funeral Rite

The Servant of the God says:

"O My beloved child, will you come with Me to a marvelous land? Full of music, and where the hair shines with color fair and the body is smooth and unblemished.

"There none speak of "mine" or "thine", white are the teeth and black the brows' eyes flash with many colored lights, and the hue of the foxglove is on every cheek.

"It is one of the wonders of this land that youth does not change into age.

"Smooth and sweet are the streams that flow through it, mead and wine abound of every kind; there men are all fair without blemish, there women conceive without blame, and the blessings of the Gods rest upon all of the inhabitants. Where all unions of love are blessed and neither shame nor pain is permitted, for nothing is more holy to the Gods than love, and They honor it without distinction.

"Rest for a while in peace and joy with Us, then return again to this life, to embrace those you have loved before. Therefore, fear not, but rest in My broad arms and let Me bear you away that your time of sorrows be ended, at least for a while, and that you may rejoin with happy tears the ones I have carefully borne there before you that you have loved, and that have loved you.

"Come, I shall carry you with the greatest of care across the Mountains of Misery to the Plains of Youth.

"He has followed the sweet voice, filled with truth and we who are left feel sorrow at the parting. It is harder for those left than for those leaving. Therefore, be at peace and know that _____ walks in peace and joy with the Gods who love him and hold him dear. He would not want us to grieve over much. Let us remember him with love, not pain, and let us do kind works in his name, for ourselves and to show our love for him in remembrance.

"Relinquish him gracefully into the arms of the Gods who can care for him better than us, and bear hope that we shall once more meet again."

Chapter Eleven: Meditation

Ecstatic States of Consciousness Through Meditation

Ecstatic states of consciousness are the inheritance of every true spiritual path. When one begins to break out of a narrow ego focus and begins to touch upon the totality of awareness, a wellspring of joy begins to flow in the heart. This is achieved by pursuing one of the eight-fold paths. You must be focused on the achievement of a goal; you must be determined.

When I was much younger than I am now, I went to visit one of my teachers and was given a meditation. I was to imagine a sphere floating in infinite space. I was asked how big the sphere was. I said how large I thought it was, and then I was asked the distance, so I said how far away I thought it was. I was then told that since there was nothing to measure it against, I couldn't know how large it really was, and since I had no way to measure the distance, since there was nothing to measure it against, I might be seeing something small close up, or something immense very far away. I found this very disorienting, but I continued to meditate upon this as I was asked to. I was then asked to introduce another sphere exactly like the other into my meditation. Again, I could not tell size or distance except in relation to the other sphere. Since the first sphere was undetermined in size or distance, the addition of the second sphere did not assist in helping me with my lack of orientation. It only gave me another reference point which was also undetermined. Again, I was asked to meditate upon this for a while.

The next day I was given concepts of what I was trying to achieve. I was told that reality was like a diamond. Everything, the chair beside me, myself, everyone I knew, every object in the universe was a facet on this diamond. Its individual existence was an illusion, as in itself, each object was the complete totality of itself. I became confused.

"Everything is a part of the totality?" I asked.

"No, no, no! Everything is the totality complete within itself!" I was informed. I frowned, trying hard to understand this difficult concept. If everything was a facet of reality, then there was only one reality behind all things which manifested as diversity, like the facets on a diamond. There are many facets, but only one diamond. I still had difficulty in truly grasping this concept. Finally, my teacher threw up his hands in despair with me. The memory is still very vivid.

"Look," he said, "meditate upon the concept of the totality, of no one thing's essence being different from any other. See all things as essentially one thing. As you do that, perform this visualization. Imagine infinity, and see a small white cloud in it. See that cloud fade and disperse into the vast blue infinity, and when it is gone, realize that it is infinity." He then got up and left me to ponder his words. Obviously, I wasn't getting this on an intellectual level, so I was given the tools to experience what I needed to experience to understand.

I left a day or two later and flew back to where I lived. I was impressed by my teacher but did not truly understand what the hell he was talking about. Nevertheless, I meditated upon the idea of the essence of all things being one as I worked through the day. In the evenings I repeated the visualization over and over and over a thousand times, and then meditated upon the concept of the totality some more. I persisted and persisted even though I didn't understand what I was aiming for. There were times I began to feel as though I were falling, and I would catch myself up short and end the meditation. Still I persisted, and then waves of fear would fill me as I began to feel like I was losing my very Self. It was terrifying. Still I persisted in doing this meditation throughout the day at work and in my leisure time. I lay in bed one evening before going to sleep, doing my visualization and meditation, and it felt like a big wave of fear, but persisted anyway. I permitted myself to fall through this fear, to lose my Self. Suddenly I found myself incredibly expanded. I was looking down at the entire solar system and seeing it as big as a dinner plate. It was as real as this book, and I was awake. It lasted for only a few moments, but when it was over and I found myself again lying in my bed, I was changed. I had not lost myself, I had lost nothing as it had felt like I would at first, I had added to it to an incredible degree. I felt such a deep pervading peacefulness that it was beyond description. It truly passed previous understanding or concepts. I was at total and complete rest, and I understood with clarity everything that my teacher had said. It all became so simple, and I laughed.

Since I had touched upon this state of consciousness, it was easy to go back to. All I had to do was remember it. Sometimes I would touch upon this inadvertently. If I would make love to someone, I would start to once again make contact with this state of consciousness, and I would start to laugh with joy. Usually my partner would be offended, and ask me why I was laughing. I replied that I was laughing with joy, with happiness, but they eyed me with hurt or suspicion thinking that I was laughing at them, instead of with them. This did lead to some misunderstandings.

So, the moral of this story and meditation is this: you are never so advanced that you should laugh out loud when you make love.

Past Life Meditation

Find a quiet place, and enter a meditative state. Surround yourself with lavender light. Take the symbol of the eight-fold path (which is an eight-spoke wheel) and place it before you where you can gaze upon it easily. This can be a symbol you have drawn yourself, or a prepared one of any substance. Start to look at the symbol as if it were a three-dimensional tube with lines extending off into infinity from the center. Become emotionally calm and extend your antlers through this tunnel all the way to the end of infinity, and mentally come out at the other end of the tunnel at the end of consciousness. Before you, see floating in space a glowing blue sphere of light. Extend your antlers into this blue sphere and let your focus of awareness travel through your antlers into this blue sphere, and turn back from that perspective and look at yourself. If you do this properly, you will see a myriad of images like a mirrored ball, each one reflecting a different scene, a different life. Pick one of these images and go into it. You will find yourself living another life, a past life. Experience it, then return to the blue sphere and back to yourself. Clap your hands and get up and move out of the area.

Goddess Meditation

Settle yourself in a place where you will not be disturbed. This is a meditation only, and should not be acted out. Visualize yourself entering a castle door, and going down a corridor, which is spiraling downwards. As you go along, see before you a hooded, silver-robed figure standing with its arms crossed before a closed door. As you approach, hear it say,

"You may not pass unless you give me your shirt." Remove your shirt, and give it to the guardian. The door is opened and the guardian moves aside. You go through the door and progress down the corridor about another 50 yards. Before you stands another guardian, this time robed in pale blue. As you approach, hear it say:

"You may not pass unless you give me the golden chain about your neck." You remove this and give it to the guardian, who then opens the door and moves aside. You go through the door and progress down the corridor about another fifty yards. Before you stands another guardian, this time robed in bright yellow. As you approach hear it say:

"You may not pass unless you give me your golden bracelet." Remove your golden bracelet and give it to the guardian, who then opens the door and moves aside. You go through the door and progress down the corridor about another fifty yards. Before you stands another guardian, this time in a golden robe. As you approach, hear it say:

"You may not pass unless you give me the clasp which holds your cape together." Remove this, and give it to the guardian, who then opens the door and moves aside. You go through the door and progress down the corridor about another fifty yards. Before you stands another guardian, this time robed in a black robe. As you approach, hear it say:

"You may not pass unless you give me your cape." Remove your cape and give it to the guardian, who then opens the door and moves aside. You go through the door and progress down the corridor about another fifty yards. Before you stands another guardian robed in purple. As you approach, hear it say:

"You may not pass unless you give me your trousers. You remove these and give them to him, and he moves aside and opens the door and lets you go through. As you progress down the corridor, there stands before you a guardian dressed in red, and as you approach, you hear it say:

"You may not pass unless you give me your hat." You remove this and give it to him, and he lets you pass the final door, totally nude.

As you pass this last doorway, stripped of all jewelry and clothing, totally naked, you enter a dimly lit chamber. Someone grabs you and ties your hands behind your back, and hobbles your feet together. Whoever ties you is totally unseen, but before you stands a figure, a man also standing totally nude except for a crown as well as a sword. He is stunningly handsome with a beautiful body and his deep voice thunders through the room and through the reaches of your soul.

"Blessed be your feet that have brought you in these ways. Stay with me, and let me place my hands upon your heart." He lays down his crown and his sword, and kisses your feet. You hear yourself reply:

"I do not love you. Why do you cause all the things I love to wither and die?" His deep voice responds sadly:

"It is age and fate over which I have no power. Age causes all things to wither. When men die at the end of their time, I give them rest and peace and strength so that they may return once again to live, but you, you are beautiful. Stay with me and do not return." Again, hear yourself answer, "I do not love you."

His seductive voice echoes once again richly through the chamber. "If you will not accept my hands upon your chest, you must kneel to my whip." You hear yourself answer, "If this is what I must endure, I accept it," while beginning to kneel. He moves around behind you and you hear him pick something up. His whip flashes against your back, and you feel it again and again. It is painful and it stings. It seems to go on and on, and hazy images of the pain and losses of men float through your mind. As you sense their loss and pain through the vicissitudes of life, feel the answering echo through the pain on your own back. See the men, women, and children loved and lost, echoing through the corridors of time, and know their loss through empathy. Because of this empathy and understanding known through your own pain, feel compassion well up, and finally love. As you feel love for all of the suffering humanity hear your voice, speaking almost to yourself, "I know the pain of love."

You feel the whip fall silent and you are slowly raised to your feet.

"You are blessed," you hear your lover say, and feel his lips as he gives you a kiss. "This is the only way you can achieve joy and knowledge." Feel him unbind your hands and feet, and lay about your neck his golden chain while you give him a cup that you find near you. He takes you in his broad arms and begins to kiss you, begins to make passionate love to you. As he enters you, you feel a moment of total ecstasy and surrender, which goes on and on until finally you forget yourself for a moment in orgasm together with him, and find yourself literally blending together as you realize your true essence is the same. When you once again stand upon your feet, you realize you both share one body, and have become together in one being, in harmony.

SPARKLES

See everything around you on a mental level filled with small sparkling lights. Recognize that each of these sparkles around you is deity. See yourself also composed of these sparkles, and slowly let your awareness drift from your own body of sparkling light into all of the other sparkles, each one being the mind of deity. The removal of dichotomy or Union also means dissolving the bonds of "inner" and "outer".

LOVE MEDITATION

Sit calmly and place an inanimate object in front of you. Imagine the object loving you intensely with an unconditional love. After a while put another object beside it and imagine it also loving you just as much unconditionally. Experience the love of both simultaneously. Build up to seven objects spread in a circle all around you beaming unconditional love at you. Finally, experience the sensation of the universe beaming unconditional love at you through every object, building, person, atom, and molecule around you.

POWER SYMBOL AND POWER ANIMAL

This is a technique to find your personal power symbol or animal. Look at your life as a golden thread. Each major event in your life should appear as a knot. Go through your life from your earliest memories, looking at each knot and seeing what memories it contains. As you come to the present in your mind, join both ends of this golden thread – from your beginning to now – together to form a circle. See in the middle of this circle a well or pit. Fearlessly jump into this hole and land on the bottom unhurt. Wait for a few minutes, or until you feel it is right, and then jump out. The first symbol you will see, or the first animal you see is your personal power symbol or animal. Write the symbol and the animal quickly down on paper.

Animal Meditation

Visualize yourself as a particular animal to which you feel drawn. See yourself enter an enclave of these particular animals. At the head of these sits a leader of the tribe. As you go before them, ask that you be taught their wisdom and love. Hear the leader say, "It will be done," and see him or her turn and go through a small doorway near you. As you pass through this doorway, look around you. Realize that you have passed through a portal that takes you into another realm, the realm of the animal that you have chosen.

See your guide before you, and listen to him teach you about being that particular creature, and about their knowledge, wisdom, and ways. When the lesson is finished, ask the leader for your new name as this creature. He will give it to you, and then return you both through the doorway. Pass from the enclave of animals, and end your meditation.

Aura Cleansing

Meditate upon a golden sphere with a violet aura glowing brilliantly above the top of your head. Slowly move it down through all of your body pausing at the places that you feel a blockage or a hindering of the energy. See the area dark with dirt and grime. As the glowing sphere enters, see the darkness begin to glow through the dirt and grime, glow more brilliantly, and finally see the dark grime slough off and fall away, leaving a brilliantly glowing sphere. Move it slowly down through the whole body, and see the glow begin to radiate out, filling your whole aura and any dark grime or dirt just falling away. Finally, see the energy field around your body begin to spin in a clockwise direction.

ACTION AND INACTION

Meditate upon the God as the active force in the Universe. Think of the Goddess as perfect inaction. To have this union within ourselves requires us to achieve perfect peace and tranquillity. It is then possible to let this serenity manifest in our actions. This is one of the reasons why Bride the Calm is named as She is. In many respects, Bride reflects our own spirits, our own souls, as Angus Og reflects the actions coming from our spirits. Thus, on a spiritual level in the Wizard's Way, the goal is to become perfectly secure, not in outward situations, but within, and to let this manifest in our actions.

CHAPTER TWELVE: WISDOM AND STUDY

SACRED AND MUNDANE

When one speaks of sexuality there is a profound misunderstanding of how it relates to the sacred and the mundane.

Generally speaking, religious communities that are intent upon social control insist that certain fundamental needs only be used for sacred or religious intent, or uses that they have authority over, and of course one of the most powerful coercions is sexuality. When an institution loses sight of the proper uses of the sacred in this way, a severe imbalance in the body, the psyche, and the society is created.

Take eating and drinking. When one eats and drinks at a communion, it is an act of the sacred. If one were to ignore the mundane uses of eating and drinking and say that they could only be used for the communion, this would create a severe imbalance as you would be able to eat or drink only once a week or month, depending upon which institution you belonged to and how often this is appropriate for them. This is illogical and unhealthy.

Take the cleansing of the body. If one uses it for baptism, it is a sacred act, but there are other health related reasons for bathing and if a person were to do it only once in their lives, their health would suffer. Bathing is mundane, but a necessity of health.

To insist that sexuality is only sacred and to be used only in a religious context also creates an imbalance. To insist that sexuality is only profane is also a severe misunderstanding. Sex is sacred in the act of Union with deity or in the creation of another human being. It is sacred when it expresses deep love one for the other. To deny it for the reason of joy or pleasure or to say that it is exclusively for the creation of children is to give the most sacred power you personally possess to a religious institution intent upon excessive social control. It is abusive to its people in its search for greatest power. This creates an illness and an imbalance on all levels of being which manifests in our society. It is important to view sex as both sacred and mundane and not strictly either as each alone would be imbalanced. Taken in balance they are health-giving and life-sustaining.

GOD AND GODDESS METAPHORS

If one objects to the God and Goddess metaphors as being heterosexist, then there seems to be a confusion of the metaphorical anthropomorphicization of an energy form used for social structure and the energy principle upon which it is based. In actuality, it transcends metaphor.

If the dominant cultural metaphor of a god form is inappropriate to the sub-cultural construct you are operating from, then change the cultural metaphor to one that will work in your personal or social construct. Do not disregard the energy principles upon which these are founded or you may end up losing power and understanding. Although you may find a metaphorical construct which is pleasing, it may be disempowering. In actuality both or either of the God/Goddess principles alone transcend sexual connotation. What they really represent are the differences in potentials.

Most everyone starts from a zero ground point as the basis of their theology when in actuality it is merely the difference in potentials by which energy moves or manifestations manifest. Perhaps by explaining this in terms of electricity I can make this clearer.

An Electric Analogy

If you have a +50-volt power point and you connect it up to a +150-volt power source, energy will move and depending upon the current involved and the gauge of the wire you are using, you may burn the wire up. There is a 100-volt difference in potential here and therefore the +150 volt source will try to bring the +50 volts point up to an equal level. One point is receptive of energy and one point is assertive with energy. Refer then to the masculine principle as being +. You can do the same with a − bias or potential below the zero point of ground as well, and let this represent feminine energy. Utilizing this idea, one can have two male deities as depicting these two principles, as long as one is receptive in concept and the other is assertive. One can also use the concept of two female deities in this context as long as the underlying principles are understood. If you were to go to the planet Dweebkins, you would find the Dwobs used Dwork and Dwink to represent these principles as they are universal principles, not giant genitalia in the sky. What exists in nature also exists on the level of deity and what the + and − aspects of deity represent is a difference in energy potential which can be used for manifestation of action of form.

Something can be totally masculine − if you wish to use this metaphor − and still work in the level of manifestation as long as there is a difference in potential. After all there are folk tales where the goddess has appeared as a young or old man. I think the key word here is "appear." Their essence is not changed but the appearance, metaphor, or look can be changed at will.

Ignoring the Essence

Disregarding the energy principles because they can perhaps relate to heterosexual analogy is throwing the baby out with the bathwater. Simply change the concepts of these potentials to a gay reference point if that is what you feel most comfortable with. After all, in some ancient point in history, someone gave them male and female appearances because that was how they personally related to these concepts. Just because it was done a long time ago doesn't mean that you can't do the same thing in your own cultural or sub-cultural context now. The reason that this happen is that most God forms, like the God and Goddess, are actually modeled on parental figures. At the same time when you were a small child you were helpless, these parental beings protected you, gave you food, and helped you survive through a time that you would not have lived without them. As adults these images become impressed upon deity, as this is how we would like Them to respond to us, helping us with our needs when we do not feel capable. When a person begins to move the deity concept away from parent to lover, one begins to touch upon the mystical aspects of a religious system, be that heterosexual or homosexual. It is the changing of parental to loving supportive partner that the true power of divinity begins to be experienced. It is not surprising then to find that gay paths of spirituality with gods which are in lover relationships with the individuals reveal views into the esoteric aspects of a religious structure. This can also be true for heterosexuals in their preference, such as a nun being married to a male god in the religious orders. It is with this melding of deity and beloved that ego identification begins to change. It is a much closer, more intimate way of experiencing deity and has to do with identification rather than parental injunctions. Ideally partners in intimate relationships see you as you really are; parental relationships often have to do with behaving in a certain way for approval. These are two very different kinds of relationships, and an intimate one is the esoteric spiritual path while the parental is the form of exoteric religion.

What's a Meta Phor?

If you wish to have a gay assertive and receptive pantheon, it is very easy, pleasing to many gay people, and effective on a universal energy level as long as the fundamental principles are kept in mind. Don't get lost in the metaphor. You will shoot yourself in the metaphysical foot and lose site of the universal principles involved. If the God and Goddess are not appropriate for your personal needs, change the metaphor but keep the universal principle. It should be remembered however, that if one forgets the principles and keeps only the metaphor, one has departed from a truly spiritual system into a dogmatic and deluded religious system in which the true principles of spirituality have been lost. If you do this you will become discriminatory yourself or you will simply echo the ignorance of those before you that you yourself are reacting to. If you wish to set up a system that is related to the gay world, why not use Apollo and Hyacinthus, or Hercules and Hylas, or Zeus and Ganymede, or any of the numerous liaisons that there were among the gods and men? You could even use Gaith and Vroiko as your primary source of energy if you wish, as Gaith is generally assertive and Vroiko is generally receptive. These two could be used in this context if that is what you personally felt most comfortable with.

As long as one aspect of the universal force is receptive and the other force is assertive as in the yin and yang principles of oriental philosophy, you can have whatever metaphor you wish. When the metaphor gains more importance than the underlying reality, corruption will take place in the system and the principles upon which it is founded will have been lost. If an anthropomorphic concept causes this, then like Islam, you can disregard images and refer to the assertive and receptive principles or intelligences or consciousness solely. However, if you do this, do not discriminate against those that do choose to use God, Goddess or other metaphors. If may be human nature to be elitist, but it is spiritually incorrect as deity is all inclusive by definition. Remember the principles, not the metaphor. This will lead you to spiritual illumination, not segregation.

WISDOM

In our society one kind of knowledge is essential. This is the knowledge of reading and writing. If someone cannot read or write often they are made to feel stupid. This is a carryover from an older time. For long periods of our history, the only people who could read or write were priests and royalty. A person who knew the Old Religion, who was perhaps a master ritualist or herbalist, was called ignorant and valueless by the priests because they were often illiterate. Often the ancient knowledge was too sacred to be written and it took twenty years to memorize it all. It was not permitted to be written down even if the person did know how to write. However, the church, because it had a monopoly on writing, condemned people who were knowledgeable although illiterate. It was a way for them to destroy the old knowledge and institute control over the populace. It was a form of psychological warfare and it was highly effective in its degradation of anyone uneducated by the church. It did not matter the personal wisdom, caring, or knowledge of the individual, they were labelled as ignorant and not to be trusted if they were illiterate. It is unfortunate that people who are not literate now should be the object of this type of attitude and discrimination today. This type of psychological warfare has also been used by the patriarchal medical profession against midwives who may have been trained since their childhood in their trade. Many midwives were also burned at the stake.

As a writer, I find literacy very important, but I want to listen just as carefully to someone for what they say and understand, not for the particular skill in writing they have. Many of the greatest realizations in life cannot be written down anyway. A person's value and wisdom should be based on who they are, not what they do or whether they can read or write.

The church extended its control when it forbade the use of national scripts, such as the runes. Someone using the runes was not usually educated by the church, and so this furthered its religious war. Such tactics were also used against the American Indian, demanding that the children go to boarding schools, where they were separated from their parents and their cultural religious and traditional values in order to learn to read and write. Underneath all of this was the desire to destroy the indigenous culture and make them vassals, dependent upon the church and oppressive state. They were forbidden to speak their language or practice their traditions. This is similar to the kidnapping of the Norwegian children by the Nazis who took them to Germany during the war to make them the perfect Nazi Aryans. When these children were returned to Norway after the war, most of them would have nothing to do with their parents. To see this done to a group of people in this country is chilling, heinous, evil, and criminal. The perpetuators should be tried for war crimes.

If it is any consolation to the American Indian, although I expect it is not, this was also done in Europe to destroy the indigenous cultures there. It did succeed in some cases and in others the people fled to America to escape this type of persecution, or went so far underground that they have not emerged yet. Many sacred things in both European and American cultures were lost in this way and cultures manipulated and destroyed by this method. If the written word is so important that it invalidates the wisdom of a person or a culture, then perhaps the importance that we place upon it should be re-examined.

Areas to Study

Astrology

Astrology is a good thing to study for several reasons. It is a wonderful tool for self-exploration. Seeing yourself can be very difficult.

This can be a good tool in learning to view yourself in an objective manner. It can also give you insights into other people and their motivations.

It can also be useful in studying the time and tides of the universe which can make your magical and mundane workings more effective. It is better to work with the tides than against them. This is why the rites are held on the full moons and the high days. It is making the most effective use of your time and effort.

Divination

Divination is a good thing to study also. You can use the tarot, the runes, the I Ching or whatever you wish. It is wise to divine beforehand to see how effective your magical workings will be and to avoid problems with them that may show up in a reading. Forewarned is forearmed and it is wise to have some foreknowledge of how things will go so that you can avoid issues with people and events. If practiced enough, it will also increase your psychic sensitivity. It is a good training tool.

Aromatherapy

Aromatherapy is useful in the physical treatment of ailments, and it is also useful in the study of the psychological effects of scents. Your sense of smell has the longest memory of all the senses – a smell can evoke memories of fifty years ago quite clearly. None of the other five senses can do this. This makes it a powerful tool in the area of natural magic in particular. Some of the best books on the subject are the *Aromatherapy Workbook* by Marcel Lavabre, *The Practice of Aromatherapy* by Jean Valnet, and *The Art of Aromatherapy* by Robert Tisserand. There are few books that deal with Aromatherapy on a metaphysical level, that are really of much effective or practical use, so I would suggest that just these basic ones be used.

Outside of the area of aromatherapy but certainly in conjunction with it, is the study of incenses. I recommend *Wylundt's Book of Incense* as it appears to be the best on the subject that I have come across.

Ecology

Ecology is important to study. It is the foundation of our well-being, and is not to be underestimated. There is more to the study of metaphysics than power and withdrawing from the world. We must re-enter the world in a healing function and step past the greed, hatred, domination, and insecurity that is destroying our planet. If our planet dies, of course we won't have the greed, hatred, domination and insecurity that we dislike, but neither will we have the beauty love, peace, and joy that also resides here. It is sanity to try and save our environment, and insanity to disregard it for purposes of greed or inertia.

The earth is our cathedral as our globes are churches. That is perhaps the best analogy of how our view of the earth is explained. Because of our recognition that the earth is the same as our own bodies, the preservation of it in a pristine natural fashion becomes imperative. Would you consider injecting yourself with toxic radioactive waste and expect your liver to clear it away and not have a problem with it anymore? Most of us would not even consider it, and I think most of us would realize that we would probably get liver cancer if nothing else. Yet if we see the destruction of our environment and do nothing, it is the same as if we let someone else jab us with a syringe full of toxic waste, inject it into us and then pick our pockets. If there is any amount of healthy self-regard, you will say no to the destruction of your environment and yourself. It is the same thing.

It is for the preservation of our cathedral and ourselves that the necessity for ecology becomes important on a spiritual and physical level. Would we wash the floor of the Vatican in human waste and oil? Of course not, it would be a desecration. Why then should it be permitted to our world cathedral? It is the responsibility of every Wizard to stop the unconscionable destruction of our environment.

Comparative Mythology

Comparative mythology is something that I was instructed to study from the earliest days of my magical training. There was no reason to feel insecure in the study of religions if you have nothing to hide, so my teachers insisted that I study all religions in general. Of course, there have been a great many teachers in this area, Joseph Campbell among the greatest, but also others. Any of Joseph Campbell's books are recommended reading as well as other works on comparative religion and mythology.

Chapter Thirteen: Psychic Self-Defense

Psychic self-defense is important for Wizards to know, especially gay Wizards. Due to the violence against gay people in general, it is good to know self-defense both physically and psychically. The physical self defense aspect is encouraged by leading forms of oriental fighting arts such as Karate or Tae Kwon Do. This is not only good physically, but is also good discipline mentally. It will help in your spiritual quest as well as increase your personal power and self confidence. A healthy mind helps create a healthy body and vice versa, so this arena should not be neglected. Physical stamina can also result in psychic stamina, so to truly be a force to be reckoned with one must physically exercise as well. The body is the battery for psychic energy, so to walk around with a dead or drained battery won't help you a lot in the process of illumination. Spirituality must be considered holistically.

Dealing with Idiots

Sometimes you run across beginners or even corrupted adepts who will toss negative energy at you; in the case of the beginner to see if it will actually work; and in the case of the corrupted adept, to see what the limits of your abilities are. These cases are rare, but they do happen, and it is wise to be prepared for them.

First

As covered under the area of familiars, they will warn you by their behavior of a psychic hit before you may sense it yourself, giving you needed time to create a protective force around yourself and those you love, including your familiar.

Second

It is wise to have charged objects around which focus upon protection. That is in case you are physically ill or in a social situation where you don't have the energy or the privacy to do much. It is probably wise to create a protective oil and wear it on yourself. Anoint an object with a charged protective oil and bless it with protective energy to wear on you, if you don't wish to anoint yourself. It is also wise to have several of these objects about your house and automobile as well.

Third

The thing to do is to learn psychic techniques which will isolate you and return the negative energy back to the originators. There are a number of ways to do this. The most powerful way is to cast the globe and stay within it. Perhaps you might do this around your bed before you retire, dispersing the globe in the morning when you rise. If however you are in a situation where that is not possible, invoke the God or Goddess that you have formed a personal rapport with. See the God clearly in your mind, telling them you need their help, and visualize Them placing a sphere of lavender light six inches above your head. With the first two fingers of the left hand, reach up into this sphere you are visualizing and see the light enter your fingers, go down your arm and into your chest. With your right hand, your first two fingers extended, reach out in front of you as far as you wish your protection to extend, and see the light flow from the left hand, through the chest area and continue out to the first two fingers of the right hand. Move in a clockwise circle, arms extended and visualize the lavender light coming from your fingers extending both above and below you to form a complete sphere when you have completed your turn. If you wish you may intone a song of your own making to fix the intent of the energy sphere around you such as:

"Sphere of light
___(name of deity)'s___ delight,
Protection spun,
Around me tonight."

Or

"Light of armor,
Protects today,
From all harm,
It's kept at bay."

When you are good enough, you can dispense with the hand gestures, but I wouldn't for at least several years. Another thing you might do is see the sphere as a glowing lavender mirror which reflects all that approaches it. You might also use the antler gesture in each of the four directions to help strengthen the work as this is an invocation to the protective power of the God. You might also put this protection sphere around your familiar by seeing the light spring from your fingers to form a sphere around your pet. If an attack is directed at you and you deflect it, it is possible that the attack energy will be bounced to whatever is closest to you, which can be friends or familiars. It is therefore wise to also protect them all as familiars are particularly vulnerable. You might also put this visualized sphere of energy around your house and car. This protection is good for about 8 to 12 hours, after which time it should be renewed.

THE PENTAGRAM

The pentagram can also be a very protective symbol to wear. They are usually made with a circle around them. They are potent symbols on etheric and astral levels and they do keep negative energy away, particularly if they are charged with protective energy or oil. If you have one of these, it is better worn under your clothes so it won't generally be seen. You might also reinforce your lavender sphere with pentagram symbols as well, making the star from the top point and going down towards the left. You might also charge some of the objects you wear with a lavender pentagram by tracing it over the object. See the lavender trail your fingers, sinking into the object you are charging. If you are under psychic attack, visualize the lavender pentagram coming out and standing in front of you. This should protect you from most forms of attack. I would encourage you to read some other books of psychic self-defense, such as the one written by Dion Fortune. The pentagram should be recharged every full moon.

BLACK MAGIC PRAYER GROUPS

If you find yourself in a situation where a person or a group of people are praying for you "to be saved" and to join their organization; in the pure sense of white and black magic, this is quite black. This is identical to someone casting a spell to make you join their group against your will. It is the direct desire to manipulate another person's will against their own best interest and desires. So, if you have a group praying for you to do something not in your best interest and against your will, but for their own desires, this is a psychic attack and it can do a great deal of damage.

Although a person or persons committing this attack and violation feel quite justified in doing so because they consider it in your best interests, the point is they may or may not be right, and feeling justified does not really give true justification for trying to manipulate someone.

For someone who does not want to be manipulated or dragged into another religious organization, this becomes a problem. A great deal of psychic energy can be directed through these types of groups even though the people in the group may not know how to effectively use their energy. This is a problem, as someone who does not know how to use a loaded gun should not point it at other people. Usually people who would do this have been so violated themselves that they have problems with proper boundaries. They are also usually people who have the "true believer" type of mentality, and who have been indoctrinated in "mindlessness", and have very few original thoughts. They have never been taught to think about their actions outside of a certain narrow spectrum. To pray for anything other than the person's own highest good and well-being becomes questionable. Anything which manipulates a person's will is black. People who have worked inappropriate love spells will know what I mean by that.

If you are under attack by a prayer group whose intent is to "save" you, then you have the ability and right to protect yourself psychically from them. Don't get me wrong, prayer groups can do wonderful healing work and I don't necessarily disapprove of all prayer groups. As long as these groups are praying for the healing of the world, then they are worthwhile. However, if their use is corrupted to manipulation then they have descended to black magic no matter what they call it and regardless of their reasons, and should be treated as black magicians. The best thing you can do in these situations is return these people's energy back to them by creating your lavender mirror globe and letting them deal with the consequences of their own energy and actions.

PSYCHICALLY CHARGED OILS

Psychically charged oils can be very useful. Take a small amount of Canola oil, perhaps 1 fluid ounce (if you can just find a one fluid ounce bottle, it makes the measurement much easier). Take this oil between your hands and visualize Bride or Angus Og or whichever God or Goddess you feel closest to, visualizing their hands about 1 foot above your head. Feel and visualize this energy coming out of their hands going down through your head and out of your own hands and into the oil. It is good to visualize this energy as a particular color which is appropriate for the purpose the oil will be used for. See the oil begin to take on the color of this energy, and take in so much that it begins to glow brilliantly. Mentally repeat to yourself that the oil will continue to hold this charge. Continue to do this for at least 10 minutes. You may add a few drops of another scented oil or perfume according to your own personal desires, but the scent should remind you of what the oil is for. While you are doing this you might repeat:

"I charge this oil in the name of _____ for the purpose of _____"

Now use the oil for the purpose that you have charged it for. If you dispose of it before it is all used, pour it out upon the earth.

Afterword

A Word for Pagans of Other Systems

If the Old Religion is to be a truly spiritual path, not just another religion, it must not be discriminatory. To be another religion is easy, people will believe anything. To cause people to have valid and useful realizations is a spiritual path, and a spiritual path does not bind with dogma, but sets free with truth, and truth is not in anything but your own evolving awareness. A truly spiritual path does not cause you to lose contact with deity or reality, but to experience it fully.

The greatest danger that the Old Religion faces at this point in its evolution is elitism caused by personal and social biases. This does not show realization of the Union of deity, but only a small bigoted misguided ego.

If someone is turned away by a supposedly spiritual teacher for being black, gay, male, female, or some other prejudicial reason, it is simply showing their spiritual path is invalid, and nothing of a deeply spiritual nature can be learned from that individual.

In the Old Religion, the first concept of deity is like that of the Hindu concept of Brahma, or a monistic type of being. It is that all-pervading essence of which we are all aspects and totality simultaneously.

By refusing someone access to a path to the realization of all-pervading deity, of which the God and Goddess are also aspects, you simply show that you have not achieved the ultimate realization of deity. If you had, you would realize that the person coming to you is also just as valid an aspect of deity as you yourself, no matter what color, persuasion, or genetic predisposition.

"All acts of love and pleasure are rituals to me" are the ritual words of the Goddess. Who then can judge that the love of someone gay is wrong and unacceptable? Their love and pleasure are just as valid a ritual to the Goddess as someone else's with merely different genitalia. In truth, the genitalia matters not at all in this respect. To discriminate along these lines against gays is usually a carryover from a "religious" background of hatred, bigotry, and greed.

If there is no role for "people like that" in your tradition, you should walk before your Gods and ask Them for one. If your spiritual path is true and pure, then you should have communion and rapport with your Gods. They will truly lead you beyond definitions, hatred, and prejudice if you let Them.

Let us not be just another religion, let us be truth. Let deity manifest in our actions, realizations, and love.

THE OLD RELIGION'S VIEW OF GAY PEOPLE

What is the Old Religion's relationship with and view of gay people? It must be remembered that there are many traditions in the surviving Old Religion. Some are old family traditions, like the ones that this is based upon, and others are reconstructed from the remnants of traditions that have faded away. Generally speaking, the old and better preserved, unreconstructed traditions do not discriminate against gays. Not every single one of the old traditions are so open, but the ones I have encountered are. The groups that are most often discriminatory are those which have been reconstructed from the remnants of traditions of an old tradition by people whose background and basic biases were Christian. Whether the people from these traditions like to admit it or not, or know it or not, they have obviously been strongly influenced by the Judeo-Christian biases against gays because it generally does not exist among the older complete traditions. Since there was usually no one left to tell the reconstructionists that it was incorrect, they often kept their bigotry and biases, and worked it into their systems. The people themselves can hardly be blamed for not knowing. Many of the traditions have been destroyed, and the ones that did survive usually preserved different aspects of knowledge of magic and the Old Religion in a fragmented form. Some of the old traditions were obviously tribal as well and insular to the others around them. To find that this information was very obscure among the knowledge that did survive was not a surprise as gays usually don't have a lot of children to pass these things onto. The information on these gay areas is due to the heterosexual traditionalist pagan community, and for this we are all in their debt. It is interesting that lore of this type survived more among the Christian inquisition records that among the general pagan community, considering how much sexuality was brought into the old trials and of how often sodomy was mentioned as part of the religious rites.

Among the old uninterrupted direct lines of traditionalist groups there is an unusually strong position for gay people. In a number of these systems, complete gay groups can be set up. This is because the feminine species of gay men are recognized. Since the feminine principle is honored instead of debased, a gay man is permitted to act as the high priestess or Servant of the Goddess, although some ritual considerations must be made. This is because the older systems recognize that it is not genitalia, but the spirit that determines the vibration, femininity, masculinity, or worth of an individual.

Interestingly enough, straight men are not accorded this right, only a gay man can take the place of a priestess. The person most suitable for this role is the passive sexual partner in a homosexual relationship.

According to at least one hereditary system, there were a number of totally gay groups, most of which were decimated during the persecutions of the 1400 and 1500's by the Inquisition. The ritual considerations and gay lore have been handed down and exist even to this day, although these systems have usually been so closed that there has been no accessibility to gay people (or much of anyone else for that matter).

What is the extent of the material that has survived? When one queen priestess of a hereditary tradition was asked this, she replied that their group honored Diana, and the Chaste aspect was honored as well. She said that heterosexual sexual initiations were not permitted because they discriminated against gay people. When asked for further information she gave legends of the Gods acceptance of homosexuality, poems, ritual considerations, advice, spells, and more. There was more of the same in at least two other hereditary systems, so it is not an isolated case.

So, if you have wondered about whether you would be interested in finding out more about the Old Religion and were discouraged or insulted by discrimination, it really was because of personal bigotry and ignorance on the part of whichever heterosexist pagan or Wiccan group or individual you contacted. Not all of the Old Religion's traditions are so corrupted.

THE ORIGINS OF RELIGIOUS AND SPIRITUAL SYSTEMS

The function of a spiritual path is the psychological evolution of awareness towards the realization and experience of Union with deity. The main function of religious institutions is to maintain social structure. This means that religions generally are the starch of social fabric. They give the guidelines as to what is acceptable in a society and what the proper social interactions and behavioral rules are between individuals. Religions are formed around standardized social behavior and are created to maintain and justify the actions of individuals in a society while maintaining the stability of the society itself. If a society is psychologically well-adjusted and integrated, it will manifest this type of religious structure. The society will use religion to maintain the current social structure. If a society is dysfunctional, it will manifest a dysfunctional religion. The basic principles are the same.

A functional religious system is paralleled by a functional family unit in its straits and qualities. Here, the family is the basic unit of society. It does not control its adherents through guilt or fear, but guides them with love, reason, and understanding. It is the growth of the individual and their care, not their control, which is the goal of this kind of system. It is also flexible and adaptable to its people's changing needs. A wholesome religious system finds the newborn child perfect, blessed, and unblemished; loved unconditionally by the Gods. It also teaches healthy boundaries by limiting its influence to spiritual matters only; while showing they are necessary for cooperation, respect, equality, communication, tolerance, and nourishing social interaction. It permits open communication on all matters while teaching respect for ourselves and all other things. It does not teach martyrdom, co-dependency, or self-sacrifice for unnecessary reasons. A religion should set forth social scripts for its people that are healthy and life enhancing, not ones based on doomsday or massive destruction. These destructive ideas are created to terrify and to maintain social control. Focusing on the destruction of the world for a lifetime is destructive to the individual and society. Whatever you focus on is what you create. This is part of taking self-responsibility because with self-responsibility there are also positive goals. Finally, it will teach that violence is wrong, and a healthy religious system will not support, bless, or commit violence in any form, psychological or physical.

Dysfunctional religious systems parallel the dysfunctional family. If for example, you have someone who was consistently beaten as a child by an abusive parent, this individual will probably continue to beat his children as he perceives this to be normal behavior. Generally, widespread religious systems are instituted by the members of the society who are in political or social control. It is this controlling individual, or group, that will create a religious structure to justify their actions. If their background has been abusive, this behavior will be justified by the religious structure. Therefore, the god that will develop out of the social fabric of this dysfunctional individual/family/society will be one that beats, maims, or destroys its adherents. Children and adherents will be punished unmercifully for the slightest infraction. Since a dysfunctional god form has unusually low self-esteem, it will probably be jealous, vindictive, angry, insecure, and intolerant of anyone who might criticize its actions or take attention away from it. These are based upon the infantile or stunted psychology of the dysfunctional people who set up the religious system.

If one parenting member of the family is unable to maintain a stable personal relationship or degrades a partner, you may find a religious system with a single differentiated god unable to tolerate a partner. Since this type of family/social system usually sets up a scapegoat to take out frustration and anger at their own dysfunctional behavior (in a family, usually the child) you may find religious systems which institute purges or persecutions against specific groups, sometimes even their own members. So thus, you know that any religious system that creates purges, persecutes a specific minority, or has discrimination in its priesthood structure is dysfunctional. Dysfunctional systems petrify and cannot accept change or challenge to their social authority. Dysfunctional families and dysfunctional society/religion ends its own growth and freezes in a set pattern that will limit any science that might cause social change or changes in thought in general. Galileo and his interaction with his church is a superb example of this.

A functional religious system permits beneficial social change and accepts new thought as it is a secure and open system, not a closed insecure one. If a religious system is unable to change with the evolution of society, it will block beneficial social change. It then becomes the enlightened individual's responsibility to step away from such an abusive religious structure and into a non-discriminatory spiritual path. This promotes healthy self-esteem, not only for the individual but also for the society, which must be allowed to progress.

If a society is not permitted to evolve, it degenerates into a structure that is abusive of anyone outside of the controlling hierarchy. It is to the hierarchy's benefit to keep its people powerless and burdened with economic pressures. The control structure can then persecute and dominate without interference. This type of social structure and resulting religion will be particularly threatened by any innovators concerned with true societal well-being.

Truly empowering spiritual paths threaten defined religious and social structures by expressing freedoms. For example, one notes the persecution of the Sufi. Gay people are most likely to be especially chosen to be eradicated as they are extremely creative individuals and the creative function of these individuals can destabilize a fossilized dysfunctional system, thereby upsetting the control structure. It is not gay people themselves that are the threat, it is the creative function that they carry which is the threat. It breaks previously set barriers based upon social control.

These misunderstandings are carried further by people who are set up or set themselves up as spiritual authorities, but who are in reality religious authority seeking to use these systems for personal gain and control. This corrupts the institution that may have been erected with the sincere and honest goal of spiritual evolution.

If you go to the very roots of a religious system you will usually find a truly spiritual founder. The problems begin with the institutions that usurp the integrity of the man or woman's name, and use it for their own greed and political gain.

But what about a spiritual path? A truly spiritual path stimulates your own evolution or awareness, which manifests in actions. It is not merely an outward emulation of what one is told that one should be. It arises spontaneously from your own heart and soul and is not false or insincere.

A spiritual path gives you the realization of compassion, not the simulated act of pity.

What is the role of gay spirituality in the world? The fact that gays are usually in the vanguard of the new should give us some clues into their function on a cultural and spiritual level. To understand this effectively, we must begin with the soul consciousness of a gay person. Let us define masculinity as red and femininity as blue. A gay person's soul consciousness or inherent way of sensing themselves would be to define this aspect of themselves as purple, the blending of red and blue. They do not sense the limitations or barriers that separate these from each other at opposite ends of the spectrum. In essence a gay person would stand in the junction between these two opposite ends. People who are adjusted to viewing only their end of the spectrum (red or blue) would have difficulty in recognizing themselves in this color, purple. It is set apart into a separate category even though this is an aspect of their very essence. This is applicable not only to masculinity and femininity, but to other split ways of living and thinking as well.

In a society split on these levels, it becomes confusing to a gay person, as what is supposed to be two polarized things (in our society) is for them experienced really as one. Gay people are comfortable with this even though society is not. It is this sense of unified consciousness that manifests as gay acts and compulsions. Well-adjusted and openly gay people are simply being true to their own soul consciousness, which is not and was never meant to be divided. It is the function of gay consciousness to cause gay acts, as the consciousness creates the acts, rather than the acts creating consciousness. This makes the arena of being gay much larger than what it may outwardly appear to be as the acts may be suppressed to the detriment of the individual. That repression makes that person no less capable of the consciousness or the desire to take action along these lines. Although the individual may deny their own soul inheritance, it does not mean that they do not carry it.

Through the Fires

The path of gay spirituality is the beauty of a unified expression of consciousness which thereby becomes available to all, since an aspect of everyone is present. The use of gay spirituality is in the discovery of higher levels of consciousness through new roads and experiences. This is the same common gay experience in many fields, such as art or design. Therefore, the gay path of spirituality is that of the scout, the pathfinder, the forerunner in achieving the awareness of deity. This is done through personal intuition and experience, not through following the dogmatic religious law imposed by a control system.

Gay spirituality was never meant to be confined to a fossilized institution; the responsibility and possibilities are much greater. It is meant to be the creative function by which institutions are established, the primal cause of spiritual systems and religious institutions. These religious institutions seek to emulate and honor the spiritual experiences of others. They do not experience this themselves as this would mean making changes in society itself instead of maintaining its structure.

If a gay soul conscious person is attempting to fit into a fossilized institution, he will be pushed away from it either by the institution or by his own sense of truth as he is not being true to his own spiritual function, or himself. The institution will immediately sense him to be a threat to its structure. A gay soul conscious person will automatically step beyond the institutions control and the institution will intuit this. To try to fit into these institutions is like trying to fit a square peg into a round hole, it is simply not possible unless irreparable damage is done to the square peg, distorting it into something it was never intended to be.

When the paths of spirituality become overgrown in the established institutions, with dogma and misunderstood metaphor, it is the gay function of spirituality to open new roads from personal experimentation and intuition to the source of being. This is why there were always so many gay shamans. When the old systems no longer functioned, due to social changes or simple losses of awareness, the gay soul conscious person could inherently intuit a complete truth from his or her own experiences. To be gay, or more correctly, to have a gay soul consciousness that manifests in gay acts, is to be the innovator or creator of religions, art, poetry, and to have greater access to all of the creative processes. Gay spirituality is inherently creative as gay consciousness is inherently creative. This is the nature of the union of opposites or Unity.

As previously stated, religions usually venerate someone else's spiritual achievements or experiences; expressed in metaphor, analogy or even history. It is the function of gay consciousness to create the new spiritual analogies, paths, and ceremonies which will be reflected as religious rite and experience.

So my friends and brothers, we are about to step on the path of the mystic. You will walk alone even though others are at your side. You shall find your deepest joys and face your greatest fears. It is not meant to be only intellectual but an experimental way. Looking at a cake does not give you the full or real enjoyment as eating it does and it is a shame to starve while looking at food. Life is not meant to be just looked at, but to be lived and experienced fully. Otherwise you miss the point and waste it. It's the difference between reading about sex and having the experience of it. It is the function of the gay existence to experience things for yourself, to try some of the exercises in this book. They can be a lot of fun. Become more aware – that's what it's all about.

REFERENCES

Traditionalist Sources
Women's Mysteries by Esther Harding
The Golden Bough by Robert Graves
Silver Bough by F. Marian McNeill
Witchcraft and the Gay Counterculture by Arthur Evans
Another Mother Tongue by Judy Grahn
The Glory of Hera by Philip Slater
Wonder Tales of Scottish Myth and Legend by Donald MacKenzie
Gods and Fighting Men by Lady Gregory
Healing the Shame That Binds You by John Bradshaw
Codependent No More by Melody Beattie

RECOMMENDED READING

The Old Religion
The Teachings of the Holy Strega by Raven Grimassi
Whispers by Raven Grimassi
Raven's Call (a magazine), Moon Dragon Publications
The Complete Art of Witchcraft by Sybil Leek
West Country Wicca by Rhiannon Ryall
Women's Mysteries by Esther Harding
Witchcraft and the Gay Counterculture by Arthur Evans

Gay
Growing Up Gay in a Dysfunctional Family by Rik Isensee
Gay Relationships by Tina Tessina Ph.D
Permanent Partners by Betty Berzon Ph.D
Another Mother Tongue by Judy Grahn

Strange Experience by Lee Gandee

Psychology
Healing the Shame That Binds You by John Bradshaw
The Self Sabotage Syndrome by Janet Woiwitz
Healing Your Sexual Self by Janet Woiwitz
Games People Play by Eric Berne
Scripts People Live by Claude Steiner
Codependent No More by Melody Beattie
Born to Win by Muriel James, Ed.D

Scents and Incense
The Practice of Aromatherapy by Jean Valnet, M.D.
The Aromatherapy Workbook by Marcel Lavabre
The Art of Aromatherapy by Robert B. Tisserand
Wylundt's Book of Incense by Steven R. Smith

Comparative Mythology
Primitive Mythology by Joseph Campbell
Oriental Mythology by Joseph Campbell
Occidental Mythology by Joseph Campbell
King, Warrior, Magician, Lover by Moore and Gillette
Tao Te Ching by Lao Tzu
Origins and History of Consciousness by Erich Newmann

Groups
A Circle of Men by Bill Kauth
Ceremonial Circle by Cahill and Halpern
The Tao of Leadership by John Heider

www.ingramcontent.com/pod-product-compliance
Lightning Source LLC
Chambersburg PA
CBHW050553170426
43201CB00011B/1681